To Light The Way

From loneliness, through fear, to joy;

One Woman's Story

by

Karen Lynne

Published by Satin Publishing

Author photograph by Louise Jacob Photography

10% of all profits made on the sale of this book are dedicated to Gloucestershire Domestic Abuse Support Service (GDASS)

ISBN-13: 978-1981242566

ISBN-10: 1981242562

Acknowledgement:

Thank you will never seem enough for all the love and support that I have received. I am blessed with so many precious friendships and humbled by those of you who invited me and my animals to stay at your homes when I had nowhere to go. I will be forever grateful for all these friendships.

Anna Sherry: For your unwavering friendship and clear solutions

Ali Soleil: For believing in me when I was still a stranger to you

Darryl Westbury: For your kindness and for introducing me to Conversations With God.

Gibby Tree: For protecting me and standing by my side.

Jacqueline Rogers: For your patience and wisdom

Laurelle Rond: For your spiritual wisdom and friendship

Lesley Beattie: For the huge amount of trust that you put into our friendship and your constant support.

Louise Evert: For your strength and belief in me

Lou Rosson, Abi Cosgrove and Tonia Simms: For being the daughters I never had.

Mini Suharwardy: For always being at the other end of the phone and always believing in me

Nadia T:For standing by my side and for allowing me to be a part of your children's lives

Nathalie Wiesperer: For getting me through all the legal stuff.

Neale Donald Walsh for introducing me to a God I can believe in and for giving me the keys that helped me to write this book.

My Thanks also goes to:

April, my support worker from Gloucester Domestic Abuse Support Service: For educating me and holding my hand.

Stroud Police: For believing me and supporting my situation

And finally to a little cockapoo named Bollie: For the absolute joy you brought into my life .

AUTHOR LINKS:

www.karen-lynne.com
www.facebook.com/thefamilyangel
karen@karen-lynne.com

Publisher Links:

Satin Publishing:

http://www.satinpublishing.co.uk
https://twitter.com/SatinPaperbacks
https://www.facebook.com/satinpublishing/

Email: nicky.fitzmaurice@satinpaperbacks.com

Author Biography

Karen Lynne is the founder of The Family Angel and the Family Angel Community. It has been her desire since she was 6 years old to create Happy Families and she is now passionate about creating an ethos of mutual understanding, respect and love within every family that she mentors.

Having developed a love of writing whilst sharing her Family Angel Blogs, Karen gifted herself, in the midst of chaos, the opportunity and time to sit down and write this book. Her inspiration came from the many teachers in her life, some of whom advised her to write her story, although initially Karen couldn't understand why it would be of interest to others.

Recently, Karen began to see the value in sharing her wisdom gained through personal triumphs over the difficulties in her life, and so this book was written with the sole intention of inspiring other women to find their strength, to step into their own power with dignity and grace, and to value their own worth.

Karen already has plans for her next book. How wonderful would it be if children didn't have to go on difficult journeys to find their own self-worth? In her next book Karen will share with parents the ways in which they can nurture their child's self-worth, and at the same time create harmony in their home.

Dedication:

To those who feel lonely and afraid,

You are not alone

You are beautiful and valuable

You can find your strength and your voice

It is time to stand up and say

You cannot treat me that way.

Table of Contents:

Chapter 1: Mum

The hospital corridor was long. I walked silently in between my Grandma and Grandad heading back towards the exit and the fresh air. My sister, Julie, skipped happily along in front of us. I was 6 and she was 4. We had just been to visit our Mum. I knew something was very wrong.

Before we were allowed to see her we were warned that she might cry, but that we were not to worry as these would be tears of joy. It was quite a shock to see her, she was so thin. She barely managed to stretch out her arms and encourage us to cuddle her. I remember all the adults were sad. It felt like they were all holding their breath, hoping and praying that the meeting would go well. Julie chatted away happily, oblivious in her innocence of what was going on, but I knew... something was very seriously wrong.

As it turned out I was right, that was the last time we saw our beautiful Mum, a lady who used to be so full of life, a lady who laughed a lot and embraced life. And now, this lovely lady had been reduced to little more than a skeleton by the leukaemia that would take her life or, as Neale Donald Walsh would say, cause her Continuation Day.

My security and child-like innocence were gone forever on that day; the laughter went out of my world. There were plenty of adults who lovingly and willingly tried to take her place, but none of them were my beautiful Mum and my life in a conventional family died with her.

I didn't realise it then, but by passing when I was a young child, my Mum gave me the gift of experiencing different parenting styles. She also gave me a connection to heaven, to use a word from my childhood, that would begin my consciously spiritual journey through this life, but more about that later.

Dad didn't cope very well with losing Mum, in fact he didn't cope at all. If my life had been a movie, then he would have had a shaky start and, we would have clashed in the early days, but somehow, he would find his inner strength and learn how to be a Mum and Dad to me, and so give the film of my life a happy ending. That is what would have happened, should have happened, if only my life were a film, but my life was not a film. My Dad didn't read the script with the happy ending. He didn't step up the way I needed him to, and so my journey through this life took me on a very different path.

At the time of my Mum's death, we lived in Yorkshire in a village outside Leeds. My Grandma and Grandad however, from my Mum's side of the family lived on the other side of the Pennines in Manchester. We stayed with Grandma and Grandad from the moment we left the hospital ward. I don't know what happened on the day of the funeral, I don't even remember a funeral because a decision had been made that my sister and I should not attend; a decision that I resented for many years of my life. The adults considered us to be too young for such an experience but, as the Americans say, that left us without a day of closure, a day to say good-bye.

I can remember the day my Dad told us Mum had passed. He picked us up from Grandma and Grandad's and drove us all the way back home to Yorkshire without saying a word about Mum. I can't even begin to imagine what that journey would have been like for him. I know that we ran into the house when we got home expecting to see her, only to be greeted by the emptiness and silence. Dad sat us down next to him, one on either side of him on the grey settee. I can remember looking at the wooden panelled wall ahead of me with a sense of dread at what he was about to say.

I don't remember the words, only the feeling of loss, the pain in my heart that felt physical, the longing to be able to see my Mum, feel her, be held by her, hear her laugh. As the words reached our ears the tears rolled down our faces. Dad was as lost as his two young daughters. We hugged, we cried and nothing more was said.

There were no words to make what had happened to us, to our family, be right. Mum was the heart of our family, like so many Mums are, and now our heart had been taken away. The house was silent except for the sounds of sobbing and it all felt wrong, very wrong but I could do nothing about it. Life had suddenly flung me onto a new path. A path without security, a path without my Mum's love, or so I thought at that time. I didn't want to live without her, but I had no choice.

Dad and I were shocked out of our tears when Julie stood up, dried her eyes and said,

"Can I go out to play now?" At the time, I couldn't believe what she was saying and by the look on Dad's face, neither could he. But, as I have since discovered, when an emotion is too hard to feel young children choose to feel it in short bursts, that is the only way they can cope. On that day, it looked like Julie had taken the news better than either Dad or myself, but she hadn't. She was just dealing with it in the only way she knew how.

I now realise that my childhood ended that day. I took on a responsibility that was not mine to take. As a 6 year old child my Dad should have done everything in his power to look after me, but his power was not very strong so in that moment, I chose to look after my sister and my Dad as best as I could. I wanted us to be a happy family again.

As I said, I was only 6 years old, so although my intention was to try to take Mum's place, in reality, we needed the help of another grown-up. Dad began a course of action that I can only describe as him seeing his responsibility to us being a need to find someone else to take care of us.

At first he tried to hire a nanny and we went through three nannies in a relatively short space of time. I honestly don't think it was mine or Julie's behaviour that drove them away as we embraced them all, especially the nanny who brought a very cute white miniature poodle with her. We so loved having a dog in the house. For me it was the beginning of my lifetime of love of animals, especially dogs. We didn't even complain when one of the other nanny's cooked baked beans all the time. She was so lovely, but she just couldn't cook so every meal would include a tin of baked beans or a tin of slippery spaghetti. Yuck! I haven't eaten either since.

Three nannies came and went and then we moved back over the Pennines to live with my godparents, my Auntie Bernice and Uncle Brian. These were happy days to be honest. Auntie Bernice was a very quiet, peaceful lady but was Mother Earth personified. There was nothing she wouldn't do for us and she made us feel very welcome.

Sadly, for us, she has now celebrated her Continuation Day too, thankfully though, many years after Mum's passing. Uncle Brian was and is a hoot, very outgoing, a character larger than life and someone who always made us laugh. Together with their two children, Linda and David, who were each a year older than Julie and me, we became part of a happy family for a short while.

I would have been happy to stay with Auntie Bernice and Uncle Brian, but life had other plans. I don't know the exact reasons for our leaving, but one day we were living with Bernice and Brian and the next we were moving in with Grandma and Grandad. My grandparents must have only been in their fifties, my age as I write this, when they welcomed Julie and I into their home, and yet they looked older than I think I do now. They looked 'old' if you know what I mean. After a recent experience of taking care of my ex's children, I can really appreciate how exhausting it must have been for them to take us on full time.

The plan it seemed was for Dad to stay in Yorkshire until he could sell the house and move jobs. So in those early days we only saw him at the weekend. Grandma and Grandad loved us dearly and this should also have been a happy place to be, but there was an underlying tension between my grandparents and my Dad.

It seemed to me that they needed someone to blame for my Mum's death, and he was it. Grandad was physically a big, powerful man and later Dad would admit that he was frightened of him. I now know that the toxic energy of the situation affected my feelings but I wasn't aware of it then. All I knew was that something wasn't right. My grandparents said horrible things about my Dad and my Dad in turn was not very complimentary about them. It was above all not a nice atmosphere to live in.

My Dad was still relatively young when Mum died, so it was not surprising that after a few years he started to date other ladies, eventually choosing a new wife, Camilla.

Julie and I had held such high hopes for this next stage of our lives. Camilla seemed lovely and kind towards us and our biggest prayer, to be part of a family again, seemed to be answered. This time we were to get a new Mum and a Step-Brother all at once as Camilla had a son, James, and he was a year younger than me and a year older than Julie. We looked forward to the wedding with great excitement and joy.

Our expectations could not have been further from the truth. Camilla clearly wanted to create a 'proper' family with my Dad and James but Julie and I did not fit into her vision. This became blatantly obvious from the minute we all lived together. Without any exaggeration, she made our lives hell. This was one of the darkest periods of my life. I was 12 years old when Dad married Camilla and 16 when I moved out. Rather than gain a Mother on the day of their wedding, Julie and I lost our only living parent, my Dad.

The signs were all there early on. I understand it must be difficult to treat someone else's children the same as you treat your own but she didn't even try. From day one James was treated differently to Julie and me. If you had seen Camilla with her son, you would have thought her a brilliant Mum, there was nothing she wouldn't do for him. But with her Step-Mum hat on, Camilla was the typical Pantomime Step-mother. Not only was she constantly mean towards us, but she made it her mission to distance us from Dad by perpetually telling him lies about us.

Here is a typical example of one such lie that she fed our Dad. At the time when this incident happened we had been living together for a couple of years and Camilla made a point of refusing to cook for Julie or me. The routine for when we got home from school was that we would find an egg and a slice of bread on a plate, this meant we had to cook egg on toast for tea. Or, if she was being really mean, a slice of bread and a small tin of baked beans which meant beans on toast for tea.

On this occasion, it was beans on toast. As I have already explained I hated beans which meant my dinner was only going to be one slice of toast. I bravely decided to cut another slice of bread out of the loaf, I say bravely because it had been made very clear to us that what was on the plate was all that we were allowed to eat. If we didn't like something that was tough! Bravely, I took the bread knife and began to cut the bread.

Now I must explain to you that the kitchen was long and thin. The door was at one end and at the other was the table and an old-fashioned cupboard where the bread was kept. The cupboard was tall and had a 'door' in the middle that dropped down horizontally to create a shelf. I hope you can get the picture. I was standing at that cupboard door with the knife in my hand as Camilla opened the kitchen door to my right. She screamed at me

"What do you think you're doing?"

I quickly turned to my right to face her and it was as I turned, that yes, you guessed it; so did my right hand which was carrying the bread knife!

No I was not threatening her. No I was not attacking her. I was simply doing exactly what my Grandma had taught me to do which was to look at the person who was talking to me. The next part of the story happened so fast. She screamed at me again, something about not attacking her and I must put the knife down. Within seconds James, her son who was taller than me, rushed into the kitchen and pushed me to the floor. He brutally stood on my arm and took the bread knife off me.

In a daze, I protested my innocence but to no avail.

I was sent to my room that night without any dinner, and when Dad came home from work he was told that I had attacked her with a knife. He believed that story for the next 30 years without ever asking me what happened!

This is just one way that my actions were distorted by my Step-mother, and Dad began to believe that I was just an unruly teenager with serious problems. He never once considered it wasn't my fault. Not even after I had moved out of the family home, and the same stories were now being told about my sister. He never once put two and two together to realise the women he had married was making his daughters lives hell.

As I have said, I moved out at 16 and I went to go and stay with a school friend called Dawn, and her Mum and siblings during a school holiday. As the holiday ended Dawn suggested I could stay. At first I didn't think that was possible, but I dreaded going home so we asked her Mum. Dawn's Mum was just the kindest, gentlest lady I know. Bless her, without hesitation she said that if Dad would pay her £6 a week for my food, then yes, she was happy for me to stay. I couldn't believe my ears.

Knowing that my Dad usually did anything for a quiet life, I asked him expecting him to say yes, but that was not quite the answer I got. It seemed he would happily let me leave, as this would make his life easier, but paying for me to leave was another matter. All he offered was £3 a week which was the child benefit he claimed in my name.

I couldn't believe it but I wasn't going back. I was already working as a waitress in a Pizza Restaurant, so I thought that with an extra shift I could afford to move out and pay Dawn's Mum. It wasn't easy, but I did it and without any sort of fight to stop me, my Dad let me go.

As I have mentioned, in my early years there were many different people who tried to step into my Mum's shoes to parent me. From nannies to godparents, grandparents and a horrid Step-parent, I had gained a lot of experience.

One other lady I would like to mention here, because she had a huge influence on my life, and that was my boyfriend's Italian Mum. I started going out with Cal when I was only 14 and he was 15. We seemed good together, although we did break up for a short while when my troubled home life got too much for him to cope with. That should have been a warning sign to me, but I didn't pick up on it. Anyway, part of the reason I loved Cal so much was being part of his noisy Italian family. As you know family is everything to the Italians and this was a wonderful new experience for me.

Cal, his full name was Calvino, had two brothers and no sisters, so both his Mum and Dad lovingly welcomed me into their home. I soon discovered that Italians love to be noisy and shout just to be heard. There's no anger in the noise, just loud voices.

Every day this lovely family sat together around the table for a family meal and you could see there was nothing that Cal's Mum would not do for her family. She was a very strong lady, both physically and emotionally, and was very much the matriarch. If anything, she probably did too much for her sons, but she made me feel at home when I was with her. I can remember the house being full of people, plants, music, food and love.

She taught me a lot just by watching her. I know now that children learn mostly by observing, and that is what I did. Even something as simple as ironing shirts. I'd had no role model growing up and Cal's Mam became the role model I so desperately needed. I spent many an hour happily chatting to her as I watched her take care of her family. I loved being with her and she loved having some female company in a very male home.

Little did I know that all these people who had once parented me, and given me these different experiences would become such a vital part of my future business . At this stage in my life everything seemed like a challenge and I ached for love and security. I always felt that I was on the outside looking in, sharing a short time with different families but always wanting to find somewhere to belong.

People described me as being brave, but I didn't feel very brave. To me 'brave' meant I had a choice, a choice to be brave or take an easier option. In truth it never felt like there was an easier option. I had to be brave. I had to keep moving forward and there were no choices that I could see.

For many years when my home life seemed so hard, so cruel and so lonely, I would imagine how the plot would work out if my life were a book. What would the next chapter say, so that it got me away from the pain and loneliness. I kept looking forward, but I missed my Mum every day.

When my Mum passed the adults around me told me that she was in heaven, that she was looking down on me and that I could always speak to her. I don't know if those adults believed what they were saying, but I took them at their word. I spoke to my Mum and I heard her reply in my head. When I was 6 everyone thought this was cute but by the time I was 14, and still talking to her, I was considered to be a little crazy.

I learned not to tell anyone what I was doing. I only met one other girl who did the same, a girl whose Mum had also passed, and like me she kept her conversations with her Mum quiet.

I realise now though, that talking to my Mum had given me a connection to the spiritual realm, it kept me open to spiritual possibilities and gave me a faith that would keep me strong no matter what life threw at me.

And the universe was not done with me yet. I had grown up experiencing what it was like to be parented by many different adults. Now I had to experience what it would be like to mother many different children.

Chapter 2: The Early Years

When I went to see the careers advisor at school, I felt excited. I was good at maths and I thought the world would be my oyster. I expected her to tell me about lots of interesting jobs that I could go for because I was good at maths, but the meeting didn't go quite as I expected. When I asked what someone who was good at maths could do, her answer crushed me. "Teaching or accountancy." she replied.

"What? Teaching or accountancy? That can't be right. There must be more?"

"No. Teaching or accountancy."

It was a short meeting as you can imagine. After that I didn't want to stay in school; I wanted to get out into the world. As I write this sentence it makes me smile. Somewhere along the way my desperate need to be a part of the world deserted me. For many years, I was afraid of the world outside, but at that point in time, I was desperate to embrace it. And as for accountancy? I couldn't imagine anything more boring than checking someone else's figures. My apologies to any accountants, I have since learned that accountancy is about so much more than this, but at 14 this was my very limited opinion.

It wasn't just the careers teacher who thought teaching would be an option for me. When my Headmistress, Miss Manley, realised I had left home at 16 but was still attending school, she started to take a keen interest in my progress. She called me into her office one day as she'd heard a rumour that I was hanging around with a girl in school who she thought would be a 'bad influence' on me. Poor Dawn, what on earth had she done to deserve that description? I didn't like to tell Miss Manley that I had moved in with the 'bad influence', so I just acknowledged her warning. Before I left her office she suddenly asked me,

"Karen, have you considered becoming a teacher?"

"No not really," I replied.

"Well I think you should consider it, Karen.' she said.

"I think you would make an excellent teacher".

It was nice to have her blessing, it made me feel warm inside to think that someone believed in me, but it would be many years before I decided that teaching was the path I wished to take.

Before that I had to suffer the boredom and frustration of working in the civil service in their VAT office. It was only after this experience that I would seriously consider that I might enjoy being a teacher more.

I found the VAT office mind numbingly boring. I was lucky in that my supervisor would give me jobs above my pay grade just to keep me occupied, and whilst I appreciated his actions, it seemed very unfair that I was doing the work but not getting promoted. Even then I had a strong sense of fairness and this simply did not seem fair. The job was better than being on the dole but wasn't the life I had envisioned for myself. I was here to do something important, I was absolutely sure of that, but what was that important thing? I had no idea. I only knew that I had potential for greatness and I was not going to fulfil it at the VAT office. I handed in my resignation and left.

The next 6 months of my life I spent twenty miles north of Newcastle with Cal, who was still my boyfriend at the time and who would later become my husband. He was studying up there and so I joined him. When the 6 months were complete, we moved back to Manchester; he moved back in with his family and I moved into a tiny bedsit.

It was a bit rough I have to say. I had to share a bathroom with six other occupants, but my room was my space and I loved it. I brightened up the settee and chairs with the bright orange covers that my Grandma had given me, and it wasn't long before I rescued a gorgeous little Collie puppy, Puch, who became my roommate. How I ever got the Landlord to agree to my having a puppy, when I lived on the first floor and he had a *no pets* policy, I will never know. Fortunately for me, there had been some thefts locally so the Landlord thought it was a good idea to have a dog on the property.

Sadly, when the bedsits were broken into sometime later, my cute and well-behaved puppy stayed in his wicker basket and did nothing to defend the property! The basket wasn't a dog bed, it had a lid attached to it. The thief found this very useful and with the lid closed,

Puch simply curled up and patiently waited for someone to release him.

He didn't even bark when the Police arrived. Some guard dog!

I wasn't home when the flats were broken into, but I rushed in when I saw the Police outside.

"Is there a dog in flat 4?" I asked.

The Police lady's face broke into a huge smile.

"Yes, he's still there," she replied, "he's safe."

We discovered that all the money in the electricity meters had been taken from each flat, and yet the money I had left on the table was still there. Better still, the most precious thing to me at that time, my dog Puch, was also there unharmed.

Puch was my first dog. I didn't go looking for him but he found his way to me. This is something that has happened often in my life with animals, but he was my first and he was very special. Spending time with Puch gave me my first experience of unconditional love. No matter how tough life got those big brown eyes would look into mine, he'd put his chin on my knees, his tail would wag, and my heart would melt, every... single... time.

During this time in my bedsit I began to rebuild my life. I gave much thought to what I wanted to be 'when I grew up'.

After much soul searching and a few years out of the school system the familiarity of the school day started to look more enticing and I turned to teaching.

One of my biggest regrets about leaving home early on was that I hadn't passed my 'A' levels. I can remember the feeling of utter disappointment when I realised that all the missed lessons had taken their toll. I wanted to hold my head high again. I wanted to prove to myself that I could pass so I enrolled at a further education College. As a person claiming unemployment benefit I could only study for 15 hours a week, but that was enough to study two subjects.

I chose Human Biology and Mathematics. It felt good to be studying and challenging my brain again, so you can imagine my disappointment, when after completing the first year, I was told that the Human Biology class would not be running a second year. It turned out that not enough people had signed up for the second year, which left me with my only other option of a 3hour evening class every week.

I was determined not to give up and to be honest I had done some of the work at school. So I set myself the challenge of being my own teacher and after another year of study I proudly added 2 A levels to my list of qualifications.

I was a little nervous about applying for a university place. I only had 2 A levels when 3 were expected, not to mention I was older than the other applicants due to my years out of the education system. I shouldn't have worried though. The fact that I had chosen to come back into education after working for a while, and the fact that I had doggedly completed my A levels under difficult circumstances, all went in my favour.

Cal was moving down to London to start working for the BBC and I was offered a place at the University of London to study Mathematics. We had a magical year; I lived in a lovely ground floor flat of an amazing house complete with turrets, an enclosed garden and a Polish Landlord who allowed us to take Puch.

It was our first time living together on our own and that was exciting. I wanted to take care of Cal the way his mother had. I can't believe I am saying this now but I loved cooking and cleaning and keeping our home nice. Little did I know the size of the rod I was making for my own back, but at that point in my life I studied and played house and was incredibly happy. In fact, Cal and I were so happy together that we decided to get engaged. We planned to get the engagement ring when we went back home to Manchester and to announce our engagement to his family on Christmas day.

However, like most things to do with family in my life, it didn't go to plan.

For some strange reason Cal's Mum, who had always welcomed me into her family and into her home, was not happy about a possible engagement. I have no idea why, but the lovely engagement we had planned did not happen. We did buy the ring from Preston's of Bolton, but I didn't wear it until we arrived back home in West

London. It was a bit of an anti-climax, but we were engaged. There was no talk of a wedding, we would have to fund that ourselves, but an engagement meant I belonged somewhere for the first time in a long time.

It came as a bit of a shock some months later when Cal came back from work and said, “We can go home”.

“What do you mean we can go home? I am just coming to the end of the first year of a three-year degree course. I can’t go home. Don’t you dare leave me here in London after I came down here to study and to be with you.”

“You can go to university in Manchester instead.”

Cal had an incredibly clear way of seeing things. It appeared the BBC in Manchester were looking for cameramen, and if Cal didn’t take this opportunity now, it may be years before they needed cameramen again. Or at least that is what he told me. I didn’t think he could possibly understand what he was asking of me. How could I just change courses? How could we suddenly uproot and go back to Manchester?

It wouldn’t be the first time that I changed my plans simply because of a decision I had allowed Cal to make for me, or the first time that his job came before mine either. It also wouldn’t be the first time where all I saw were problems and he saw possibilities.

He told me to stop saying I couldn’t go and find out if I could, and he was right! Because I had only done a year of my maths course UMIST, that’s the University of

Manchester Science and Technology department, were happy to offer me a place. The decision was made, our bags were packed and our first adventure living together in London was over. We headed back up north and moved in with Cal's family.

The next few years flew by. After 3 months living at Cal's family home we bought our first house, a 3-bedroom semi-detached in Didsbury. We moved in with a new hob that we carefully balanced on a cardboard box in the kitchen, a new bed and a settee that we had been given, which frankly looked like something out of Doctors waiting room.

We didn't have much, but we had our dreams and hopes. It was Cal and I against the world, we were on our way up and we were happy. Sadly, our dreams and hopes didn't work out as planned. Our wedding the following year was spoiled by his Mum's lack of enthusiasm. With hindsight, it could have been because we got married in a Registry Office, not a Catholic Church as his Mum would have expected. However, Cal was determined he was not getting married in a church.

At the time, I accepted his decision. His Mum cried throughout the short service and when I went up to her afterwards to pacify her, she spoke to me in Italian, which I didn't understand, and then she walked out of the Registry Office. To this day I don't know what she said.

The rest of the afternoon passed and was sadly filled with many an argument from his Mum, before we finally had a fun evening with our friends. It was not a conventional wedding by any imagination, and it certainly was not the wedding of my dreams. I have no photographs to mark the day and we did not have a honeymoon afterwards, but at the time I was very happy to be Mrs Karen Lynne Delmonte.

It took another 2 years after my wedding day before we spoke to Cal's Mum again. At that time, I unexpectedly found out I was pregnant. Cal and I had always wanted children and it had been my only desire in life at this point. I wanted to create the family I thought I'd never had, and I wanted to create a home where my children would feel safe and loved. I wanted to give my children the family life I had never experienced for myself. I guess this is what every parent wants.

However, at the time I'd become pregnant I had completed my degree and was on a post grad course to become a teacher. Cal was working away when I first realised that my exhaustion was due to my pregnancy and not down to my first practical experience of teaching.

I was nervous about telling him, as it was not really a 'good' time to start a family but I needn't have worried; he was delighted. So was his Dad, who didn't know whether to sit down or stand up when we told him. Cal's Dad insisted that we to go to a pub to celebrate and surprise, surprise his Mum turned up too. I was happy that the family 'feud' was over, although I felt a little uncomfortable that I was only worthy of being in the family now I was carrying a potential grandchild.

Sadly three weeks later, my happiness at being pregnant turned to despair when I suffered my first miscarriage. Words could never be sufficient to express how distraught I felt. I was taken to hospital for confirmation that the pregnancy was over, but I already knew. I knew the minute my Doctor said,

"I know this will sound like a daft question but do you still feel pregnant?" I didn't. It was over. My child was lost and I didn't even know if it was a boy or a girl.

I was told the foetus had probably passed in the bleeding. I had nightmares that I had flushed my child down the toilet. As I waited for my D&C on the hospital ward I overheard the conversations between two women who had chosen to have their pregnancies terminated. How cruel is that? There was only one other lady on the ward who had suffered a miscarriage and she already had a 4 year old child. I couldn't imagine that her pain could be as great as mine. I was lost.

My pain continued for some time. No one knew what to say to me. Cal tried to be supportive by saying we could try again, on purpose this time, but I wanted him to show his grief, show me he was hurting too. I don't know whether he couldn't, or simply thought that by hiding his feelings he was being strong for me. Either way it was not helpful.

It was just before Christmas. There were babies and families everywhere and I couldn't stop crying, couldn't pull myself together. I felt very isolated and alone with my grief. Eventually I decided to attend a meeting for women who'd had miscarriages and still births. I felt nervous as I approached the building where the meeting was being held, and when I found the meeting room it was full of women. I was shocked at how many women were there. We were split into groups of 8 to 10 women. and we sat around in circles and shared our stories.

As I listened to the horrendous situations some of these other women had been through, I started to feel a bit of a fraud. I had only had a miscarriage at 12 weeks, it wasn't uncommon. Some of these women had gone full term or at least well into their pregnancies. They had pictures of babies who were still born or born with deformities that meant they didn't live for long. My heart went out to every one of them and I was struck by their bravery in being able to share.

When it got to my turn I started by apologising. It wasn't to be the first time, or the last that I would apologise for the experience I was having, as if somehow my grief wasn't valid, but I was overwhelmed by the love and support I received from these ladies who I had never met before.

I shared how I felt and they listened and empathised. It was what I needed to move forwards. When I left the meeting that night something inside me shifted. I could hold my head high again, not for long as it turned out, but that night I thought if all these women could cope with all that had happened to them, then I could handle a miscarriage at 12 weeks. I picked myself up, started to look forwards again and re-engaged with my life.

Chapter 3: I am a Teacher

I began my teaching career with enthusiasm and in trepidation. My first job was at a school in a relatively deprived area of Stockport, where my dream of inspiring children to love maths was brought down to earth with a severe bump. There was little room for the innovative ideas I had learned whilst I was training to be implemented into the classroom. Instead much of what I did was teach a specific mathematical technique and then get the children to do lots of examples. No wonder those who struggled with maths found it so boring!

After a few months at the school the Deputy Head asked to come and watch one of my lessons. At the time when he was free, I was teaching the bottom set in year 9 and just to make things worse, I was teaching fractions. These children struggled to understand fractions in years 7 and 8 and now I had to go over the same 'stuff', as they put it in year 9.

The children were bored with a subject they did not feel they could do, and were at pains to point out that there was a perfectly good button on their calculators to do fractions! Frankly, I was tempted to agree. I liked that these children had a habit of speaking their minds.

I explained to the Deputy Head what I would be doing with them, but told him he was still welcome to watch. Feeling my frustration, he asked me what I would like to do instead with these children? Instantly I felt excited and motivated. I shared with him a problem-solving exercise that I had learned at university and would love to try with this class. He gave me his blessing to take this one lesson and do whatever I wanted to do.

What I really wanted to do was prove to these children that they were not 'thick', their words not mine, as far as maths was concerned.

The Deputy Head came to join us and I explained to both him and the children that in this lesson we would be looking at one problem which was this...

There are 30 children in a class, 15 boys and 15 girls. There are 31 chairs in a row. The children sit on the chairs so that all the boys are on the left, all the girls are on the right and there is an empty chair in the middle. The boys can only move to the right. The girls can only move to the left. And they can only slide into an open chair or jump over one person to get to an open chair. The question is how many moves does it take to get all the girls to the left and all the boys to the right?

Now for those of you who are not mathematically minded, you maybe losing the will to live just reading this problem! Please stay with me and remember, as far as mathematics was concerned, I was teaching the bottom set of year 9 and every child in the group, without exception, thought they were rubbish at maths.

For the first 10 minutes after I gave the children the problem, I left them to it, without any further instructions. Immediately there was a buzz in the room. They naturally split into groups of 2,3 or 4. After a while they were starting to rip pages out from their exercise books. Not great when my Deputy Head was watching!

I stopped the class and offered them some coloured counters or coloured sheets of paper to work with. The buzz returned. After a while the energy in the room started to change into an air of frustration, so I stopped them again.

"What would make the problem easier?" I asked.

"Less kids," was the immediate response.

After a short discussion, we decided it would be easier to start with smaller numbers of boys and girls and off they went again. The buzz was back. One boy and one girl was easy. Two boys and two girls was soon conquered. Three boys and three girls became a bit tricky, but interestingly they didn't want help, they wanted to do it for themselves. The lesson soon ended with the original question unanswered.

Can we do this tomorrow they asked? I looked at the Deputy Head and he nodded. Surprisingly, he also found time to return the following day. I hadn't set the problem as homework, but that night every child worked on the problem at home! The next day they came into the room already chatting about what they had done. The problem for three boys and three girls had been cracked. Already they were seeing patterns and symmetry in the moves. With a little encouragement, they realised that they needed a formula because the number of moves was growing very quickly. It wasn't long before they had created a formula that suggested with 4 boys and 4 girls the problem would take 24 moves. It took some time to prove, but suddenly they were on a roll and had solved the original problem.

"Can we try it?" one small voice asked.

"Of course," I replied.

I was not going to stop them when they were so excited and focused and to do this physically they would really have to work together. This was a bit risky on my part as it could easily collapse into a series of arguments, or it could become a moment of inspiration.

I took the risk and we all went out with our chairs. My heart sang; there were no arguments and they worked together well. They shouted out the moves together and when they had got all the girls and boys to the opposite chairs, they spontaneously cheered and applauded. They were really pleased with themselves and they had a sense of achievement. This was maths that they could do and their pride was written all over their faces. The whole exercise had been a resounding success.

The next time I walked into the classroom they were alert, excited and waiting for the next problem to solve. Their thoughts of being rubbish at maths had gone, they were eager and ready to go. This is how every teacher wants to be greeted when they walk into a room, but my heart sank. I knew this was what I wanted to do; to inspire, to build self- belief, to get them working together and believing in themselves and each other. Instead I had to go back to the curriculum, which we both found mind numbingly boring. This experience stayed with me.

I instinctively knew that teaching was about inspiring children to be the best that they could be, not simply teaching them to pass an exam.

I spent my first year of teaching at this school. I had dreamed of being a teacher that inspired children and yet my first year was as demoralising to me, as forcing the children to go back to 'normal' maths. I don't blame the school, they were working within government guidelines in an area where poverty challenged academic success.

I wanted to make a difference, but discovered instead that what I really wanted was to 'save' every child and I ended up going home every night with a headache. It took a long time before I realised I couldn't save the children, and in fact as a teacher, that was not my job. It took many years of my life to realise my job was to share what I knew and then hold a space for each child to grow into; that is when the magic happens.

The magic happens when you share what you know
And then hold a space for the child to grow into

At the end of the academic year I was told about a job that was becoming vacant at a private school. To be honest I'd never seen myself teaching in a private school, but the job was recommended to me, so I applied for the position.

When I walked around the school, I found this was school as I remembered it. There was an atmosphere of possibilities in Stockport Grammar School, the children were polite and the staff were friendly. Suddenly I wanted the job. This was the sort of school I wanted to teach in and I had an advantage. The wife of my current Head of Maths used to work at the school before her death. A reference from him was highly valued here and he believed in me. The interviews seemed to go well and I was over the moon when I got the job.

Life at Stockport Grammar School was completely different. Here I could focus on teaching Mathematics instead of spending half my time focusing on discipline. I was not the cleverest Mathematician in the department, in fact, I was surrounded by very bright and very talented Oxford and Cambridge graduates. Sometimes I would sit in the Maths Office and listen to their conversations and wonder what they were talking about.

I loved teaching at this school, but I did feel that I was 'not good enough' for quite some time. Like many people, having confidence in my own abilities is one of my life challenges, and that challenge was highlighted in this school. It took a couple of years to understand where my strengths lay.

I had a policy for the children I taught which said, if they paid attention but still didn't understand, then their lack of understanding was my fault not theirs. I emphasized to them that it was my job to teach, and sometimes I might need to explain things in a different way if they had not understood. The rule was that I would explain 3 times the same way and if they still didn't understand, then I would change my approach. This took the pressure of understanding off the children's shoulders and meant that they felt able to tell me when they were struggling.

I can remember one day when a young girl in my class repeatedly told me she couldn't understand. I'd explained 3 times in 2 different ways and she still felt able to say,

"No sorry, I don't get it." I was starting to wish the floor would open up and swallow me, it was at this point she said,

"You are the most patient teacher I know."

If she'd known the thoughts going on in my head she wouldn't have said that! However, on the surface I was proud to remain calm. I set the rest of the class some work to do and explained with yet another approach and she finally got it. We were both relieved.

I share this story not to tell you I was a patient and understanding teacher, but because this approach led to a personal understanding of my strengths. After a couple of years, children who had been in my lessons but moved onto different teachers, started coming back to me asking for help.

They would say "Mr X, or Mrs Y, has explained this 3 times and I still don't understand. I daren't ask again, will you explain it to me please?"

I was flattered. My heart went out to these children, and yes, I took time out of my day to help them. This didn't happen every week but it happened often enough for me to start questioning why. Suddenly it dawned on me even though I wasn't a brilliant mathematician like some of the members of the Maths Dept., my skill was that I understood why the child didn't understand.

I could empathise with them and then the challenge to me was to find out how I could explain so that they would have clarity and understand. I was, and am, a good teacher. If you cut me in half like a stick of rock, I would have teacher written right through me.

Whether it is in Mathematics, or as would follow; horse riding or parenting skills, or communication or spiritual practices, I am always at my best when I am sharing my knowledge and experiences. The joy is when I am teaching what I know, but finding a way to present that knowledge in the most understandable way for my pupil or client.

At this point in my career, and my life, to suddenly realise that I may not be the cleverest mathematician in the world, but that I have a true and natural gift for teaching was mind blowing.

I am a teacher. I am a *brilliant* teacher. I would say it to myself in my head over and over. It made me smile, and it made me stand taller. It made me accept that mathematics was not my gift but that teaching, and intuitively knowing why someone was struggling to understand, that was my gift. The brilliant mathematicians, who incidentally were all lovely people, were not better than me, they simply had a different gift. Suddenly I felt I was making a valuable contribution to the strengths of the Maths Department and amazingly, I felt that I belonged; it was a lovely feeling.

Life took on a surprising turn and I found myself teaching horse riding, instead of Mathematics. It wasn't something I had dreamed of doing, or even wanted to do, but it had come my way.

I had a horse, a beautiful bay mare called Rosie. She was on a livery yard and so was looked after by other people, however, I did try and see her three or four times a week. The problem was that this was not enough for Rosie. If it had been a couple of days since I'd last seen her, when I arrived at her stable she would instantly turn around and put her rear end in my direction. Who needs words!

She made it very clear she was not impressed. Then I had a bright idea of moving to a house with a couple of acres of land where Rosie could live at home with me. That way even if I didn't ride her every day, I would at least see her. Well you know what they say. Be careful what you wish for.

Cal and I searched for 18 months to find a house with some land, but with little success. One day he came home and said,

"I've found a house."

It seemed there was no brochure or at least not one he was prepared to show me. He'd made an appointment to see the property which was in a small village, just outside Knutsford in Cheshire. The house was an old farmhouse built in 1716. It had low beamed ceilings and windows with small panes of glass. It had a huge farmhouse kitchen and was very quaint. It needed some work but at that point in my life I thought it was my dream home.

However, what my dream house did not have was a riding school attached to it and this one did, complete with indoor school. As lovely as the house was, this was not for me. I wanted a small amount of land for one horse, I didn't want to run a riding school. In fact, I knew nothing about riding schools, absolutely nothing. I said 'No', but Cal took no notice. He thought it would be nice for me to be at home and run this little riding school.

"You can ride, you can teach, and you're doing the books for my company, so what is the problem? Of course you can run this riding school."

I should have known that what Cal wants Cal gets, but I said no and for the next 3 months nothing was said of it. Then one day I received a call from an estate agent.

'Karen, does your offer on Holly Tree still stand?" 'Offer, what offer?' I thought.

"I'll have to talk to Cal and get back to you," I heard myself say, and I phoned Cal straight away.

"Did we put an offer in for Holly Tree?" I asked.

"Yes," he replied, without any hint of an apology. "But I knocked a lot of money off the price so they won't go for it."

"They just have!" I replied.

As I write this I am embarrassed that I allowed Cal to push me into something that I didn't want to do. However, I know what came next, I appreciate that I learned a lot through the horses and the children for the 10 years that we were there. May be fate had a hand in me finding myself in charge of Holly Tree Riding School. There is much I can say about the riding school, in fact, I could write a whole book just on my experiences at Holly Tree, but for now there is one life lesson I want to share with you.

Holly Tree was very run down when we bought it and for the first three months I was busy still teaching at Stockport Grammar working out my notice whilst also trying to run the riding school. We moved in the week after the summer break had ended. In the October half term, I decided to ask for some volunteers from school to help clean up the riding school. There was lots to do ranging from brushing away years of cobwebs to painting the indoor school.

I promised nothing in return as far as riding was concerned, so I didn't expect many volunteers, and yet I was pleasantly surprised to get ten or so children who volunteered to help. Now these children were from a private school, but to be honest they were the more challenging kids who had signed up. I couldn't say 'thank you, but no thank you, you maybe more trouble than you are worth,' so I welcomed these children with open arms.

What a surprise; I couldn't have asked for harder working kids.

Inside the four walls of a classroom they did not necessarily excel but outside, surrounded by dogs and horses and nature, they came alive.

They worked so hard; they were polite and willing and worked well together. No job was too dirty or too difficult. I saw a completely different side to these children and I learned a big lesson. I was a teacher, I believed in an education system, but that week I realised that the education system was great for left brain children but not so good for predominantly right brain children. These children needed to be actively doing, they needed to be outside and they needed someone to see passed their challenging behaviour.

As I said before, these children were from a private school so their behaviour in the overall scheme of things was not that bad, but when they were put in a different environment and treated in a different way, they blossomed.

The interesting thing was that once they got back to school, these same children worked harder for me in my maths lessons all because of the time they spent with me at the riding school.

Some children need to leave the confines of the classroom in order to come alive and shine

Chapter 4: Holly Tree

Holly Tree taught me so much, where do I start?

To be brutally honest I was out of my depth when I started running the riding school. I'd acquired 7 horses and 7 ponies with the school, and on each of the first four days after I moved in, a different horse or pony went lame.

It was a steep learning curve and just as well that the lesson diary that showed full classes of seven was a far cry from the truth. Otherwise I would have been out of business by the end of the first week. It was also the first time in my life when I consciously 'faked it until I made it'. The staff and the teenagers who helped were all looking to me for leadership. A response of; "I don't know" was never an option. I had to work intuitively, do it my way and work out what my way was as I went along.

On the first day that we moved into Holly Tree, I travelled from my previous home in my little red Nova. It was bursting at the seams with both mine and Cal's stuff and poor Puch was squeezed into the passenger foot well. I couldn't even see out of the rear window as I had a spider plant swinging from the central mirror. Not sure it was legal to drive like that but we were safely making our way to our new home.

When I was nearly there the phone rang. It was Cal telling me the riding instructor needed the key to the tack room. 'What key?' I thought, 'why wouldn't the instructor have her own key?'

Then Cal added that I needed to sort out the money for the school float. I was not getting off to a good start. It had never dawned on me that the instructor would need my help. I thought the school would pretty much run itself. How wrong was I?

I turned into the driveway and was a little surprised to find the gate open. With children and horses on the yard and the yard so close to a main road, it seemed ludicrous that the gate was not shut to protect them. Note to self, make a sign to say the gate must be kept closed. I think this was the first thing on my 'To Do' list, a list that started that day and grew every day. I don't think I ever got to the bottom of that 'To Do' list for the next 10 years!

That first morning I drove in to the yard, I found a small rotund lady down the far end surrounded by children, parents and ponies. She had short bobbed hair framing her very round face and was wearing a brightly coloured jumper, the sort your Grandma would knit for you.

She was the calm in the eye of the storm.

This lovely lady was Linda my instructor and over the years I came to love Linda dearly. She was a real character, fiercely loyal to the school and a great instructor for building up confidence.

On that particular day, she was trying to work out how she could teach, without any saddles, and yet in such a way that the children would have fun and their parents would still think they had value for money.

Bless her, it never dawned on her to send the clients away. She was looking for a solution when I drove through the open gate.

The huge smile that broke onto her face as she saw me, let me know how relieved she was that I had arrived.

"Hi, I'm Linda. You must be Karen." she said, "Karen I need the key to the tack room."

"Hi, Linda," I replied, "I'm sorry, but I haven't been given a key to the tack room?"

"Oh, that's okay," she laughed. "It's in the safe in the house."

"But I haven't got a key to the safe!" I replied, getting more worried by the minute.

Her smile grew even broader. "That's okay," she said, "the safe is always open!"

'Of course it is, I thought!' Linda followed me into the empty kitchen of my new home and sure enough, there in a corner was a huge safe, the sort bank robbers used to blow up in the films I'd watched as a child. It was very big, and very solid, and the door was wide open.

Inside was a money tin and the tack room key. I handed the key over to Linda who rushed back to the clients, while I made a start at emptying my purse of change for the float. That sorted, I followed her to the indoor school and took the payments from parents, while

Linda and the 2 teenagers who were there to help, tacked up the ponies. Crisis over. The riding lesson began.

With a sigh of relief, I wandered back to my car.

It would be a while before Cal and his brothers arrived with the van we'd had loaned to us for the house move. I decided to unload my car, find the kettle, cups, and coffee so that I could make a drink, then go and sit down in the gallery of the indoor school and watch the lesson.

Fortunately, as it turned out, no-one knew who I was that day as I sneaked into the back and sat down. Linda was teaching what I later discovered, was the hardest class to teach. The children were relative beginners, but had just moved up from lessons where they had constant support from leaders who walked alongside them, to this lesson, where they were on their own. From an instructor's point of view, it was like trying to spin plates. Not only were there 7 unique children, there were also 7 ponies, each with a mind of its own.

When I sat down the ponies were following each other nose to tail around the school and Linda was giving the children instructions about what they were going to do next. It seemed they were going to take it in turns to trot from the front of the ride to the back.

Linda was sitting in a corner of the school when at that moment she decided to eat a tangerine. Now the instructors were in the school for long stints, so it wouldn't be unusual for them to eat as they taught.

However, in this case, the peeling of a tangerine started a sequence of events that I could not have predicted.

As the smell wafted across the school, one cute little pony called Blaze decided to leave the parade of ponies and trot across the school to get some of Linda's tangerine. The child on board Blaze had no control and started to cry.

The pony at the front, an old flea-bitten grey who was the most reliable school master continued to lead the ponies around the school. However, the ponies behind the newly created gap now had to decide whether they followed Blaze or trotted to catch up with the rest of the ponies. The riders were little more than passengers at this stage. They were learning to take control of their ponies but it was a steep learning curve.

Suddenly there were ponies everywhere. Some took advantage and turned into the centre of the school, as if the lesson had finished. Some took the opportunity for a quick trot but cut the corners to catch up with the rest of the ride, and Nicky bless him, the flea-bitten grey, just kept following the track around the edge of the school.

It was at that moment that I realised that teaching 7 children on 7 ponies would be harder than teaching 30 children in a class room.

Linda was amazing. She remained calm, laughed as she called Blaze a cheeky pony, and slowly got all the children and ponies back into the right order, as they once again followed Nicky around the school.

A good leader stays calm in a crisis

Undeterred, Linda continued with the lesson. The first couple of ponies trotted beautifully from the front to back of the ride. However as the third pony, Beauty, set off the fourth pony, a black fell pony called Jubilee undercut her and cantered to the back of the ride.

Jubilee put the brakes on a little late and so she went into the back of Goldie, a small palomino pony who hated anyone touching her back end. Goldie bucked, the child fell off and the parents began to grumble.

Chaos ensued once more and once again Linda calmed everyone down, checked for injuries and soon had all the ponies and children back in order. It wasn't long before there were smiles on all the children's faces again, although there was still a lot of grumbling about certain ponies in the gallery.

I was glad no-one knew who I was! Linda was amazing and the children loved her. At the end of the lesson they greeted their parents at the door of the school with happy faces.

In the ten years that followed, I learned a lot about the horses and that in turn, taught me a lot about the children. Horses are sensitive creatures. They don't respond to your position in life, they don't care if you are the Queen of England, or living on the streets. All that horses respond to is your energy.

I always used to think it was sod's law that after a tough day teaching mathematics, when all I wanted to do was sit on my horse and have a quiet hack around the country lanes, that would be the day my horse decided to jump at everything and the ride would be anything but quiet. At the time, I blamed my 'temperamental' mare Rosie.

Once I started to live and work with more horses, I realised that Rosie was not the one to blame. It was my energy and my frustrations that caused my beautiful equine companion to jump at everything she saw. I was not respectful, or even aware of the energy I was bringing into her space. It was many years later that I heard Oprah Winfrey say something similar; that one of the most important lessons she'd learned from her television shows was be aware of the energy that people brought into her space.

"Be aware of the energy that you bring to my space"

Oprah Winfrey

Many years later, I was reminded of this when I was divorcing Cal. At the time, I was living on my own in a huge 6 bedroomed country house in Buckinghamshire which we had recently bought together, although Cal had already left me to live with the lady he would marry next.

The white rendered house with huge sash windows sat in thirty acres of land and from my kitchen I could see my horses in their Monarch Stables. The setting was beautiful, and yet I didn't have any friends. I only knew the farmer and his wife who helped with the land, the gardener, the farrier and a lady who lived down the road who was a friend of the previous owner.

This house was supposed to be our fresh start, but it had turned into a gilded cage. On this particular day, Cal was back home because his new lady was away and he hated being on his own. Although his affair and our following divorce had pulled the floor from underneath me, we were still on talking terms and were trying very hard to remain good friends.

The sun was shining and Cal suggested I rode one of the horses. I wanted to ride but I hadn't ridden for ages, mainly because of the move to the new house and then finding myself getting divorced. Instinct told me to spend the time grooming the horse and not to ride but Cal challenged my instincts.

"You always put obstacles in the way, it's a nice day. Just get on the horse."

I wanted to, but I felt anxious, not about the horse, but about life in general. Anyway, as was my pattern at that time, I did as I was told.

Jim was a full 17 hands of Irish Draught horse. He was under normal circumstances, a gentle giant whose eyes melted your soul. On this day he was restless as I tried to groom and tack him up. My plan had been to ride in the manège, but he wouldn't stand still long enough to let me get on. I should have read the signs but I got frustrated with him.

Cal came out to see what I was doing and offered to hold onto him so I could get on board. I accepted with some relief and soon I was walking with Jim around the school. I asked him to trot and he duly picked up speed. Normally he was pretty laid back but not this day, his trot got faster and faster and I couldn't slow him down. Soon we were cantering around the school and yet faster and faster he went. I panicked. I did everything wrong.

He was a big horse and I was scared of falling off. He was getting so fast and unbalanced I feared that he would fall over as we went around the corners. To this day, I don't know how or why he slowed back down to a trot and then a walk. All I know was that as soon as he stopped, I jumped off. As my feet hit the floor, my knees gave way and I sobbed as I sat on the ground. My tears weren't about Jim, my horse, but in that moment my anxieties about my divorce had all been transferred into a very real fear about getting back on board.

Wisely, I decided not to get back on board that day, although many instructors will probably say that is exactly what I should have done. It took the support many months later of Sue, a kind and knowledgeable instructor, to get me back on my horse. She pointed out what I already knew, but had simply forgotten. Jim had reacted the way he did because he was trying to get us both away from my frenetic energy. I had never sat on him before and felt so anxious. He hadn't recognised my energy that day, and it hadn't felt good to him so he'd literally tried to run away.

Sue reminded me how horses are constantly reacting to our energy. Working with her that day also reminded me that sometimes, when we are amid a crisis, we need a friend or mentor to support us, to help us see clearly ahead and to remind us of what we already know.

Sometimes we need a friend to remind us of what we already know

That day, Sue said to me, all the things I would say to someone else if they came to me for help. She started by making me take simple steps. Again, something I would do for a client, but that day I couldn't do for myself. It isn't a weakness to be blinded when you are in a fog, the weakness is not to ask for help.

You have probably heard the expression 'you cannot see the wood for the trees?' Well, when we are in an emotional state this will often happen and it is times like these when we need support. Whatever the reason for our loss of confidence, a problem with a relationship, a parenting problem, a loss of someone we love, a lack of self-love, a problem at home or a problem at work, whatever the problem the strongest step we can take is to ask for help.

Whatever the problem the strongest step we can take is to ask for help

When I first arrived at Holly Tree, the horses and ponies looked very sorry for themselves, their coats and eyes were dull. Yes, they were old, but they were also merely going through the motions each day, they had no joie de vivre. They may have been loved by the teenagers over the weekends, but there was little time for TLC when the instructors were on the yard. In fact, I was surprised at just how little care and attention they were given. I'd been told the riding school pretty much ran itself but that was clearly not the case and the school's best assets were not being well cared for.

Over the weeks and months, I started making life for the animals much easier. I purchased some hard feed and they started to get two feeds a day as well as their hay. Despite my husband's disapproval, I started to buy one stable rug and one turn out rug for every horse and pony in the school. I also started to muck out each stable properly every day. Slowly, but surely, they started to come alive, their characters started to show through and we started to get to know each other. It took a long time for them to learn to trust me, but I was building that trust by:-

- Treating them with respect
- Treating them kindly
- Fulfilling their basic needs
- Setting clear boundaries

At the time, I didn't realise that this approach with my equine employees would be a philosophy that the riding school would become well known for. It was, and is, a philosophy that not only applies to my relationship with my animals, but also my relationship with my clients, my colleagues and my friends. It is also a great philosophy for parenting children.

This philosophy of how I should treat people and animals, which partly comes from my beliefs, formed the framework of how I chose to run the riding school and became the foundations upon which I built everything else.

Chapter 5: Freckles

When I realised that the horses responded to our energy, life began to change for me. I developed a thirst for knowledge about how this energy 'thing' worked. I was constantly asking questions, not for anyone specifically to answer, or so I thought at the time, but questions that came into my head. I wondered about the animals, about why children behaved the way they did around me, and about how my faith and the belief that there was more to life than we understood, fit into the whole picture. The riding school gave me a 10-year journey of research and experience.

When Cal and I bought Holly Tree, the horses and ponies that came with the school were all very old. Amazingly one or two, like Nicky, stayed with me the whole 10 years but, I did have to say goodbye to many over the first few years of being there.

As I write these words, I feel regret over some of the horses and ponies that I allowed to leave the school with people who at the time I thought I trusted, but who with hindsight may not have treated them very well. I hope they lived out their lives with lovely people, but my instinct says that may not have been the case. At the time, I did the best I could with the knowledge I had.

At any point in time, we do the best we can, with the knowledge we have

When I eventually sold the school, I spent a year finding homes for the horses and those I could not find homes for I took with me. Unfortunately in those early days, I chose to take people at their word and I let some of the horses go to a dealer, who I later then realised had just told me exactly what I wanted to hear. As I said it was a steep learning curve and a period where I started to recognise and trust my intuition, but it all took time.

Some months after we'd bought the riding school, I came out onto the yard at 8am and as always, with my 3 collie dogs, walked across the yard to the feed room, but something felt wrong. Normally as I came out of the house the horses began to whinny at me, but not that morning. I thought it was strange, but I continued on to the feed room. As I started to rattle buckets and make up feeds there was still no noise, the yard was ominously quiet. Nothing stirred. I stopped making up the feeds and started to walk around the yard to find out what was wrong.

I entered a small barn called the 5 block. Unsurprisingly it had 5 stables inside, but I could only see 4 heads over the doors. As I approached the fifth stable I found Freckles, a flea-bitten grey mare about 14 hands high, lying on the floor in her stable. I went into the stable and tried to move her, but she couldn't get up. She wasn't responding. Her legs were so cold, she must have been down for some time. I phoned the vet as another member of staff arrived and we both tried to get her to stand, but still no success.

The vet soon arrived and said she must have been down for a long time. He was quite blunt, if we couldn't get her to stand he would have to put her to sleep. The vet left and the horses all around remained silent.

How could I save her?

At the time, Cal and I were having building work done on the old farmhouse and as the builders started to arrive, they came over to see what was the matter. No sooner had I explained the situation than they were problem solving. We had a large pulley for pulling bales of wet hay out of the water trough and they decided to use that. The 5 block was a bit rickety, so they used extra supports to hold up the beam they'd attached the pulley to.

Somehow, we managed to roll Freckles onto a horse blanket and then pulled her out of her stable. it was all a little undignified, but we were taking action.

The horses on the yard were still standing in silence. If you are not a horse lover, I really want to impress upon you that their silence was not a normal reaction to seeing so many people on the yard. The builders attached the horse blanket to the pulley and slowly they started to pull her up. Freckles remained quiet and trusting throughout. Not once did she panic. She simply allowed us to help get her out of the mess she was in.

As Freckles became upright the vet returned. He told us to give her some time still supported by the blanket and pulley so that the circulation could return to her legs. As we massaged Freckles legs to help the process there was a quiet wicker from Laddie, the woolly cob in the stable next to Freckles. Laddie was Freckles loyal friend. They always walked around the edge of the field together and clearly, he was happy to see her standing again. As Freckles came back to life, so the horses and ponies began to move in their stables and quietly whinny for their breakfast. It seemed as her life was rescued, the yard came back to life too.

I thought about all this afterwards, and what surprised me was how all the horses knew that Freckles was in trouble. Obviously, the horses in the 5-block could see her, but none of the horses in the stables outside could. Also, the yard was split into two with a huge hay barn in the middle and even the horses down the far end of the yard somehow knew that Freckles was in trouble. They were clearly not using any of their more obvious senses. They couldn't see or hear her, I cannot imagine that they could smell any change and yet somehow they just 'knew'. They used what we would call a sixth sense, some sort of energetic link between them to remain quiet until their 'friend' was rescued.

My awe and respect for these beautiful creatures grew immensely that day. Freckles would never go back to working in the school. Her back legs were weak for the rest of her life, but she trusted us enough to allow us to help her stand up every morning. I retired her from the school that day and allowed her to enjoy the time she had left. She enjoyed her retirement before playing a part in my next unusual experience at Holly Tree.

About 6 months after Freckles rescue by the builders, it became clear that her quality of life was slipping. I walked into her stable to help her get up only to find her lying in her own faeces, my heart sank. She looked so undignified lying there waiting for help to get up. I knew it was time to let her go. The vet was surprised that we had helped her to live as long as she did. He smiled when I told him we helped her to get up every morning, but he also agreed that it was time to say goodbye.

The school was closed on a Friday and so we arranged to let her go the following Friday. She would have a few more days before I had to say goodbye. Those days were torture, it was like she was on Death's Row, and of course, she made me question my decision by rolling in the field and managing to get back up all by herself. It was her swan song which was both lovely and painful to watch.

I had never made the decision to put a horse to sleep before. It was a very stressful and sad time, made even worse by the question of whether I wanted the vet to use a lethal injection or a gun. As a gentle person who hates violence and guns, shooting her seemed almost barbaric, but I asked the vet which method he preferred and why.

As you have probably guessed he wanted to use a gun. He said it was kinder on the horse as they literally did not know what hit them. I had asked the question and he had answered. Was I going to respect his experience or allow my emotions to get in the way? I decided to put Freckles first and allow the vet to use a gun but I wanted to be there.

I know that sounds strange, but I felt I owed it to this little horse to stand with her, and if I could keep my emotions in check she would be not be afraid if I stood by her.

As you can imagine my choice caused some controversy. Looking back, I don't know why I told anyone but I have a habit of wearing my heart on my sleeve and so when asked, I told the truth. Everyone had an opinion. Some were supportive but some, like one of my instructors, were not. This instructor told me quite bluntly that I was murdering my horse by shooting her and so it became a very long week. When the day arrived for Freckles to be put to sleep I was emotionally drained, but I had made a decision that there should be no tears until Freckles had gone, and it is one I managed to stick to.

As we led Freckles out of sight of the other horses, my heart was beating loudly. I deliberately took some deep breaths to slow it down so that Freckles would not pick up on my anxiety, she however, remained calm throughout. I was not allowed to stand next to her for safety reasons, but I stood just behind the vet and still in her line of sight. BANG. Freckles dropped to the ground.

I knew in the instance that it happened, that I had made the right decision. It was so fast, there was no time for her to fear what was about to happen to her. As she dropped, so did I, and the tears flowed down my face as I sobbed and watched the blood trickle from her nose. The vet put a reassuring hand on my back and then stepped away. He gave me the time I needed to say goodbye. I put my hand on her warm neck and secretly said to her,

"Thank you, Freckles, for all your work in the school. I hope I made the right decision for you today."

I didn't expect a response to my question. I believed in a life after death for humans, and it was the first time I'd found that I hoped animals went to the same place when they died, too.

It only took a week for the answer to my question to start to come to me. The following Friday, when Cal and I had gone to bed, we both heard a horse trot passed the house. Now to be honest it was not possible for a horse to trot passed the house because there was a small wall in the way that would stop them. At the time, we didn't think about that.

"Your yard, your horse, your problem," Cal said. This clearly meant he didn't have any intention of coming out on the yard with me.

"What if there's someone out there?" I asked.

"You'll be okay if you take the dogs with you," Cal replied.

Twice more we heard the horse outside the farmhouse, so up I got. I put my dressing gown on, my wellies and with the help of the dogs and a torch, I ventured out onto the yard. It was pitch black as we had no street lights near us which was perfect for seeing the stars, but a little scary when you are wandering around on your own. I didn't want to disturb the horses so I didn't put any stable lights on, I simply focused the torch in each stable in turn to check all the horses were alright.

Eighteen stables later, we had gained a few horses since we moved in. This time it was clear they were all safely in their stables, so I went back to bed. That night it was a mystery what had caused both Cal and I to hear horse's hooves outside the house, but after sharing the story on the yard the next day I didn't think much more about it.

Until the following Friday that is. Yes, the same thing happened on the following Friday. Only this time with hooves cantering passed the farmhouse and me venturing out in pj's, dressing gown and wellies with the dogs and a torch. A quick walk around the yard in the dark only proved to find all the horses safely tucked up in their stables.

When it happened the third Friday, even Cal said to me,

"I don't suppose there's much point you going to check the yard," I agreed, but I'd started to wonder. Could it be possible that somehow Freckles was coming back to tell me she was okay? Could it be possible she was answering my question?

We never heard the hooves again after that third night, and it took some time before I was given possible confirmation that she was trying to reassure me. Now I am sure at this point you maybe thinking I was going a little crazy. I'm not offended if that is the case. I have believed in a life after death since my Mum died. I have talked to her since I was 6 and heard her voice talk back to me in my head. I had never ventured too far away from my Christian upbringing, except for talking to my dead Mum of course, but I secretly wished I could talk to more of my relatives who had passed. I was curious about all things spiritual, just not brave enough to let my thoughts be known.

As often happens in life, I was soon given an opportunity to get my answer. One of my adult clients, Yvonne, who also helped on the yard, said she went for 'readings' to a clairvoyant in Macclesfield. She said this lady didn't charge you, just simply take flowers or chocolates, or donate to the spiritualist church. I plucked up courage and asked Yvonne to make me an appointment for a reading.

It was early spring when I went for my first ever reading. As I got into the car I felt nervous. I was either going to find out it was my Mum that I had been talking to all these years, or that I was crazy. As you can imagine my anxiety rose as I drove. If you know Macclesfield you will know there are lots of small roundabouts as you approach the town. In a flower bed alongside one of these roundabouts was a whole bed of snowdrops. They were the first snowdrops I had seen that year and as I drove around the round-about, I fleetingly thought 'how beautiful'.

I found the lady's home, it was a little terraced house and so I carefully parked the car, picked up the flowers I had taken as payment and knocked on the door. The sweetest little old lady came to the door. She was just like your grandma with a warm smile and twinkly eyes.

"Come in dear, come in," she said.

Before we had even walked through the hallway, she said to me, "Now normally I take a while to get you seated and relaxed before I start, but there is a lady here who insists that I say to you right now,

'Yes, the snowdrops were beautiful'!"

I wanted to cry tears of joy, I didn't need any more proof. There was no one else in the car with me as I'd driven passed the snowdrops, and even if there had been the thought was in my head. At that moment, I knew my Mum was with me and giving me the proof of her existence that I so desperately needed. I hadn't been crazy all those years. I really did hear her voice.

The reading was magical. There were tears of joy, tears of sadness and so much proof that this lady was genuine, although after that first comment I didn't need it. After a little while the answer to my thoughts about Freckles came. This clairvoyant described Freckles to me, she reassured me that animals live on as well as human beings, and then she said,

"This horse wants you to know you made the right decision."

The relief I felt at that moment was enormous. In those days I had been a real worrier, I worried about everything and I had continued to question my decision long after Freckles had passed.

As I continued on my life path, I would learn how much worrying is a waste of energy and how detrimental it is to the life we are trying to create, but at that time, this lady had taken one of my biggest worries from my shoulders.

On that day, my faith that there is life after death for both human beings and for all our animal companions became very real to me. It also struck me that there was a lot more for me to learn.

> ***"There are more things in heaven and earth Horatio than are dreamt of in your philosophy"***
>
> *Shakespeare*

Chapter 6: The Teens at Holly Tree

Life at Holly Tree was busy. My favourite days of the week were Saturday and Sunday because the yard was full of children.

When I arrived at the riding school there were two teenagers who helped out on a Saturday, and a different two on Sunday, however, no other children were allowed to stay on the yard. As time went by more and more teenagers and then younger children asked to spend at least one, if not both of their weekend days on the yard. For many of them they didn't even get a free riding lesson for their efforts. They would arrive at 8am and not be picked up until at least 5pm, sometimes later if we were doing a children's party. They just wanted to be there, to be near the horses, to be a part of the Holly Tree family and their parents were happy for them to be with me.

In the early years, I did not do much teaching, so I spent the weekends supporting my clients and working on the yard with the kids. My favourite moments were to see some of the children grooming horses and plaiting manes and tails and to watch the teenagers mucking out and helping the clients with their ponies.

There would be wheelbarrows, spades and forks all over the place and piles of muck outside stable doors all waiting for a spare wheelbarrow because we never did have enough. There would be children making shapes out of our huge muck pile because I always told them it had to be neat and tidy and sometimes the muck pile would be so high the children could see over the roof of the stable block! It would be considered a health and safety nightmare now.

There was often music and laughter on the yard; it was a sort of organised chaos as kids worked with each other to take care of the horses. I used to stop for a moment and take it all in and my heart would sing. Yes, sometimes there were tears and arguments too, but I could usually dissipate those and the yard would go back to its happy industrious self. I was proud to see the children working together, taking orders from teenagers higher in the pecking order than themselves and always working as a team. That was my Holly Tree Family.

Even as I write this now, it brings a lump to my throat as I think of how special all this was. I often wished I could save those moments and bottle them up to revisit when life got tough and to remember when the jobs were finished and the yard emptied of children and dogs as they disappeared off together for lunch. I would often find them all huddled in a corner eating pot noodles and packed lunches which they shared with each other and my dogs. I dread to think of how much chocolate and crisps my dogs ate in those days but they all lived to a good old age. My days were truly happiest when I was surrounded by the teenagers, the younger children, the horses, ponies and dogs at Holly Tree. It was a magical place in many ways.

I learned a lot about teenagers during those years, and observed a mandatory transition that all our teenage girls seemed to go through where they were just plain miserable. The first time it happened, I wondered why the teenager kept coming up to the yard. Ellie had changed overnight from cheerful and helpful to stubborn and lazy. I really liked her and it saddened me at first. However, I soon realised that she kept coming because she still wanted to be with us.

It wasn't a quick process but eventually she came out of her teenage fog a more grown up version of her cheerful and helpful self. Ellie went on to pave the way for the other girls and eventually it became acceptable that, when these teenage girls went through their miserable phase, it was nothing to do with the rest of us. We would ignore their moods, not take their comments personally and wait for them to emerge out on the other side. It was true that the rest of the children had to 'carry' them through, but they trusted my judgment and did just that.

It was amazing how these teens and younger children adapted to the teenage journey of one of their mates. It was also great to see how they allowed the teenager in question the space to be miserable as they passed through their transition. The kids rarely commented on the lack of effort or reliability, but simply worked around them and allowed them to feel whatever it was they were feeling.

It would take months for a teenager to come out through the other side, but I believe our faith in them helped protect the friendships they had made with the others on the yard. It was always a joy to see a teenager emerge from their period of misery.

On top of this general teenage misery phase, I experienced all the usual teenage problems on the yard. From teens with no self -confidence to teens who were going out and getting drunk, from the teens with food issues to teens who claimed they were being abused, and above all, we had a yard full of teens who all at some point or other said their parents didn't understand them. Well, in their parents' defence they probably didn't. The teens didn't understand themselves, so really their parents had no chance. However, these were great kids on my yard and throughout all their teenage angst I found the greatest gift I could give them was to listen.

One teenager comes to mind, I will call her Jane, this lovely girl bounced onto the yard one day. She was a whirlwind of cheerful energy. Always smiling, always loud, and it was hard not to like her. She loved the horses, loved being at the yard and threw herself into the care of our animals. To this day Jane is a joy, but in those days her cheerfulness hid a troubled child. I honestly do not know how much of what she told me was true but she made wild accusations about what was happening to her at home. Her parents seemed lovely, but just to be on the safe side, I informed her school about what she had told me and asked them to keep an eye on her.

I knew that for her own safety it was important for me to share what she had told me in confidence. I hated doing this as I wanted to honour the trust that she'd put in me, but if there was any chance that she was in danger then I had to break that confidence.

At this point in time Jane loved being at the yard, but did not like going to school. It had become a rare occurrence for her to attend school every day of the week. I liked Jane a lot but wasn't quite sure I could believe everything she was saying. Eventually she said she was pregnant, this was incredibly difficult for me to hear as Cal and I were having real problems getting pregnant.

At that time we were in the middle of a round of IVF. That would be just typical I thought, Cal and I had been sensible and had waited until we had a home and a good regular income to start to try and conceive, only to find it wasn't that easy. I will return to this a little later, but suffice to say that it took every bit of my self-control not to break down in tears when Jane announced her news. After I had done all the 'poor me' thoughts, a small nagging thought came into my head could she be lying to me?' I decided to go along with what she was telling me and acknowledge her pregnancy.

My first action was to stop her from riding. I know many pregnant women ride well into their pregnancies, but the policy of the school was not to knowingly allow a pregnant client to ride. If for any reason she fell off and then miscarried, we could possibly be blamed and the client would definitely find it hard to forgive herself. I personally knew the kind of questions that go through your head when you have a miscarriage and I know I tortured myself with the question "Was it my fault?" Jane pleaded her case magnificently. It would be okay. She would be careful, she wouldn't do anything daft, she wouldn't fall off. I heard her words but stuck to my decision and wondered how the whole thing would play out.

The next week when Jane arrived at Holly Tree, she asked an instructor to allocate her a horse. I noticed her leading the horse into the school so I questioned what she was doing.

"It's okay" she said in a matter of fact way, "I had a miscarriage this week!"

I smiled inwardly as I accepted her explanation. I later gently questioned her about the events of the week and having had two miscarriages I knew that her related sequence of events bore no resemblance to the truth.

Clearly Jane had never been pregnant. I could have been angry with her, but she had no idea of the pain that her fake pregnancy had put me through.

However, I understood teenagers well enough to know that the lie was to get attention, which meant there was something not quite right in Jane's world. I hoped this new revelation meant that the things she had said about her family members were also not true. I decided not to get angry with her but to try and help her.

From where I was standing she seemed a bit lost and I wanted to help her find her way.

As Jane's time at the yard continued, it became clear she had a great connection to the horses and her sunny personality meant the clients loved her. If she would not attend school regularly, I knew she was giving herself a hard start in life. I asked her what she wanted to do when she left school? Her immediate response was to come and work for me but I steered her desire to work with horses towards courses she could study.

In all our discussions, all I did was listen and tell her I believed in her. When she asked where she could learn about horses, I advised her to have a look on the internet. When she found 3 different colleges and wanted to know what was the best course, I advised her to do some research. When she asked which college I thought was best, I suggested she should go and visit them to see which she liked best. Like a game of tennis her ball kept bouncing back into myside of the court and all I did was gently hit it back to her. She did all the research, all the running, she made all the decisions. Eventually she decided on a college and a course.

One of my clients tried to put Jane off saying there was no money in working with horses. That was true but this was about more than money. I knew that if Jane could find something to study that she was interested in, then she would stick at it. If she could complete one year at college, attend every lecture and hand in every piece of course work, her self-belief would grow and she would know what it was like to complete something. I knew that no matter what was going on in her world, the key to making things better was for her to feel good about herself and proud of what she had achieved.

No matter what the issue, the key to solving the problem is self-belief

Jane's story has an incredibly happy ending. She did go to college and complete her studies. In fact, she ended up doing a degree in equine studies. As part of her dissertation she did a presentation on horse licks where she singled out one particular company for selling the best licks for horses on the market. She did such a good job that her tutors suggested she make the same presentation to the company in question. When they heard her presentation, they immediately offered her a job selling the product. Now at the time Jane did not have a driving licence, but undeterred she accepted the job. She passed her driving test the day before she started her new job and was given a company car!

Amazingly, Jane was aware of the part I had played in helping her to get her life on track. For many years, every time something good happened to her she would tell me about it and thank me. Every time her gratitude touched my heart but I had to also remind her that she had done all the hard work herself. I wanted Jane to value herself and believe in herself and that is what happened.

My role had been like a small ripple in the pond that was her life, but our connection at that time had huge consequences for this young women. I saw Jane very recently at a horse show and she looked just the same as she had at the riding school 15 years before. She was selling a different product but was still cheerful, still full of energy and very content with her life. It was wonderful to see her.

I have followed the process that I used to help Jane many times with other teenagers. The biggest gift I have found that you can give any child, is the time to listen to them without ever judging their opinion. We all of us base our opinions on the given knowledge we have at the time, this means our opinions can and often do change as we travel through life, but this does not mean our opinions are not to be valued. Often the teenagers would see thing differently but I would always tell them,

"I hear what you are saying"

I wouldn't necessarily agree with them, but I would always acknowledge their right to have an opinion. After all, as they grow up we want them to have opinions so they can make good choices for themselves. We want to nurture them in a way that encourages them to think for themselves.

The biggest gift you can give to your child is the gift of your time, and that time is best used when you listen actively

The process that I used to help Jane can be summarised as follows:

- Take time to listen.
- Encourage action but let them decide what action to take.

- Congratulate them for each action they take, whether they get the outcome they desired or not.
- Brainstorm with them to help them decide what is next.
- Remind them how far they have come.
- When they reach a decision, or complete a task tell them how proud you are of them.

Teenagers want to find their independence, but at the same time they are desperate for your love and support. The main difference in parenting a teenager, to parenting a smaller child is that you have to stand back and let them learn by their own mistakes. This is a tough lesson for a parent, of course you want to protect them, you have protected them for many years but as they reach the pre-teen years and then become teenagers it is time to start letting go a little at a time. It is time to start helping them to learn how to stand on their own two feet I call this a **Circle of Trust**.

Your child stands in the centre of this Circle of Trust and you stand on the circle itself. When they are little, the circle is so small you can wrap your arms around them and keep them safe. As your child becomes older the circle gets bigger when you start to take small steps back from them and they learn to do more for themselves. In the early years, it could be tying a shoe lace, pouring a drink, riding a bike, playing in the garden without you watching them all the time. Your Circle of Trust grows quite organically in many ways.

One of the first times you may feel the circle growing could be when you let them go to the shops, or a friend's house by themselves. You know it is time to let them but my goodness, the very first time you do, you almost feel sick with nerves until you know they are safe again. Your Circle of Trust just became bigger.

When your child becomes a teenager, that Circle of Trust keeps growing as you give them more and more responsibility. As a teenager's frontal cortex, the decision-making area of the brain continues to develop well into their twenties, it can be a challenging time to help them learn to make good decisions. We expect them to think before they act but again because their brain is still growing, this is a skill that they must learn and every parent of a teenager knows the process is as painful for parent and child alike.

All this growth takes place within your Circle of Trust which gets bigger all the time. That circle will always be there no matter how old your child becomes. Even when they have children of their own and are starting a new Circle of Trust with their children; your Circle of Trust still grows. It is filled with your love, trust, respect, and pride in the adult your child has now become.

Chapter 7: Renovations

When I first moved into Holly Tree, I had high hopes that Cal would want to be involved with the riding school. Not necessarily by helping run the school on a day to day basis, but in my mind's eye, I could see him sitting on a small tractor harrowing the fields, or wandering along the boundaries with a hammer and nails mending broken fences. He was, and is, a very practical man and I believed, wrongly as it turned out, that he would love to be involved.

However, even though it was his decision to move there, it wasn't long before the riding school became an issue between us.

As I have said before, when I moved in I had no idea how to run a riding school. I came to horse riding late in life and whilst I had a beautiful horse, Rosie, I was not an experienced rider.

In the early days, I used to sit in the school next to the instructors as they gave the lessons so that I could learn how to teach horse riding. It's one thing to know how to give the instructions for walk, trot and canter, but quite another to know all the drills and exercises that the instructors used to teach a group lesson.

I was a teacher by profession, but teaching maths and teaching horse riding were very different. However, once I had learned the exercises, and then applied what I knew about teaching, it wasn't long before I was able to competently teach a riding lesson. In those early years, I only ever taught when an instructor couldn't come to work but by the time we closed the school some ten years later, I taught both Saturdays and Sundays and had found the children and adults alike all enjoyed my style of teaching.

In those early years , I would spend many hours in the school watching and learning and this caused lots of arguments with Cal. He was the one who had decided that I could run a riding school, but I believe he thought it would be a nice little job that would keep me at home.

Once we had moved to Holly Tree cracks started to appear in our relationship. As I built the school up, he hated the number of people coming and going on the yard. He hated the amount of time it took to care for the horses. He hated the knocks at the door and the constant phone calls, but most of all he hated that all these things revolved around me. He moaned at me for talking to my clients too much and suggested I would get more done if I stopped talking.

As stupid as this now sounds, I did try, but I soon realised that the clients came to my school because I was warm and friendly. They liked that I knew who they were and that I welcomed them onto the yard. I did, and do like talking to people, but I soon learned it was not simply a perk of my business but integral to it and so it was not advisable to stop, no matter how much time it saved me!

The riding school had put stress on my relationship with Cal, but added to this was also the extra stress of living with builders as we renovated the farmhouse.

When we had moved in, I never dreamed that we would practically rebuild the place. I must admit though when I first walked into the empty rooms on that first day, the ceilings had seemed claustrophobically low.

We had always intended to 'do up' the kitchen and bathrooms, and then to open up the staircase, but that was before it became apparent that Cal had to duck to get underneath the ceiling beams. Not a problem for me, but a very vocal one from Cal. He was not a man that swore, well not in front of me anyway, but it always amused me when I could hear him cursing as he hit his head on the beams when he walked from one end of the house to another. That sounds a little cruel, but even now I find myself smiling as I think of him swearing at the beams.

The decision was made that the ceilings had to be elevated by 18 inches so that Cal could live comfortably in our home. The consequence of this decision was that the roof had to be taken off and the first floor taken out.

At one point the house was only four walls and if the tarpaulin canopy had not been firmly fixed above those walls, you could have stood in the house and looked up at the stars. I mention the stars because they were amazing at Holly Tree. There were no street lamps or other light pollution, so on a clear night the sky shimmered with twinkling lights, they looked magical and I loved them. Getting back to the house, which was originally built in 1716, when they took the tiles off the roof the beams underneath looked a little like the Mary Celeste.

Cal had an amazing eye for detail, he was a cameraman after all. When the house was still only a shell he would ask me where I wanted light switches and sockets etc. At the time, I struggled to visualise what the rooms would look like when they were finished. I struggled to see where the stairs would be, where the furniture would go, where I would want to place lamps and therefore need sockets, or where I would want wall lights. Yes, when we started rebuilding Holly Tree, I struggled to visualise the end result but Cal could 'see' it all.

I guess this was what made him a great cameraman, he could always visualise the shot before he had created it. I have since learned that visualisation is a powerful tool in the process of creation. We often use it inadvertently when we imagine/visualise all the things that can go wrong. The Universal Laws of creation work whether we are focused on what we want or what we don't want, but it is our focus that is a vital part of the process. So those people who look on the negative side are always proven right by their fears becoming reality. It is literally a self-fulfilling process.

But I digress, at that point in my life I had no idea how powerful visualisation could be, and at that time I struggled to do it.

Visualisation is a powerful tool in the process of creation

As builders demolished and rebuilt, Cal rewired the whole house, always adding a few 'just in case cables.'

Actually, there were a lot of 'just in case' cables pushed and pulled through walls and under floor boards!

"Just one more" he would say. I grew to dread those words, as it was never an easy job to thread yet another cable in the tight space between the floor boards.

When we had done up the kitchen in our first house, we'd had to wait until we could afford the units that we wanted. That first kitchen was a galley kitchen, so we planned to do one side before the other giving us time to save up for quality cupboards and fittings; we had come a long way since then.

Cal had always wanted the best and now his income meant we could do all this work without waiting, which was both a blessing and a curse. Renovating Holly Tree was a huge undertaking and we lived in a mess for months. I say we, but to be honest, Cal's work regularly took him away from home, so he had periods of respite. During the time he was away he expected me to keep an eye on the builders, but to be fair, I had no idea what I was supposed to be keeping an eye on. He understood what they were doing, I was not so clear. From the early days of our move to Holly Tree the stress of the riding school, the builders and Cal's time away from home were all putting a strain on our marriage.

When the student is ready the teacher will appear

Another pressure came in the form of Christine James. Christine came to my yard as a client but she would soon become my teacher and my friend. I'm sure you have heard the saying that *when the student is ready the teacher will appear*. Well, I was ready, and the beautifully eccentric and individual Christine arrived.

Christine was already an accomplished horsewoman, in fact she had done a lot of riding in her earlier years, so she didn't want lessons, she simply wanted to hack through the beautiful country lanes. Riding with Christine was always an experience, I can remember riding out with her one day. I always put her on Brandy, my most faithful school mistress. Brandy was a 15.2hh cob who had been there, done it and got a whole wardrobe of t-shirts. Her reputation spread far beyond the riding school. People would phone me and ask if I still had Brandy and then usually go on to say that they were nervous for some reason and had heard that she was good in helping people rebuild their confidence. Her reputation was spot on, everyone who rode Brandy loved her and she remained part of the Holly Tree story for most of the time I was there.

As I said, Christine was an accomplished rider but she had her own way of doing things. She always rode with very loose reins and had a conversation with the horses through telepathy rather than body language!

One time when I rode out with her she was on Brandy as always and I was riding a chestnut gelding called Marcus. We always imagined that if Marcus had a voice he would speak in a very posh British accent and sound like he had been a Major in the Army, if you know what I mean. There was one thing that Marcus did not like, and that was to have a horse out in front of him. If anything went passed him at speed he was always up for a race. On this day, Christine and I were on the quiet country lanes with Christine who had been strolling slowly behind me, when suddenly I heard her say in a very firm voice,

"Brandy, this is not the speed we agreed!"

As she finished the sentence she flew passed me and Marcus. My heart jumped into my mouth. Marcus was always up for the challenge. I had no idea how I would stop him from racing with Brandy now she had passed him. His ears shot forwards. I shortened my reins. He snorted. I sat deep and took long deep breaths to try and hide my thoughts. He was on his toes but somehow I stopped him from breaking into a canter. I couldn't help but shout to Christine to shorten her reins, but she wasn't listening. She was however, continuing a very vocal conversation with Brandy and much to my amazement Brandy started to slow down. As Marcus and I caught up with them Christine threw her head back and laughed.

"There is life in the old girl yet!" she beamed, loving the spirit of this usually trustworthy horse. We were all okay, no one had been injured, but I had been anxious whilst Christine had blissfully surrendered and allowed Brandy to enjoy her freedom. As always, I learned a lot that day. Christine and I laughed and chatted all the way home, revelling in the beauty of Brandy showing us a spark of the horse she had been in her youth. We were honoured that she would share her true spirit with us in a place where she could have some fun without putting us in danger. Brandy's eyes were bright, her head held high as she ignored the limitations that her aging was causing on her body, and she had a spring in her step as she too seemed to enjoy the moment.

So, Christine, my next teacher burst into my life very loudly. Her job or purpose in life was to connect people with their loved ones who had died, she was what we would call a Medium.

Cal would say that she looked like one of 'those sort of people'. As you can imagine, having talked to my Mum since I was 6, I was fascinated by the possibility of talking to people who had left their human bodies, but Cal was not. In fact, not only did he not like it, he was very vocal in his opinion that it was all rubbish. I think he must have felt frightened by the whole idea; he never had a nice word to say about Christine or her appearance, and in my experience people often lash out when they are frightened or boxed into a corner.

As I said, Christine was an eccentric in the best of ways, so her outfits were usually very colourful, her shoes often had stars on them and her hair was dyed a deep jet black. I agree that you could not miss her, I agree that she was very loud, but neither of those things gave me any reason to fear her. Far from it, I felt drawn to her. It wasn't long before Christine was teaching me to do some healing and to embrace my own abilities as a psychic medium.

When Christine was on the yard everyone knew about it. The children were drawn to her and the animals took notice of her. She would go to the gate of a field and get a specific horse to come to her without making a sound. She simply called them telepathically and over they came. We often told the children not to be too noisy around the horses and ponies because they are sensitive creatures, but all that seemed to go out of the window when Christine was around. And when one of my cats fell off a stable roof the teenager who rescued it didn't run to me but ran to Christine to get healing for the cat.

Happily, with a little help from Christine, and giving up one of his nine lives, my cat survived the experience. As Christine came to Holly Tree more and more often Cal complained that people would be calling us a spiritual riding school. He said this as a criticism but I thought that sounded lovely.

One of my first 'aha' moments when I was learning to do some healing involved a horse called Colin the Cob, who was a magnificent horse. He was 16hh and looked like he was a Shire cross somewhere along the way. He had one very gentle looking eye but also one eye that because of the markings on his face, made him look quite angry. He was a real character. One of my clients who loved Colin very much said that he would be a 'biker with a heart of gold' if he were human. She used to have picnics with him and make him a cake with ingredients that are good for horses. Sometimes she put a drop of Guinness into his cake until the day she added a little too much and I was worried that he was getting drunk!

Colin was a big bulky horse. He had strong solid legs with white socks, large feathers and a broad white blaze down his nose and a huge sense of humour. When a rider tried to get on him he would often move his front leg and place his hoof gently over the riders boot so they couldn't get their foot off the ground! You couldn't help but love this horse.

Colin had come to me from a horse dealer. I was wary of dealers in general but this lady used to let me try before I bought, so the horses would come to the school for 2 or 3 weeks before I had to decide. Despite not liking the vet and therefore failing his vetting, Colin fit into the school straight away, so he stayed and became a Holly Tree horse.

There was an air of sadness around Colin. He was physically very healthy when he came to us, but he had a huge scar down one of his legs and he was frightened of bright shiny objects and loud noises. Even the light shining on his water trough would be enough to stop him from drinking in the early days, and when I tried to use a metal tape measure to measure him for a rug he nearly had a heart attack. Christine 'communicated' with him and told me he had been working and was in a nasty accident. She wouldn't tell me the details as she said it would upset me and stop me from seeing the horse in front of me. However, she did say that someone had paid for the care Colin needed to get his physical health back, but the psychological damage meant he could no longer do his job and had to be sold. Christine's version of events rang true because without his scar Colin would never have found his way to my riding school.

We worked hard with Colin to help him overcome his fears and Christine decided he would be a good candidate for me to practise my newly acquired healing skills. Colin loved receiving healing energy. His head would lower, his eyes shut and his back-leg bend in a relaxed position. I could see he was enjoying the time that I spent with him and I could feel that the energy in his stable was calm and peaceful but I had no idea if I was doing the healing thing right!

Anyone with a perfectionist streak will understand my need to do something right. I could never understand how anyone could call me a perfectionist, because from where I was standing I never got anything right. Then one day the penny dropped and I realised; the very thought that I never got anything right was because I held myself up to some ridiculously high expectations.

Two miraculous things happened when I was healing Colin's leg. Firstly, I was with him in his stable one evening and it was dark outside, so I had the lights on in his stable. Everyone had gone home but I was determined to stick to the daily healing sessions as Christine had suggested. On this evening, just as my usual thoughts of 'am I doing this right' started to surface, I suddenly saw a network of purple light across the floor of the stable. It was like a mesh of hexagons and I was fascinated. The light went around Colin's legs and my legs too for that matter, across the shavings bed and over the concrete floor. It was beautiful and I had to stop for a moment to take in its beauty.

Although it was an odd occurrence, I wasn't afraid because as I saw the lights I also felt the most gorgeous feeling of love. I didn't see anyone or anything, just these purple lights across the floor but tears rolled down my face as I connected with the intense feeling of love. A bit confused about what was happening, I phoned Christine. She laughed and said,

"Good. I asked them to give you a sign tonight."

When Christine referred to 'them', she was always talking about our spirit guides or our loved ones in spirit, I was amazed. I never did see the lights again when I was healing. It was like that was a special sign to help me believe.

What I did see though, was the hair starting to grow back on the scar on Colin's leg. That in itself would have been a miracle to me, but there was more.

Anyone with horses will know that when a horse is injured, the hair that grows back over the wound will be white. However, the scar on Colin's leg was about 10 inches long and although some of it went over the white sock area, the rest was surrounded by brown hair. The miracle in this case was that when the hair started to grow back it was white as expected in the sock area, but brown on the rest of the scar. I was so impressed, not that I had caused this to happen but that by working with universal energy the scar on his leg was able to heal.

I told everyone; the staff, the teenagers, my friends, everyone that is except my clients and my husband. It was acceptable not to tell the clients, after all, this was the beginning of my journey and I wasn't confident enough to share with them, but it saddened me that I couldn't tell Cal.

As my curiosity with all things spiritual began to grow, the distance between myself and my husband also began to get bigger. I thought I was doing the right thing by keeping quiet in order to keep the peace. Now I know that keeping quiet had stopped Cal from seeing who I was, and my holding back in this way would contribute to me eventually losing my own identity.

When you don't speak your truth to prevent upsetting someone else; the person you hurt is yourself

Chapter 8: Goodbye Mary, Hello Rebecca

Holly Tree became my life. All of life was represented in this one relatively small community which consisted of myself, my staff, the teenagers and children who helped on the yard, the clients, the horses and ponies, and the dogs and cats. I don't think we ever had a Holly Tree wedding but there were births and deaths. There was laughter and tears and there were arguments and resolutions.

Cal always said I attracted some strange people to the yard, and to be honest, at one time I did think he had a point. With hind sight however, I think all the 'strange' people that I attracted were my teachers, although I didn't recognise them as such at the time. And maybe, just maybe, they were also lonely and looking for something, the same something I had always looked for... a place where they felt they belonged.

After 5 years at Holly Tree I think I was finding my feet. I had learned an awful lot about horses and human nature in that time and I had started to feel a little more confident, although the feeling that one day I would be found out stayed with me until the day I left.

I lost my main instructor because although she was happy to be my main adviser regarding the school, when I had begun to trust my own judgment and wanted things done differently to her, our relationship became challenging.

It saddened me to think this lady had helped me to build Holly Tree, but rather than celebrate our success and continue to work together; the more confident I became, the more difficult our relationship was.

One day the tensions became too much and we argued. I had an ear infection that day, which for obvious reasons made it difficult for me to hear. I was in the school leading a pony in a beginner's lesson which this particular instructor, I will call her Mary, was taking. In those half hour lessons, the riders were about 6 years old and every pony had an adult or a teenage leader with it. When I was at the far end of the school I couldn't hear Mary, who was sitting in a corner at the opposite end.

At this point, the children were learning to trot and it's always a little tricky at this stage because the riders don't have much balance. We used to take their reins off them and tie them in a knot so the rider wouldn't mistakenly think that holding onto the reins would keep them safe. Also, the riders couldn't hurt the pony's mouth by pulling on the rein to get out of the saddle for a rising trot. Anyway, I made the unforgivable mistake of not hearing my instruction from Mary to let my pony and rider trot to the back of the ride. She raised her voice and asked me again. This time I heard, not the exact words but I knew she was shouting at me. I requested a minute to finish tying the reins up and making sure my rider was safe.

Suddenly, Mary screamed at me across the school. Her words were angry and cutting and I felt them in every part of my body. I couldn't cause a scene in my own school because all the parents were watching, so I made sure the rider was safe and we trotted to the back.

"At last," she commented. No encouraging comment to the rider, just a sarcastic remark aimed at me. As the lesson continued, so did the sarcasm. No matter where I was in the school, she kept repeating everything to make sure I had got it. I was getting more and more angry but didn't want to cause a scene. Seeing my distress, another friend, who regularly helped with the yard, quietly offered to lead the pony as I passed the main door. I accepted and exited the school.

I was embarrassed and furious. How could she show me up in my own school? Her behaviour was totally disrespectful. I decided to speak to Mary after she had finished the last lesson of the day. I had one more half hour lesson to go, so I made myself busy. When Mary eventually came out of the school, the clients had all gone and only the helpers were left on the yard. Mary marched towards me furious. I was calm but ready to speak my truth. I had no intention of arguing, no intention of sacking her. I simply wanted to stop her from ever treating me like that again.

Surprise, surprise, Mary didn't see the situation the same way that I did. She decided that I'd embarrassed her and screamed at me,

"Don't ever treat me like that again!" For most of my life I am proud to state that I am not an angry person. I did not 'do' anger. I now know how damaging it can be to bury my anger but this was not a problem on this day, I saw red. Me? Treat her like that? How dare she? My anger exploded like Vesuvius. I couldn't control the words that came out of my mouth, and whilst I can't remember exactly what I said, I am very aware that I didn't use any of the mediation skills that I now have.

My anger would have continued except for one thing. To the right of where Mary and I were having our confrontation there was on old wooden shed that we grandly called the feed room. It was very run down and there was no door. Inside the feed room were 6 helpers ranging in age from 8 to 15 years old. They were shocked to hear the shouting, and like a scene from a film, they looked around the edge of the door frame.

As I glanced in their direction, all I could see was one face above another, 6 faces in a vertical line wearing expressions of absolute shock. I so wanted to laugh. Seeing the kids like that, they completely disarmed me but I couldn't lose face. I quickly brought my argument with Mary to a conclusion. She exited, throwing a final comment that she was not coming back.

As Mary left the child and teen helpers fell out of the feed room and I burst into laughter. They cheered when they heard Mary was leaving, mainly because the atmosphere on the yard had not been very comfortable in recent weeks, and that was probably because my approach was much softer than Mary's.

I will always be grateful for the help I got from all the Holly Tree kids. Being surrounded by them week in week out was bliss for me, and if I could have run the riding school solely with teenagers instead of the adults, it would have been a lot easier.

I know that thought may shock you, but in my experience the teenagers who came to the yard were hard working, respectful and fun. Yes, we had our ups and downs. Yes, I had to set my boundaries but working with the teenagers and younger children and the horses was an absolute joy for me. I don't want to offend the many loyal Holly Tree staff that I had over the years, as they were also amazing, but I did have some who really challenged me, like Mary. Have you ever heard this saying?

A friend may come into your life
for a reason, a season or for life

I believe that many people have come into my life as friends, but the friendship has challenged me because that friend was there for a reason, a reason that would help me to grow.

As you will discover, I have had issues with many women who I believed were strong women but, at some point in every one of those difficult relationships, I've had to learn to put my boundaries down. It always amazes me that as a teacher, setting boundaries was something that came naturally. However, with adults, I've had much more of a problem learning to value my opinion and stand my ground.

Have you ever had someone tell you that you just needed to toughen up? Me too, often. Like my 'not talking' experiment I did try to toughen up, but with little success. It didn't feel like me so I made a conscious decision, if being nice meant that from time to time someone would take advantage of me and cause me pain, then that was okay with me! I would rather be nice than tough.

I smile when I think back, how on earth can it ever be okay to allow someone to cause me pain? I now understand that being nice is perfectly acceptable, but if you cannot learn to know your boundaries and state your boundaries, you are not respecting yourself. In fact, every time I took bad behaviour from another person I was saying I DO NOT MATTER.

I couldn't have been further from my learning and understanding. In truth, I had stood my ground with Mary when she had pushed me so far. I had felt righteous indignation at how she had treated me. We will come back to that phrase, as I now know it is part of my pattern, but in the Holly Tree days I was clearly choosing to learn the hard way.

Learning to set our own boundaries is one of the most important lessons in life

So, I was choosing to learn the hard way at Holly Tree; Cue Rebecca, not her real name. Rebecca arrived on my yard in 1999 like an angel sent from God, or so I thought at the time. I needed a new Yard Manager and before I even advertised she had arrived on my doorstep. Nothing was too much trouble for Rebecca. In those early days, she always said yes. Whatever I asked her to do, the answer was yes. She handled the horses, the clients, and the kids on the yard and she seemed to do it in an amiable and knowledgeable way. In her early days at Holly Tree she was a breath of fresh air and we had a lot of fun. What followed though was incredibly unnerving.

At the time that Rebecca arrived, I was going through a really difficult time in my marriage. 1999 was my annus horribilis as Cal and I were drifting further and further apart. He was working away a lot and whenever he came home, he found fault with me or the house within minutes of arriving.

I realise now that when he walked in, I was always holding my breath, waiting to see what would be wrong. This wasn't a great way to greet him. I didn't welcome him so he always found fault; it was a vicious circle. No matter what I did, it never seemed to be enough. I was struggling behind closed doors, and Rebecca clearly took advantage of this. She saw me as weak and easy to manipulate and what she was doing crept up on me very slowly.

She started to put barriers down between me and my staff/helpers on the yard. She would stop people from coming to the house, telling them not to bother me as my marriage was breaking down. She even told clients that I was getting a divorce.

The reputation of my riding school was built on me. and spreading lies that I was getting divorced, was not good for business. Things were bad with Cal but at that point we hadn't considered divorce. That consideration did come later in the year, but not at this point. Cal and I were childhood sweethearts, whatever the problem was between us, I believed and hoped that we could work through it. Slowly, slowly my contact with people diminished. Even when I tried to go out onto the yard, Rebecca would stop me and say she had everything in hand and I wasn't to worry. And sadly, I allowed her to do this.

Rebecca also targeted my friends. First of all, she would socialise with me and my friends, then I realised she was socialising with my friends without me. I felt a bit like a kid at school for thinking 'she's taking my friends off me.'

It felt ridiculous to be having such thoughts as an adult, so I kept pushing them to the back of my mind, but no matter how hard I tried I began to feel left out. Rebecca became inseparable with one friend and then she caused a permanent rift with another. This friend, who I will call Ida, was a local business women who had originally come to the riding school with a group of her friends. Slowly, but surely her friends stopped coming to the lesson, but Ida and her partner continued riding and Ida started to help on the yard when she could. We became friends, close friends. I enjoyed her company and we spent a lot of time together, mainly on my yard. Ida and I had known each other for 4 years when Rebecca turned up at the yard. To this day, I don't know what Rebecca said to Ida, who she had only known for a few short months, but whatever was said it caused a catastrophic rift in our friendship.

In the beginning, there was just an uncomfortable feeling between us. You know the one. You can't put your finger on it, but something feels different. Suddenly you are conscious of the conversations you are having and thinking about the words you are using. Communication becomes stilted and difficult.

Eventually I decided I had to talk to Ida about the situation, and so I called in at her house to speak to her. It was hard to say some of the things I had to say without sounding childish, but I did think I had managed to clear the air that evening. However, one phrase stuck in my head; Ida had said that she couldn't repeat to me what Rebecca had said because she'd promised Rebecca not to! I naturally questioned this quite strongly. Why would it be okay to believe something 'not very nice' about a person you had been in a close friendship with for 4 years? Why wouldn't you want to talk to your friend about that? Why would you trust someone you had known less than 6 months? There were lots of questions in my head.

I couldn't understand why my friend Ida would be loyal to someone she hardly knew. However, on the evening that we 'made up' I let that one go. I was so happy to think that Ida and I were back on amiable terms, that I just filed the anxiety that I felt around the whole loyalty thing. I should have known I couldn't let it go. For me friendship, in fact any healthy relationship, is based on honesty and trust.

A healthy relationship is based on honesty and trust

My 'why's' simmered under the surface, until one day when we were having yet another difference of opinion, I threw it back at her quite strongly. Ida was genuinely shocked. Of course she was. She had released the thought months ago. She thought I had accepted her loyalty to Rebecca because I had silenced my truth.

This was not one of my better qualities at the time. I often backed down, did anything to prevent confrontation but then something that didn't sit comfortably with me would always eat away at me. I would then either get angry, which as you know I do not often do, or walk away feeling very hurt, which was my usual choice.

As I have now learned it's not a healthy situation to deal with my feelings in this way. I love the wisdom that comes with life's challenges, but it isn't easy to appreciate the personal growth at the time. My challenge to Ida's lack of loyalty to me was the beginning of the end of our friendship. I did end up buying a beautiful mare because of the break down in our relationship, but that is another story for later. At that point, Rebecca had succeeded in her plan to isolate me from my friends so that she could step into my place.

What followed was quite scary to think about. To be honest, I can now see very clearly when people are manipulating me, or others, but it took a long rocky road before I was able to do that. At this point in my life I had no idea what this 'angel' who had come into my yard was doing, and even now I am not sure that she consciously set out with a plan to take my life.

In the following months she continued her manipulation. She isolated me from my friends and my business, she moved into my house, she encouraged me to drink a lot more than I was used to so she could spread rumours about me not coping. I found it increasingly difficult to stand up to her. Eventually she went after my husband and it was only at that stage that I said NO MORE.

For the next few months she used the drama in her life to manipulate me. Do you know anyone who does that? Are you allowing someone else's drama to affect your life? Unless you can see how these people manipulate you, it's very easy to get drawn in. Gosh with hindsight it's so easy to see, but when I was treading water in this situation, it felt like a nightmare that I couldn't wake up from.

Chapter 9: The Messenger

As I have said 1999 was one of the worst years of my life. My marriage was going downhill and no matter what I did, I didn't seem to be able to fix it. In September of that year it was Cal's 40th birthday and I wanted to do something special for him to show him how much I still loved him.

He'd always wanted to go to New York, so I chose to arrange a surprise trip. Now this was not easy. In all the years I had known Cal, he was a bit of a workaholic. He was always frightened that he would miss an opportunity if he turned work down.

I can remember in the early years, when he was thinking of leaving the BBC to go freelance, his justification was that he could work less hours for the same money and we would get more time together. What a joke that turned out to be. Initially he was nervous of making the jump from the safety of the BBC so when he first left he took a job with Sky news. I have to laugh now when I think about it. He spent the first few weeks of his freedom stood outside Strangeways prison in Manchester watching the prisoners on the roof! He was not happy. There wasn't much creativity being a news cameraman and we never really adapted to a phone call at 4 or 5 in the morning telling him where the news story was that day.

It didn't surprise me when after 3 months he handed in his notice.

We'd made a conscious decision when Cal left the BBC that we could afford to live on my teaching wage until his work started to come through. It wasn't long before that happened and he was offered work on a drama called Prime Suspect. Life took off after that. He was always in the right place at the right time and seemed to go from one quality drama to the next. Little did we know in those early days of good quality television dramas that he would one day work on big budget films such as Troy, Gravity and the Harry Potter films. Cal's focus and skill got him where he is, but he was not great at holidays.

In fact, at that point we had only had one holiday abroad together in the 25 years I had known him. So, with hope in my heart, I booked New York and got one of his friends who was a Director, to book him for a job that didn't exist. That way I could be sure he was free to go to New York.

How we kept New York a secret until the very last minute, I'll never know. Two days before we were due to fly out, the Director who was in on the secret said he may have to tell Cal to protect his assistant. Evidently Cal was giving the assistant a hard time for not sending him a call sheet. I held my breath.

The next day I told Cal he didn't have a job because we were going away, but I didn't say where. It wasn't until we got to the airport and walked into the Business Class check- in for the flight to New York that he knew where he was going. The delight on his face was worth all the effort. When Cal smiled his whole face lit up and his eyes sparkled. He could change the atmosphere in a room when he was genuinely happy, just by smiling. Sadly, I'd seen little of that smile in 1999, but I now had high hopes that our trip could rekindle the love we clearly had for each other.

I had spared no expense on this trip. As I have already stated we flew business class. I had chosen a Hotel that overlooked Central Park. There was a helicopter ride booked and a trip to Niagara Falls on his actual birthday. This was a fun packed 5 days. Time for us to be together and have fun and that is what we did. I'm not a great fan of big cities but I loved New York. Every day we laughed and joked together as we discovered all that New York had to offer. We held hands as we walked from one tourist attraction to the next.

I felt like we were a couple again, we were comfortable in each other's company, and we agreed about which parts of New York we wanted to see. During the day I felt proud to be standing next to this amazing man, my husband, but at night as we arrived back at the hotel Cal would play the 'I'm tired' card and the physical side of our relationship was never rekindled. I was tired too and very disappointed that Cal would hold my hand during the day but didn't want to touch me when we were behind closed doors. The reason for this would become clear the following March but at this point I felt hurt and confused.

The holiday was good fun but we were more like brother and sister than man and wife.

When we returned home, things didn't get any better. When I booked the tickets to New York, I also booked 2 tickets to St Lucia because my sister was getting married there in the December. Cal refused to go. I begged him to but he dug his heals in.

"Why would I want to go to St Lucia with your sister and her friends?" he asked incredulously. Did he really want an answer to that question? I didn't understand. We didn't have to spend all the time with Julie, but we would get lots of time together in the Caribbean. What's not to like? How could he say no? Well he did, very vehemently, so I marched back to the travel agents. It may seem strange now but in those days we didn't book our own holidays on line!

"Is it possible to trade 2 economy class tickets for one business class ticket?" I asked. If I was going all the way to the Caribbean on my own I was going in style! I explained why I needed to make the change and suddenly the ladies in the travel agent were buzzing around me, happy to be a part of my attempt at self-empowerment. It was soon done.

I went home with a smile on my face to be greeted by an incredulous Cal. "What, you're going without me? You've paid for business class? You can't go on your own. I won't let you."

Seriously? He expected me to miss my only sister's wedding because he didn't want to go? I couldn't not go. Except for our Dad, who I knew would not go, I would be Julie's only relative at the wedding, I had to be there. I wanted to be there. And yes, I was capable of travelling all by myself. That last statement did make me a little nervous but I wasn't going to admit it to Cal.

As I sat on the plane in my business class pod, I felt sad that Cal didn't want to be with me. What does it say about your marriage if your husband doesn't want to go to the Caribbean with you? I hadn't asked him to go to Blackpool, no disrespect to Blackpool. I had asked him to go to St Lucia. I seriously began to think that my marriage was over and my stand for my freedom now had a bitter sweet taste. However, I chatted to the man in the pod beside me, who ironically was a wildlife cameraman, as we waited for take-off and I made a conscious decision to enjoy my trip. Little did I know what my trip had in store for me.

At this point I think I need to tell you about a psychic reading I had been given earlier in the year. Since my first trip to a psychic medium, I had grown to love the experience of having a reading done, and so I ventured to receive readings from other psychics that had been recommended to me.

The reading that year came from a lovely elderly gentleman, I was really enjoying my reading until he told me that I would have an affair. What?? Me?? I don't do that sort of thing! I was so insulted. I didn't believe in affairs. I was loyal. I loved my husband. I would never do that to him. Or would I? When I got very upset at what this medium had said this elderly gentleman took hold of my hand in a very grandfatherly way and said,

"Okay, can you accept that a messenger is coming your way? Will you be open to his message?" I backed down.

"Maybe," I replied. 'Okay, I can be open to a message." He went on to say this messenger was about 10 years younger than me, he was in one of the Forces; he was tall, had broad shoulders and a lovely smile and that when I met him the conversation would feel effortless, as if I had known him before.

"Okay," I replied, "I'll take that." A message from a younger man I could accept.

Your thoughts maybe way ahead of me at this point, but yes, that messenger was at the wedding. He was in a relationship too, but was on his own in St Lucia; fate had thrown us together. Most of the people at the wedding were in couples, so this lovely young man and I drifted towards each other. We talked a lot, we laughed a lot. and he listened to me. Isn't that just the classic statement from people who are in tough relationships and fall for someone else? Being heard is just so attractive.

We all want to be heard

It took until the day of the wedding before I made a conscious decision to cross the line.

The wedding day was unconventionally lovely. At the end of the night there was just my sister and her new husband, my young messenger and myself left, when this young man suddenly said to my sister,

"You can't be the last to leave your own wedding!" My ears pricked up at the statement. What would I do? I instinctively knew where this was going, but my head was not sure I dare go there.

As Julie paused to answer the question, her new and slightly inebriated husband lent back on his chair and fell backwards into a hedge. We couldn't help but laugh. He was not hurt but clearly it was time for them to go home.

My young messenger then made it clear he would make sure I got back to my hotel safely. I didn't object, so Julie and her husband left. I bought myself a bit more thinking time by agreeing to another drink and then by making this kind man walk me back to my hotel.

It was a lovely walk, but not after a whole day of wedding celebrations. My poor feet were complaining all the way home. They had been squeezed into the same shoes all day, and although for the most part were comfortable, they were definitely not after 12 hours in the heat.

As I walked and talked to my messenger, I was also having a conversation with myself. What were my instincts saying? My body surprisingly had no problem with the idea, it was my head that was stuck in the 'rights and wrongs' of what I was about to do. I honestly felt my marriage was over. Actions speak louder than words and Cal's decision not to come out to St Lucia was screaming at me. Who wants to be in a relationship with someone who doesn't want to go on holiday with them, not even to the Caribbean? The closer I got to my hotel, the clearer my answer became and the more nervous I got.

By the time we had reached the hotel door, I had already justified my decision to invite my messenger in because the room had a lounge area where we could sit and talk!! Right, as if that was all I was saying when I invited him in. The door was opened. The line was crossed and there was no turning back.

My head was still fighting with my decision as I made my home situation clear, but my body was ahead of me as I let my fears go and opened up to the joy of being held, kissed and caressed. As the daylight approached, we fell into bed and snuggled together as we allowed sleep to wash over us, free from the guilt which didn't surface until later that morning.

I woke rather abruptly to a knock on the door. It was Julie and her husband calling to walk me to breakfast. What should I do? What could I say? This was their wedding and this man, my messenger, was related to my sister's new husband. I was letting her down. As my mind went into over drive there were a couple more knocks on the door and then silence.

"Have they gone?"

"I think so," I replied.

We looked at each other and giggled. it was like being two naughty school children and I was nearly forty!

The pleasure of being with a man who could see me and wanted to be with me, followed by the guilt of breaking my marriage vows and letting my sister down, weighed heavily over me throughout the holiday. We tried to hide our connection, but Julie's new husband soon guessed and with his Yorkshire sense of humour gently ribbed me about it. My sister's reaction when she eventually found out was a relief. She was surprised but quite amused to find out that I was not quite so perfect as she'd thought.

The relationship brightened up my trip to St Lucia and as I sat on the plane to go home, I wondered how I could have found my value and self-respect by doing something I did not approve of! The message was clear; I deserved to be treated better, but that would only happen when I started to respect myself and value who I am. I had put Cal on a pedestal; he was good at everything he did, which made me feel a bit of a failure. Well a lot of a failure to be honest. My self-esteem had taken a battering and it was time to do something about that.

The message from my messenger was to value me.

Know your own worth

I had heard that message once before many years ago, but I hadn't quite known what it meant. At the time Cal and I were living in London. Cal was in his first year at the BBC and I was at the University of London doing my first year of a degree course in Maths.

We had lived on the ground floor of a lovely house on the edge of Ealing and it had everything we needed except a washing machine, so I'd visit the launderette over the road. On this day when I entered the launderette there was only one man sitting in there alone and he smiled at me as I walked through the door. I instantly felt safe with him. He was a little dishevelled but seemed harmless.

I put my washing in the machine and started to talk to him. It seems he was an out of work actor waiting for his next job. He was older than me, I would say he was probably in his 50's. Anyway, as his wash cycle came to an end he picked up a small black bag that looked like an old-fashioned doctors case and put the still wet washing into his bag and headed for the door. It all seemed a little surreal and then he shared his parting gift. As he was about to leave he turned back to me and said,

"If you don't remember anything else from this conversation remember these words; know your own worth," and with that said, he turned and left the launderette.

I was a bit surprised, but I never forgot his advice. It took years for me to understand the importance of what he had said to me that day, but I have carried his words with me ever since. I have often wondered if that man was real, or if he was an angel sent to share a gem of guidance with me. I know when I was with him I felt incredibly safe. Whoever he was, he was the first messenger that told me to value myself, and now it had taken a second messenger to remind me of that advice.

I headed home on the 23rd December 1999 with the intention of asking Cal for a divorce, but I decided to get through Christmas and New Year first. Little did I know how the next few months would play out.

I know my psychic reading had told me only to expect a messenger and not a new partner, but the emails from the Caribbean kept lifting my spirits, reminding me how someone else could see me not as a constant irritation, but as a beautiful human being.

Christmas and New Year came and went and then the s*** hit the fan so to speak. I was at a friend's house when the phone rang.

"You'd better come home. I have found your emails." My heart raced. He couldn't have found emails; I deleted them and then I had cleared all the deleted emails. How on earth could he find emails? Oh God, I said things in those emails that I would not want Cal to hear. Things that would hurt him. I did want a divorce, but I wasn't cruel.

The hour's journey home was a blur. I felt afraid of how Cal would greet me, but relieved that I could now ask for the divorce. I was shaking from head to toe as I tried to drive home safely.

Cal had pages and pages of printed emails in his hands. As I looked at the words, my words, they were surrounded by symbols and gobbledegook. How had Cal got these emails? Somehow he must have gone into the hard drive of my computer to find them. What had I said or done to make him think he needed to look?

He was furious. He screamed and shouted at me but I quietly stood my ground. I apologised for the way he had found out and told him I wanted a divorce, but I hadn't thought it was fair to ask for one at Christmas. Even as I said the words, I realised how hollow they sounded.

The truth is, there is no good time to ask for a divorce. It hurts like hell whatever time of year you ask for it. Cal was incensed, over and over he kept asking me how I could do it. He was stuck on the thought of me jumping into bed with a man I hardly knew. This I didn't get. Why would he want me to lie and cheat for longer so I would have got to know this man better before I slept with him? Where's the logic in that? It was a long night.

He called me all the names under the sun, but he didn't want me to leave him. In fact, when I tried to walk out, he grabbed me by the ankles like a scene from a film and begged me not to go. I was confused.

It took until March before I was brave enough to seek the advice of a family solicitor. I sat in the big black chair and admitted the terrible thing I had done. He looked at me and said,

"Are you sure your husband hasn't done this to you first?"

"Yes, I'm sure," I replied. Of course, hearing that Cal had broken our marriage vows first would ease my guilt, but no I didn't believe he had. I thought Cal was honest, he couldn't lie. If he ever had an affair, I felt sure that he would come home and tell me.

Later in my life another man would tell me that no man is that brave. It made me giggle when he said it, but at this point in my life, I didn't equate honesty with bravery.

The solicitor told me to go home and check Cal's mobile phone bills. He wouldn't go any further with our meeting until I did.

Reluctantly I got the bills out. The itemised sections had become so big in recent months that I'd filed them in a separate place to the invoices. How stupid could I be? The tears rolled down my face when the same number appeared on the pages over and over. Phone calls and text messages, day after day in the early hours of the morning and late at night. I checked the days that we had been away in New York and even then, when Cal was encouraging me to go for my morning run in Central Park, he was using the time to phone his mistress. He had been cheating on me for a whole year! A whole year! No wonder 1999 was so horrible and no wonder he wouldn't come to St Lucia with me. No surprise either that he thought it would have been better for me to get to know my messenger before sleeping with him.

My honest as the days long husband wasn't very honest at all. He had kept this up for a whole year. I phoned him.

"Are you having an affair?"

"Yes," came the reply. No denial. No explanation. No softening of the truth. Just the fact; I saw red.

How could he have given me such a hard time when he had been cheating on me for so long?

In a strange way, having done what I did helped me to understand how Cal could have fallen into this relationship, but the same did not seem to be true in reverse. And not only was he having an affair, but clearly some of my friends knew about it.

One friend had asked my advice about telling a 'good' friend that her husband was having an affair. I could remember the moment and my advice. I should have said 'I would never shoot the messenger, but a lot of people do,' Instead, I said, 'be careful, lots of women shoot the messenger' I had ended the conversation. She couldn't share the truth after my advice, but I suddenly knew she had tried to tell me. Another friend had told me,

"Cal is shitting on his own doorstep," I asked him to tell me more, but he wouldn't.

Clearly the only person who was not getting this was me. Did it make me feel less guilty knowing what Cal was doing? Yes, a little. Did I feel any better? No, I felt worse. I felt a fool, a stupid fool. While I was trying hard to fix our marriage he was playing carefree bachelor with another woman in our second home. I say another woman. In truth, she turned out to be a child, a 23-year-old child, the daughter of a Monty Python actor.

With hindsight, I realise this was the first time I had seen how clearly Cal put his life into little boxes. The reality in one box didn't affect the reality in another. In every part of his life, in every box, he could only ever see his own point of view. I was exhausted.

Chapter 10: A Foal Saves My Marriage

Strangely my problems with Rebecca started to override the problems I was having in my marriage. Rebecca had been warning people I was getting a divorce before I even considered it. Now I was on the verge of that very divorce. Surprisingly, Rebecca's next crisis turned my marriage around in a way I could not have fore seen.

The crisis came in the form of the birth of a beautiful foal. I know that sounds like a lovely experience and in many ways it was, but Rebecca used the situation to her advantage. It was Rebecca's mare that gave birth to the foal. The mare was in a farmer's field over the road from Holly Tree and my beautiful schoolmistress, Brandy, was keeping her company. Brandy had been retired from the school but had worked there for most of her life. I decided that we would keep her and let her enjoy her retirement in the place she knew best, surrounded by her horse and pony friends. She was an amazing mare and was happy to keep Rebecca's mare company.

I'd not experienced the birth of a foal before, so as the due date arrived, I questioned whether we should stay in Rebecca's horsebox in the field so that we would be on hand. Rebecca gave me many reasons for not doing this, she pointed out that horses had been giving birth for centuries without needing human help and also, we had no idea when the foal would be born. I had to respect her decision, although maybe my intuition had been trying to warn me that all was not well.

The morning the foal was born, I awoke to a phone call from Rebecca saying one of the Holly Tree kids had gone passed the field and seen the foal. I was so excited. Rebecca said she would arrive soon, but could I go over and check everything was okay? Could I? Just try stopping me!

I leapt out of bed, jumped into my clothes, grabbed my phone to take some pictures and went to see the youngest foal I had ever seen. She was beautiful. Oh my goodness she took my breath away. All legs and big eyes, soft baby fur and a tiny fluffy tail. Such breath-taking moments are what I love about being in nature and sharing my life with animals.

The foal was beautifully clean. Mum had done her job well and was lying down having a well-deserved rest. I wandered over to her to see how she was doing but even as I approached, I instinctively knew something was wrong.

The mare struggled to get back on her feet and as she turned, I could see there was still something hanging from her back end. Having never seen the birth of a foal before I didn't know if this was the afterbirth or not. It didn't feel right. She didn't look right even though I wasn't sure what right should look like.

Thank goodness I had taken my phone. I know that statement seems odd now, as we carry our phones everywhere but at that time in my life I was a bit lackadaisical about having my phone with me.

I immediately phoned Rebecca and told her I thought we needed the vet. Rebecca made the call and of the two she arrived first. News had travelled about the birth of the foal so one or two other friends of Holly Tree had started to show up.

The vet arrived and the news was devastating. The mare was not going to survive. To add insult to injury, in order to give the foal a fighting chance, we needed to extract colostrum from the mare. It seemed so cruel to milk her before she was put to sleep, but that is what happened.

The absolute joy of the arrival of this beautiful foal was marred by the devastating sadness that her mum had done everything she could for her, but ultimately the birth had caused the death of the mare. Such mixed feelings, but we also had a huge problem standing, if a little wobbly, in front of us. How could we take care of the foal?

Brandy came into her own here. Bless her, she stepped into the role of surrogate Mum with ease and grace, not unlike my Grandma when she took care of me and my sister. The only thing Brandy couldn't do was feed the foal; that department was our problem. Fortunately, the vet didn't tell us at the time that the he rated our chances of keeping the foal alive at zero. We soon found out that goat's milk was the next best option to the mare's milk, so I was sent off for baby bottles and goats milk.

Poor Tesco's, they must have wondered what had hit them when they had a sudden demand in the sale of goat's milk. Then just as they were probably thinking they needed to order more, we discovered the local goats farm.

One of the Holly Tree kids had mentioned the goats farm, so I phoned them to see if we could buy the milk directly from them. They were amazing. When they heard about the foal they generously offered the milk for free. This began a routine that went on for weeks, where every other day one of us took a large tea urn to the goat's farm and they filled it up with fresh milk for us. When it was fresh the milk didn't seem to smell much, but because it wasn't treated it could whiff a bit by the end of the second day!

I fell in love with the goats at the farm. They were so cute and so curious. Every day as I drove into the yard, a dozen or so goats would stand up on the gate at the end of their barn to see who had arrived. All I could see was 12 heads and 24 ears sticking out at 90 degrees to their heads. They made me smile every morning that I went.

Feeding the foal was a blessing. At first, we had to put one arm over her and hold the bottle with the other to simulate the body of the mare, but our foal soon got to grips with being bottle fed. We slept in the horsebox with her for the first few nights because the weather was so bad. We needn't have worried so much though because when we weren't there Brandy would stand over her and protect her from the elements; it was a time-consuming job keeping this foal alive. Initially she needed to be fed every couple of hours, and in the early days we had lots of volunteers. But as the novelty, together with the visitors started to disappear, even Rebecca started to lose interest.

Her suggestion to me was that she could go back to running the yard, if I was happy to take on the responsibility of feeding the foal. How could I resist? I was blind to the way that Rebecca was manipulating the situation, and completely wrapped up in giving the foal the best possible start in life; so that is exactly what I did.

It turned out that the foal hadn't received enough colostrum at the start of its life, so had to have a blood transfusion, which we did in the field, but apart from that she thrived. When the vet came back to check on her, he admitted how surprised he was to see a healthy foal in front of him. Not one of the vets at his practice had thought the foal would survive, and he congratulated us on keeping her alive. I will always feel proud that I was integral to the foal's survival, but without Brandy and the generous people at the goats farm this story may not have had such a happy ending.

There was also another ingredient to this success story. It never dawned on me once that she would not survive and as I have since learned; that was a very powerful thought.

Now to tell you that this foal also saved my marriage at that point may sound a bit far- fetched, but that is exactly what happened. Cal and I were so far apart emotionally but this little foal provided a bridge.

Every night at somewhere between 11pm and midnight, I would take a torch and 3 bottles over the road, climb through a hole in the hedge and into the farmer's field. I would call the foal, hear a rumble of hooves and suddenly she would be next to me pushing for her feed.

The foal was growing fast, she was going to be a big horse when she was fully grown and since she had been surrounded by human beings since the day she was born, she had no fear around us, which sometimes spilt over into no respect. It was always hard to drag myself out of our warm cosy farmhouse so late at night, but the rewards were outstanding. Just me, the foal and the stars. Okay, not always the stars, but somehow it was always magical feeding her at this time of night.

One day I asked Cal if he would like to join me. I have no idea why I did this, we weren't really speaking, but with everything that had happened I was too exhausted to even contemplate divorce... so I hadn't pushed my divorce forwards.

Surprisingly Cal agreed and he absolutely loved feeding the foal. Our shared joy, the conversation, as we stood in the dark and listened to the foal slurping the milk had somehow opened up the lines of communication between us again. There was a glimmer of hope, a hint of the connection we'd once had when life was simpler, when we'd had nothing but big dreams. That foal and the problems that I had with Rebecca saved our marriage at that point. Not forever as it turned out, but she gave us another 5 years together that we wouldn't have had.

My learning curve within my marriage was not yet over, but Cal and I had started to rebuild our marriage and for a while, I was proud that we had managed to survive the affairs.

The problems with Rebecca however continued. She showed little interest in taking care of her foal unless someone else was watching her, or unless she was pulling rank on decisions that could be made about the foal. Then, just as the foal was beginning to need far less attention and therefore life was starting to get back to normal, Rebecca broke her collar bone. I was furious!

Let me explain why. Rebecca was a free spirit; she wanted to ride her horses without the proper clothing. I had no problem with her riding in jeans instead of jodhpurs but I was not happy about her riding in shorts and a t-shirt, and I made it very clear she was not allowed to ride without a hat.

There was good reason for this. As a riding school, we couldn't let our clients ride without a hat and so we needed to follow the same rules ourselves. This was a good rule. An arm or a leg that breaks will heal, but if you fall and hurt your head the outcome could be life changing. I made it clear to Rebecca she must wear a hat, and as per normal Rebecca took no notice of me. I was still finding it very hard to lay down my boundaries with her.

The day she broke her collar bone I arrived back at the yard to be greeted by 3 little girls with ashen faces. One of these children was Rebecca's daughter Charlie.

"We are waiting for the ambulance," she told me, "I think my Mum is dying." Bless her, my heart went out to her. I found out where her Mum was, reassured her and promised to see how her Mum was doing.

It turned out that Rebecca was bringing one of her horses in from the field. It had been a beautiful summers day so she was dressed in shorts and a t-shirt. The school was closed that day, but we had Ida's partner Dan doing some work in a tractor on the premises. Rebecca's horse was at the furthest point from the gate so rather than walk back next to her horse she decided to ride.

She had jumped on; no saddle, no bridle, just a head collar and lead rope. Rebecca trusted her horse, what could possibly go wrong? Well, Dan just happened to come around the corner onto the yard as Rebecca approached the gate from the field. Her horse spooked and took off.

Rebecca managed to stay on board, but as her horse was cantering towards the wooden 3 bar fence Rebecca decided to bail out. She deliberately decided to dismount, hit the ground hard and broke her collar bone in the process. Like her daughter, Rebecca's face was ashen when I got to her. Dan was with her and the ambulance soon arrived.

I swallowed my anger and told her not to worry. Dan took the children back home with him and I drove to the hospital behind the ambulance. We sat in A& E for hours. All the time I put on a good act as a supportive friend whilst inwardly I chunnered about how yet again Rebecca was making my life difficult. I smile at that comment now. I was so caught up in the blame game in those days that I claimed no responsibility for my part in this whole scenario.

If I had been firmer with setting my boundaries, with making the rules that I expected everyone to follow clearly, if I had stopped allowing life to happen to me and started taking control, this would not have happened. In truth, it would not have needed to happen because I would have been wise to the truth that my thoughts and actions, or in some cases lack of them, were creating my chaotic reality. There was still a long way on my journey for that penny to drop.

Life happens through you, not to you

Rebecca was a tough cookie. Despite having her arm in a sling, she said she didn't want to let me down. She said she could still work on the yard, not the physical stuff but she could deal with the clients and organise the yard, the only problem was she couldn't drive!

Rebecca then suggested she stay at Holly Tree while her arm was out of action, and although I was not excited about the idea, I couldn't see another way out. If she didn't stay, I would have to do my job and all of hers. If she stayed, at least she could relieve me of some of that.

It was all presented to me in such a way that it was best for me, but in truth this got Rebecca into my home.

I would be lying if I didn't say there was a lot of laughter while Rebecca stayed with me. In many ways, she was good company, but she was taking me down a path that I didn't really want to go and with her help I was becoming something that I was not.

Rebecca liked to drink, any excuse brought the alcohol out and while she stayed with me she slowly worked her way through our drinks cabinet. I've never been great with alcohol, that doesn't mean I don't like to have a drink or that I don't drink, but that I get drunk very easily. I loved to share a bottle of wine with a friend but one bottle was definitely enough for me. Not so for Rebecca and I was not strong enough to say no. I allowed her to take over and until she made a play for Cal I didn't see what was happening. It was innocuous enough.

We were all sitting in the kitchen having a coffee. Cal as usual was recounting some brilliant shot that he had recently done. In all the years I heard him talk about the film industry, I never heard him praise anyone else. He never came home and said 'oh my goodness, so-and-so acted their socks of today'. No it was never about anyone else, it was always about how he'd changed the shot to something amazing and everyone was really impressed with what he'd done. This particular day was no different.

At that time, I didn't even realise that Cal only ever shared what happened on set to tell me, or anyone else who would listen, how good he was at what he did. I can't deny that he was good, he was the best Steadicam operator I had come across. It would just have been nice if he'd had some humility about the fact, it would have made him more attractive.

As it was he was bragging and she lapped it up and then came the fatal words,

"I would love to come with you one day and see you in action Cal, if that would be okay?" she'd massaged his ego and he'd fallen for it.

'NO! NO! NO!' I could hear in my head. 'Over my dead body. This is enough. She is not going on a film set with him.'

Suddenly the fog lifted and I could see clearly what was happening; this woman was taking my life. She was running my yard, had taken my friends, was living in my house and now she wanted my husband and all the time she had done it with a smile on her face, pretending to put my interests first... and I had allowed it.

I had allowed it? How could I have allowed it? Why would she want my life? It may look great from the outside but I was struggling. As Cal and Rebecca continued to chat, I sat at the table questioning my integrity and not for the first time that year. Why was I so gullible? What was wrong with me? What was I doing wrong? Why did someone think they could just walk in and take what was mine? The answer was simple... because I had let her.

I was devastated, life was just too hard. I wanted people to be like me; I wanted people to treat each other with respect, to be kind and fair, but this was not how human beings seemed to behave.

I sat in my despair and shouted at God; life was too hard. I didn't like it. I didn't want to be part of it. I was exhausted with trying so hard. I was exhausted with helping people who then threw my kindness, my niceness back in my face. I could see what was wrong but my self - esteem was on the floor.

"You cannot treat me like that"

It would take many more years before I would be strong enough and brave enough to say the words 'you cannot treat me like that', but at least at this moment in time, I had started to realise that I was part of the problem.

Chapter 11: Rebecca Leaves and Blaze Says Goodbye

Fortunately for me, although Cal was enjoying the attention from Rebecca, he had no intention of taking her on a film set and like me, he wanted her out of our life too. Over the next few weeks as my relationship with Rebecca nose-dived, Cal was very supportive. As Rebecca's collar bone healed, she had no reason to stay at Holly Tree and I was relieved when she left voluntarily.

The situation on the yard soon came crashing to my attention. Some weeks earlier Rebecca had informed me that Louise, originally a helper on the yard but who now worked for me full time, wanted to do some teaching. I was surprised to hear this because at that point in her life, Lou was not that confident. I voiced my reservations but said if Lou was happy to take some lessons I was happy for her to do so.

Lou was a great rider and was wonderful with the customers. I had no doubts about her ability to teach only her willingness to do so. It was settled and Lou started to take some private lessons during the week. It didn't seem long until Rebecca came to me saying that Lou wasn't happy with my decision that she should do some teaching. What? It had never been my suggestion she should teach. I had only agreed when I was asked if she could.

Rebecca continued with her attitude that this situation was my fault, but she could fix it. I'd had enough. I went to walk out of my kitchen door to talk to Lou and Rebecca attempted to block my exit. Not this time. This time I was not going to allow her to stop me. I loved Lou like a daughter and I was hurt that she hadn't come to me to discuss the whole thing.

I brushed passed Rebecca and marched up to Lou.

"I don't understand, Lou. I never said you had to teach, I only agreed when Rebecca said you wanted to. Why didn't you come and talk to me? I thought we were friends."

Her reply shocked me, but also woke me up.

"We aren't allowed to," she replied.

What did she mean? Why isn't she allowed to talk to me? That seemed ridiculous. I soon found out that Rebecca had been stopping anyone and everyone from coming to the door of the house. She had told all of them I was not coping now and that they weren't to bother me. As Lou told me the truth and the current reality of her life on my yard, tears rolled down her face. I hugged her, and I cried too.

"Darlin', you are so much more than an employee to me. There will never be a reason when you are not welcome at my door. You are my friend and I love you dearly."

We held each other tight as the reality of my strangely quiet life suddenly hit me. It was time to put things right. Despite Rebecca's protests that Lou had misunderstood what she had said and that she was just protecting me; the game was over.

I made it clear to all the staff and the Holly Tree kids, that Cal and I had gone through a tricky patch but things were getting better, and there was never a reason why they couldn't come and talk to me. I also made it clear that from that moment on, I would be spending much more time on the yard like I used to. Once again, the yard became divided between staff who supported me and staff who were still influenced by Rebecca. However, from this point I didn't allow Rebecca to keep me behind closed doors. It was my yard and I started to make my presence known again.

As you can imagine this was not a part of Rebecca's plan and she wasn't happy. The atmosphere between us became frosty, but I couldn't find a specific reason to sack her. What's more I had to be careful as her brother was a solicitor. If I put one foot wrong I felt sure she would sue me for unfair dismissal.

I needn't have worried. Once her power was curtailed, she had no more desire to be at my yard. As I took back ownership of the yard, Rebecca started to take back ownership of her foal. She still didn't work past 3pm, when she had to leave to pick up her daughter, so I still cared for the foal from mid-afternoon, but she had started to make decisions about how the foal should be looked after.

By this time, the foal's goats milk diet was being supplemented with hard feeds. I assumed, that having decided to leave the yard, Rebecca wanted to wean the foal off all her goats milk feeds before she left, especially as she told me to stop giving her the late-night feed. I was horrified. This would mean that the foal went over 12 hours without a feed. Surely the last feed at night should be one of the last to go?

I didn't know for a fact that this was the case, so I asked the herdsman at the goat's farm. He confirmed my instincts that the late feed should remain and be the last to go, but this was Rebecca's foal, what could I do? His advice was to continue without telling her. That thought put me between a rock and hard place. On the one hand, I thought it was cruel to the foal to take away the feed, but on the other hand, it was Rebecca's foal and I didn't like lying to her. The foal made the decision for me. As I lay in bed that night, having followed my new instructions and not fed the foal, I could hear her whinnying from the field.

Initially, her whinny just said, "Where are you?" but it wasn't long before she became more indignant and much louder. I couldn't lie there and listen to her heart felt cry any longer. I got up and with dressing gown, wellies, torch and goat's milk made my way over to the field to feed her. I continued to do this for the next couple of weeks until the day that Rebecca left.

There was no warning that Rebecca was leaving, just a flurry of activity as her horsebox arrived to take the foal and her other 2 horses. The foal's life turned upside down on that day. This poor little horse had lost her Mum the day she was born and knew nothing else but the field that she lived in, Brandy her surrogate Mum and the humans who fed her.

I heard a commotion as Rebecca tried to get Brandy out of the field and Brandy was becoming as distressed at the separation as the foal. I ran over to the field to rescue my beloved Brandy.

"I've got her," Rebecca insisted.

"No you haven't." I replied, as I took Brandy's lead rope. My heart was heavy; I desperately wanted Brandy back with the Holly Tree pack because I think she was missing them, but not like this. Her joy at seeing her friends was marred by her pain at losing the foal. Brandy nuzzled the other horses who joyfully ran up to greet her, but then she stood at the gate and called out to the foal.

In the meantime, Rebecca and her friends were fighting with the foal to get her into the horsebox. It was heart breaking, and the tears ran down my face as I watched from a distance. It took them 2 hours to get that 12-week-old foal into the horsebox. She valiantly put up a fight, but it was a fight she could only ever lose and all that time Brandy stood at the gate of the field she was now in. A road separated the farmers field from my field and Brandy couldn't see the foal, but she whinnied to her all the time.

The cruel way this foal was moved didn't surprise me. I had offered to buy her. I hadn't been looking for another horse, but after all the quiet evening feeds I had bonded with this foal, and at the time I thought she had saved my marriage. I wanted to bring her into the Holly Tree herd. I wanted to let the horses teach her a few manners as she was getting rather boisterous. I wanted her to grow up with respect for human beings. Also, she was desperate to play and she was growing so fast it was getting a bit dangerous for us to do that with her.

However, despite her previous lack of interest, and her lack of care, Rebecca was not going to give her up. She was determined that the foal was going in the horsebox no matter how long it took.

Once Rebecca left, a quietness descended on the yard.

Brandy spent the next 24 hours standing at the gate desperately looking out for 'her' foal. She'd been crucial in that little foal's survival, but now all she had left for her efforts was the pain of losing the foal she'd nurtured. There was also another shock in store for me. About a week after Rebecca had left, the farmer whose field the foal had been in came over to ask me to settle my bill. What bill?

It seemed Rebecca had paid the farmer for her foal being in the field but had told him that I was paying for Brandy. I was horrified. She'd told the farmer that Brandy was old and I had wanted her to be in his field instead of mine because it was quieter; no mention of keeping her mare company, no mention of helping to save the life of her foal.

When I explained the truth to the farmer, he did say he had been a bit surprised that I wanted to pay for grazing when I had perfectly good grazing at my yard. I told him I couldn't pay him but I would try to sort it out. I have no idea why I rang Rebecca, as it became clear she had no intention of paying. She stuck to her story that I had wanted Brandy to be in the field. I then had a brain wave. I still had Rebecca's wages for the last week she'd worked. I spoke firmly and clearly as I told her that I was not paying for Brandy but I would use her last week's wages to pay the farmer.

"Whatever," was her reply, and the conversation was over.

I thought that would be the last I heard from Rebecca, but a few weeks later her daughter Charlie phoned me. Charlie reckoned she was doing a school project on the foal and she wanted me to send her copies of the photographs that Cal had taken in the first few days of her life. I bought myself some time to make a decision and told Charlie that I would see what I could do.

I knew what Cal's response would be; no way would he let Rebecca have the photographs, but her daughter's plea pulled at my heart strings. Of course it did, that was the point. Rebecca could have taken photographs of her foal but she wasn't interested and now she wanted to recapture the time she'd missed.

I began to doubt that there ever was a school project and began to see the request as another form of manipulation. I felt sorry for Charlie but my answer was "No".

I did meet up with Rebecca many years later, when I went back to her brother to represent me in my divorce. She was working for him at the time and was incredibly friendly towards me, so I decided to leave the past behind us. After the way she'd behaved I have no idea why I thought it would be good to ask her brother to represent me in my divorce. As it turned out, he had no better morals than she did, but that was another lesson I had to learn later.

Today, I can see people who manipulate others very clearly. In fact, so clearly that I wonder how I was ever so blind, but as you will discover it took me a long time to gain that clarity. I don't believe that we are here to learn lessons, as such, I believe we are here to remember who we are and experience who we are. I had an 'aha' moment when I heard Dr Michael Bernard Beckwith say,

God doesn't give you what you want,
he gives you what you need so that
you can grow into what you want

I love this motivational quote. It seems life has given me many opportunities to learn to value me and stand up for myself. Rebecca was just one of those many opportunities, and whilst I may have stood up for myself in the end, I had allowed the situation to go on for far too long. I didn't trust my intuition and as a result I got hurt, badly hurt.

Rebecca had kept manipulating me and my situation until I stood up and stopped her. It felt very uncomfortable for me to do that as I run a mile from confrontation, but I now understand that when I didn't lay down my boundaries, there would always be someone who would come along and try to take advantage of me. And when they do, as hard as it is to accept, I am as much to blame as the person who is manipulating me.

I have also learned that I don't have to be aggressive to set down my boundaries. I can set them down quite gently. The trick is to be consistent with honouring them.

You may be wondering how Brandy got on. Well horses do mourn the loss of another horse so she was very quiet for the following week, but slowly she started to integrate back into the pack and by the end of the month was happily grazing with her Holly Tree family. You will be pleased to know that Brandy had another 2 years of retirement ahead of her at that point.

Some people told me it wasn't good business sense to keep her at Holly Tree because she was costing me money and earning nothing in return. Try as I might, I couldn't run my business based on the figures, this was a sensitive animal not a commodity. Besides, many of my customers had a soft spot for Brandy, so I think it did a lot of good for the reputation of the riding school to say we took care of our horses, even after they could no longer work in the school. Brandy wasn't the first retired horse that I kept there.

That memorable little pony who liked tangerines also stayed with us until his final day. Blaze was a character, but as he got older he became more frail and we had to retire him. He was eventually diagnosed with a growth inside his private bits. Bless him, you would never have believed he was so poorly, although when he walked he looked a little bit like John Wayne from behind.

During his years of retirement, Blaze became like the yard mascot. We would let him out of his stable in the morning and while there were people and children on the yard he would happily mooch about with them. I cannot tell you how much fuss he got at the weekends, as parents waiting for their children would go up to him and stroke him, talk to him and cuddle him.

Once there was no one to give him any attention, he would stand at a gate and whinny to let us know he was ready to go out into the field. That little pony made friends with everyone and you couldn't look at him without smiling. As his illness took hold of him he lost so much weight that I had to put a note on his stable door saying...

"I am poorly but I am under veterinary supervision, and I am not in any pain. I know I look thin but I am fed much more than any other horse or pony on the yard!! Love Blaze".

We used to keep Blaze rugged up at all times because he became so thin, you could almost use him for an anatomy lesson. In fact, at one point we had so many rugs on him that we did start to worry that the rugs may weigh more than he did! We needn't have worried; Blaze's body was getting weaker but his spirit remained strong. This beautiful little pony had eyes that remained bright and alert until his final day and when he didn't want to go back into his stable there was nothing we could do about it.

It didn't matter how many of us tried to push him or encourage him back into his stable, if Blaze said 'no' the answer was no. We adored him for his inner strength. He was living proof that when the body begins to deteriorate there is still a part of us that is very much alive. Blaze loved being retired. He spent time with children and parents, grazed with his horsey friends and stole carrots and tangerines whenever possible. We became so used to seeing his frail body wobble across the yard that we almost started to believe he would remain with us forever. Of course that couldn't happen and in typical Blaze fashion he chose the day.

On the morning that Blaze passed, after breakfast Lou let him out of his stable to wander around the yard as usual.

"What's he doing?" she suddenly said. I looked up to see that Blaze had wandered down the far end of the yard. One by one he was going from stable to stable. A knot appeared in my stomach. I suddenly had a bad feeling about what I was seeing. Could he possibly be saying goodbye? Lou and I watched as this frail elderly pony visited every horse and pony at the far end of the school. He then walked passed the smaller row of 4 pony stables and stuck his nose over each stable in turn. Onto the 5 block, a greeting to me and Lou and lastly to the stables attached to the house. Yes, this little pony had acknowledged me and Lou and every other horse and pony on the yard.

As he entered his tiny stable, he took one last look over his shoulder before he lay down and had a stroke. We rushed to his side but for the first time his eyes were dull. His body was still reacting but it so felt like his soul had already left. I called the vet and she brought his body to a peaceful end. The tears rolled down our faces at the loss of such a special pony but we were also moved to be a part of his final ritual, his final goodbye. It was so typical of Blaze that he had departed this world on his terms, when he was ready and in his own way.

I know many people question whether animals have emotions like we do, but I don't think you can doubt it once you spend time with them. At Holly Tree we didn't separate the mares from the geldings when we put our horses and ponies out in the fields. We put them out in friendship groups. I watched one horse, Marcus, go through all the human phases of grief when he lost his companion. He got so thin I thought we were going to lose him too until a little palomino pony called Tubby worked her way into his heart. As their friendship grew, he became stronger physically and I was able to put him back into the school. As I practiced my healing skills on the horses I could feel their emotions when I stood next to them, sometimes it would be sadness, sometimes fear.

sometimes joy. The most gorgeous moments were the moments when you connect with a horse and felt their love or their gratitude. Those moments of bliss can be so overwhelming in a lovely way that they can take your breath away and reduce you to tears of joy.

There is something very spiritual, very special about horses and the day Blaze died, it was an honour to be a part of his journey.

It would be a couple more years before it was Brandy's turn, but her death was integral to my decision to leave Holly Tree.

Chapter 12: Selling Holly Tree

From the moment Rebecca left, Cal started to make suggestions that it was time for us to leave Holly Tree too.

We'd decided not to get divorced and to work on our marriage. By this time Cal was doing a lot of work 'down south', as us Northerners choose to call anywhere below Birmingham. Cal made a good argument that part of our problem was that we didn't see enough of each other. I thought he probably had a point, but wasn't ready to move away from everything I knew. I tried to stall him by suggesting we should buy a second property, so that when he was working at any of the London film studios or the surrounding areas, he had a place to call home. I also promised that if we did that, I would come down south more often and stay with him in the new house. My promises were genuine at the time, but I do admit I never visited as much as I had intended.

After much searching we found a mews house in Virginia Water in Surrey. It was in a gated community and was one of the last houses to be built. It was probably one of the smallest houses too, but it still had 3 bedrooms, 2 with en-suite, a kitchen, family bathroom, lounge/dining room and a small conservatory. All the houses were built around an old mental institute that had been painstakingly restored to its former glory, and then turned into very expensive apartments.

I hadn't known at the time that the main building was a previous mental institute, but I never felt comfortable in the house. You could see the tower of the main house in the distance as you turned off the M25, and as the tower came into view, I could always hear the music from the film Psycho.

To be honest, I didn't really want this house so I was in no hurry to make an offer, but the look on Cal's face when the estate agent said all the properties on the plot were now sold changed my mind. He was crestfallen, and when all was said and done, Cal would live in this property more than I would.

I quickly got back to the estate agent, told her the truth about Cal's reaction and asked her to get back in touch with me if any of the sales fell through. As luck would have it that is exactly what happened and we were soon the proud, or not so proud in my case, owners of a property on the Virginia Park estate.

The house was perfect for Cal. All the owners had access to a beautiful swimming pool, gym, badminton courts and tennis courts. There was plenty for Cal to do when he was home alone. It's funny how you perceive your reality through your own filter. At this point in my life, I honestly thought this house would help save my marriage. I now realise I was finding a property where Cal would be happy without me, not exactly a great idea when I was trying to save my marriage. Clearly, I didn't have the clarity and wisdom that I now have.

Wisdom and clarity come with experiences

I probably need to tell you that I do now believe that our thoughts and feelings do create our reality. I think at this point in my life I hadn't quite come to that conclusion otherwise I would have understood the situations that I was creating.

I did honestly intend to go down to Virginia Water and stay with Cal, but every time I planned to go something came up! On one occasion, I had my red BMW packed and ready to go when one of my staff asked if I could help harrow the school before I went. Normally we would do this by using a very old and very dinky tractor that one of my clients, Kevin, kept at the school. Kevin had a horse on working livery but as she was only young and couldn't work too many hours, Kevin used to help us out on the yard. At this point, Kevin's little tractor was not working and we had watched him tie the harrow to the back of his car many times to harrow the school. How difficult could it be?

Well, believing that us ladies are perfectly capable of doing such jobs, I happily agreed to wiz around the school before I left. Lou and Sharon, another member of staff, came with me. We tied the harrow to the back of my BMW and I started to circle the indoor school. It wasn't long before Lou was waving at me. It seemed the harrow was just bouncing across the top of the school base. What we needed was a bit of weight, so the 2 girls volunteered to sit on the harrow! Initially all went well. With the extra weight the harrow was levelling off the sand and rubber base nicely until... I was at the corner of the school, the car seemed to be stuck so I gently, very gently, put my foot down on the accelerator.

The car jumped forwards. I looked in my rear view mirror to see Lou and Sharon flying into the air in different directions. As I took my foot off the accelerator there was a loud crash and the harrow hit the back of my car. This time when I looked in the mirror all I saw was the shattered glass of my rear window.

The car came to a halt. I jumped out and ran to the girls to see if they were okay. as they were lying on the floor surrounded by glass, but no one was hurt. There was a pause as we looked at each other before I said,

"I guess I'm not going to London today." The ice was broken, the giggles began, and we couldn't stop laughing. What a stupid thing to do. I should have known the whole idea was very dangerous. After the giggles came the clear up; in 4 hours there would be horses and ponies and children in the school. Somehow we had to clean up all the glass and then I had to admit to Cal and my male friend at the BMW garage what I had just done. When Kevin eventually heard he calmly said,

"Oh, I never tie the harrow too close to the car just in case it does that." Okay, maybe we will remember that for next time. Actually, there never was a next time. Once again, I had somehow sabotaged my trip to London to stay with Cal. This was the third time in a row that I'd made arrangements to go and something had happened to stop me.

Our thoughts and feelings create our reality

Do you think that my thoughts and feelings about going down south were somehow creating each crisis that stopped me from going? As I said, I now believe this to be true, but it was not a belief I had at the time.

So, we already had a house 'down south' and now Cal was putting pressure on me to leave Holly Tree and move down south with him. To be honest I did think he had a point. If we were going to remain married we should live most of our time under the same roof.

As the time passed, I thought a lot about what Cal was saying. As much as I loved the riding school, it was hard work and the Holly Tree kids, who had been with me for so long, were starting to grow up and leave. I was getting tired and I couldn't imagine the yard without this core group of teenagers.

One Friday night, while Cal and I were sharing a bath, I told him I would agree to move. I can remember the shock and delight on his face even now. I thought I was buying myself some time to get used to the idea by adding that I couldn't move until Brandy had died, but once that had happened I would agree to sell Holly Tree. Brandy was by now a very old mare and I just wanted her to enjoy her final days at Holly Tree. I couldn't find another home for her and I couldn't in all conscience have her put to sleep just because I wanted to move.

Well, the speed of what happened next was shocking. It was Friday night when I said those fateful words. On

Saturday Brandy was kicked in the field and was so lame I called out the vet. The vet said she thought it was just a nasty bruise, but in the worst-case scenario Brandy could have a hairline fracture underneath. In all the years of owning horses I was used to vets giving me the worst-case scenario which never happened. In this case she warned if it was a break it could get worse.

Brandy was put on box rest for a couple of days and all seemed well. How wrong could I be. On Monday morning I found my beautiful old school mistress lying in her stable in agony. The leg clearly had been broken and nothing could be done. The vet was called and Brandy was released from her pain and allowed to pass to her next life. I sat in the stable on the floor next to her and sobbed. What had I done? Had I really put a death sentence over her head. My trusty collie Riff lay next to Brandy's now dead body as I leaned my head against her and cried. To add insult to injury, Cal who never believed in any of my spiritual stuff, then came into the stable and said,

"You are the one who believes in signs. If that isn't a sign that it's time to leave Holly Tree, I don't know what is."

I did believe in signs. I had a hard time accepting this one because it felt like I'd caused her death, but I couldn't argue with what he said. By the end of the week Cal had a For Sale sign up on Holly Tree.

Angels and spirit guides communicate through signs

It took 12 months of arguing with the future owners and finding homes for my loyal horses and ponies before we were able to leave Holly Tree. I closed the school within a couple of months of Brandy's death and put all the horses except mine and Cal's, Ella and Jim and 2 old ponies, Nicky and Tubby, up for sale.

Selling the horses was emotionally very tough, but once I had closed the school I felt a huge load of responsibility fall from my shoulders. I seemed to be walking a couple of inches taller. The teenagers continued to come to the yard and I kept on one member of staff to help with mucking out.

My good friend Anna bought Bonnie, one of the horses from me, and although lots of people wanted the star pony of the school, Toby, I chose to let him go to Anna too, for her daughter Imi. There was one proviso; Anna had to promise to give Toby a home for life. I needn't have worried. My special friend gave both Bonnie and Toby a home for life even though Imi grew too big to ride Toby within a year of getting him.

Fate took another helping hand here. Anna needed to build stables on her field before she could take Bonnie and Toby, so they stayed at Holly Tree until their new stables were built. This meant that Anna came to the yard every day to muck out her horse's stables, and because she is a very kind and generous lady, she also started to muck out the other 2 stables attached to Bonnie's and Toby's. Little did she know the number of stables she would eventually muck out because she had offered to help her friend in need.

We had 26 horses when I closed the school. Granted I did start to find homes for the horses, but there were always a lot of stables to muck out. My staff member would get 5 done in her morning shift and it wasn't long before Anna and I were splitting the rest. I cannot tell you how much I owe this wonderful friend. She never received a penny for all her help, her only reward was the laughs we had while we were mucking out and a walnut and maple syrup pastry that we treated ourselves to every Friday morning. It will probably come as no surprise that some 15 years later, Anna is still one of my most valued friends. She has a heart of gold and is incredibly practical.

I cannot miss this opportunity to tell you a quick story about Anna and I, that happened some years later.

Anna's Mum was very ill in hospital in Guildford. At the time I was living in Kimblewick, Buckinghamshire which was closer to Guildford than Cheshire where Anna was at the time. It made sense for Anna to come and stay with me for a while so she could visit her Mum.

One day we had a little time on our hands, so before we went to the hospital we decided to go into Guildford town centre. I was driving my trusty Freelander through Guildford when Anna suddenly said,

"there's a space!" Now you should know that I'm not so good at parallel parking; I'm the sort of person who is more than happy to park a little further away to find an easier spot and then walk. Nowadays I always ask the parking angel for a parking space that I can get in and out of easily, but I hadn't started speaking to the Angels at that point in my life. There was traffic behind me and the parking spaces were hard to find.

I turned to Anna and said, "If you want my car in that space you need to park it." Completely unsurprised by my response, as she knew me well, Anna laughed and suggested I should get out so she could slide over into the driving seat and park my car, which is exactly what she did!

Finding homes for the horses and ponies was hard. Some of my clients wanted to buy a pony for their child but couldn't afford to, some of my clients wanted horses or ponies that really weren't right for them, and some of the clients fought over the same horse or pony. Sadly, there were others horses and ponies no one was interested in.

It was a nightmare making the right choices and even more so when I had to start advertising, as the potential buyers were then people I didn't even know. As the process continued over that 12-month period, it was the horses and ponies who started to make the decisions. I will give you an example, one that reminded me not to judge a book by its cover.

Never judge a book by its cover

The horse that was being looked at on this day was a coloured cob called Cowboy. From the day I had bought this little horse, he'd gone into the school and not put a foot wrong. Facially he wasn't the prettiest of horses because his top and bottom jaws were not quite in alignment but he was a sweetie.

On this day, we had a family who were coming to see him. I'm embarrassed to admit my thoughts as Anna and I, we stood and watched this family climb out of their old car. If any of you can remember the Beverley Hillbillies on television this family looked like the Clampits that day. Anna and I murmured comments to each other about them when they arrived.

As the family fell out of the car, there seemed to be loads of them; there was Mum, Dad and 4 children ranging from the youngest who was about 6 to the oldest who was 19, although he didn't look it.

This older boy was the one who wanted Cowboy. As it turned out he was not the son of this couple, but they had taken him in because his parents couldn't or didn't want him, I cannot remember which. This boy clearly had some problems, he didn't seem his age but he was proud of the fact that he had a little job that would pay for Cowboy's upkeep.

My heart sank as they got out of the car, not least because this lad looked a bit too heavy to ride Cowboy. However, a small miracle then took place.

The young lad loved the look of Cowboy and wanted to ride him straight away. We took them all into the indoor school to see how he would get on. Now I must tell you that another rider had tried Cowboy earlier in the day and Cowboy had refused to go into canter. This was not like Cowboy at all. We'd checked him over afterwards to see if he had a problem but could find nothing wrong.

As this young lad, who I worried was too heavy, sat on Cowboy, Cowboy seemed to grow a couple of inches. First he walked on both reins, that is both ways around the school. Then he asked for a trot and the boy rode lightly and in tune with the horse. I couldn't believe what I was seeing. The lad then asked for a canter. Cowboy made the transition smoothly and the boy sat quietly on the saddle. They were made for each other. Cowboy just seemed so happy to let this boy ride him. It made no logical sense but I couldn't deny what I was seeing.

The young lad then wanted to see how Cowboy behaved on the road, so Anna and I volunteered to walk out with him. It wasn't long before Cowboy and this lad were trotting ahead of us and completely wrapped up in each other. Anna looked at me and said,

"I think Cowboy has just chosen his new owner." I had to agree. It was so lovely to see the joy this young lad was getting from riding Cowboy. After a chat with the surrogate parents who assured me that Cowboy would be going to their yard and they would take responsibility for him, the deal was made with the proviso that we would visit them at their yard.

I couldn't have been more wrong about this family on my first impressions. They had very little except each other and their horses, but the horses were their life. Everything revolved around the horses and they were one of the happiest families I have ever met. In the end not only did Cowboy go and live with this lovely family but another pony called Cracker went too. Cracker was not at all balanced when she went around the corners of the school and consequently I'd tried to sell her once at a horse sale, but the whole experience was so traumatic that I'd brought her home. All my staff had smiled knowingly as I drove through the gates with Cracker still in the horse trailer. After that I was worried about finding a home for her, but this family only wanted her to hack out, so they weren't worried that she was likely to fall over if she took a corner too fast.

I visited Cowboy and Cracker a couple of times after they moved to their new home. On the first occasion Cowboy was out in one of their fields when I arrived. The field sloped upwards from the gate so we couldn't see him when we went to the gate, but this young lad only had to call him once. Suddenly, Cowboys ears, then his full head and then his body appeared at the top of the slope. He cantered down towards his new friend. This young lad flung his arms around Cowboys neck laughing as Cowboy nuzzled into his shoulder.

It was like a scene from a movie and I must admit there were tears in my eyes as I watched their reunion.

My heart rested easy knowing that Cowboy was with such a loving family.

Chapter 13: Time to Look Forwards

We moved 'down south' lock, stock and barrel, or should I say horsebox, horsebox and trailer, in 2003.

I surprised myself that there were no tears when I finally left Holly Tree. Maybe I'd had time to get used to the idea, or maybe the process of leaving was so exhausting that I was too tired to be sad.

The bulk of the furniture went into storage and we went down with our clothes, some ornaments and pictures. Oh and 4 dogs, 2 cats and 6 horses. Or if I was going to be more accurate I should say 4 horses and 2 ponies.

I'm sure you'll understand that I had a very good reason why I had to take each one of them; Jim and Ella were mine and Cal's horses and they were always going to come. Marcus, the old chestnut gelding had to come because of his age, mind you I had no idea at the time that he would live another 12 years and be over 30 when he eventually died. He seemed to thrive once he reached retirement. And I've no idea why no one bought Colin the Cob, but I must admit that we'd brought him such a long way from the horse he was when he arrived at the yard, that it was hard for me to give him up. Maybe I didn't try too hard to find him a new home.

We also had little Nicky, he was also very old. I knew he didn't have long in this life but I had already had to make the decision for one old pony, Tubby, to die because of our move. She had bad laminitis and couldn't travel. She passed away very gracefully so I am sure it was a good decision, but I couldn't honestly look into Nicky's eyes and make the same decision. His eyes were bright and full of life and as old as he was, he was very much alive and had worked in the school until the day we closed, so Nicky deserved to come too. Then finally there was Magic, and he was not supposed to come. He was a gorgeous Welsh Section A pony who moved so beautifully that he should have sold easily. However, when the for-sale sign went up Magic suddenly went lame. Bless him he would be poorly for the rest of his life but he was the strongest and cheekiest pony I knew. We didn't know he had Cushing's at the time but because of his illness he became my pet pony, so he came too. You'll read much more about this special little pony later. How I ever got Cal to agree to taking 4 horses and 2 ponies, I will never know. Needless to say, he played no part in their travel but he did help to secure stabling.

I prayed to my spirit guides to help me find stables for all the horses. I thought it would be difficult and, let's be honest, any yard with 6 spare stables wasn't going to be so nice.

That said, a stuntman that Cal worked with knew of someone with stables only 5 minutes' drive from the house in Virginia Water. It wasn't great, but all my horses could be stabled next to each other, I was given a field just for them and all 4 of my dogs were allowed on my bit of the yard which was a bonus.

The owner had 3 stallions kept at the yard but they were kept in stables inside a barn. Those poor stallions hardly ever saw light of day. They never went out and it was dark in their barn. The stables had cobwebs on the cobwebs, and the man that looked after them, Jim, only skipped them out each day as he was told to do. The living arrangements of these stallions broke my heart, but being at this yard did teach me that I had to focus on the animals in my care. As my friend Christine said to me at the time,

"Karen, You can't save all the horses."

I was nervous when I first got to the yard. I'd been told Jim was an alcoholic but if I ever needed help just to ask him. That was not the most reassuring introduction I'd ever been given for someone who would keep an eye on my horses when I wasn't there. Again, Alcoholic Jim was another learning curve.

It took 2 horseboxes and a small trailer to transport the horses, ponies, dogs and cats and all their 'stuff' down to Surrey, which we did the day before we finally moved out of Holly Tree. I had a small army of friends and teenagers who helped me that day.

Anna drove the trailer with the ponies in. Pat, who was the boyfriend and now husband of Abi, one of the Holly Tree teenagers, drove my horsebox, and I drove a smaller horsebox that I'd borrowed from Linda, a very generous client.

The idea was to travel down with all the animals, leave Abi and 4 other teenagers in the house with the cats and dogs so that they could look after them and the horses. Then Anna, Pat and I could drive the horseboxes and trailer back to Holly Tree. Cal was supposed to drive my horsebox back down the following day with our belongings in it.

If any of you know my time keeping skills this was a rather ambitious plan. We did do it, but it was 9pm and very dark by the time we found the yard in surrey. And it was about 4am when I eventually arrived back at Holly Tree.

When we arrived in Surrey Jim greeted us very warmly. As we started sorting out the stables we let the dogs stretch their paws and Jim bent down to stroke Sasha, one of my border collies.

"Jim, you need to be careful with Sasha, she is a bit wary of men." I said, worrying that Sash may turn around and snap at him at any time.

"Don't you worry about me girl," he replied, "I know dogs."

Well I thought, I've warned him, I can't do any more. I was sure Sasha would need time to get to know Jim but I was wrong, very wrong. Sasha soon changed my preconceived ideas about Jim. Far from being wary of Jim, she loved him and loved the attention he gave her. It wasn't long before she was lying on her back with her paws in the air getting her stomach rubbed. She was in doggy heaven. In fact, when I started to go to the yard last thing at night to water and hay the horses, Sasha would lie outside Jim's door. Believe it or not, Jim lived in one of the stables that had been converted for him into a room with a proper door. It sounds horrible, and looked horrible to me, but every day the owner of the yard, Tony, or a member of his family, would bring Jim 2 bottles of cider and 2 meals. And Jim was grateful.

Gratitude is the attitude

Jim was more than grateful. Knowing he was addicted to alcohol, Jim was quite content with his lot. It was thought provoking to see how someone with so little could be so content. Watching Sasha the day we arrived, I trusted her judgement. I knew that whatever circumstances had caused Jim to turn to drink, fundamentally he had a good heart.

I spent much time talking to Jim over the next 12 months. He talked in cockney rhyming slang which was a bit of a challenge. It was like learning a new language and Tony and Jim used to laugh when I had no idea what they were saying.

However, I soon learned that Jim took his rosy lea with a carpet of sugar. I have no idea why a carpet is 3, but he said it to me so many times that one day when Cal asked me a question instead of answering 3, I said a carpet!

I also learned that sometimes when Jim talked about a pony he was referring to £25, not Nicky or Magic! It was never a dull moment with Jim around. If you wanted to have a conversation with him you had to watch EastEnders and follow the horseracing.

I soon learned to trust Jim. Whether I asked him or not he would always top up the water buckets in my stables.

"Those horses can manage without food girl," he would say, "but they're no good without water." Actually, he didn't say water he said 'parni'. My friend Lou and I spent a whole day trying to work out what parni could rhyme with to get water. Jim laughed out loud when we asked him. It seemed parni wasn't a rhyming slang; Jim used to work on a building site with some builders from India and they used to call water parni!!

It wasn't only Sasha that made herself comfortable on our new yard. My old pony Nicky adjusted amazingly well, although you would never have guessed it the night we arrived. To be honest poor Nicky hadn't been in a horse trailer for many years before we moved him 200 miles down south. He'd lived at Holly Tree for a long time. He did travel very well but we'd had a few problems getting him in the trailer. We almost lifted him in and once installed next to Magic who loved travelling, and set him in front of a large hay net he was happy.

I had assumed, quite wrongly as it turned out, that Nicky would be in a rush to get out the other end. We opened the jockey door to let light into the trailer and then lowered the ramp at the side. Magic trotted out quite happily but Nicky wouldn't move! It wasn't a problem I had encountered before. Normally if there is an issue it's getting the horse loaded onto the trailer, not trying to encourage it to get off. We talked to him, offered him food, tried to push and pull. Nothing was working until Lou arrived.

At this point, Lou was working down south. It had been over a year since she'd left the riding school to follow her passion for camera work. and what happened next when she arrived was so touching. Nicky hadn't seen Lou since she'd left Holly Tree.

As she put her head into the trailer she said,

"What's up Nicky?" his ears pricked up, his eyes lit up and he whinnied loudly in recognition of someone he loved, who had taken care of him for many years. Thank goodness for the delight that little pony felt when he saw Lou. He would have followed her anywhere, so following her off the trailer was no problem, which is exactly what he did.

My first few months In Surrey were awful. I felt like I'd walked out of my life. I was living on a gated estate that felt like something out of the film Stepford Wives. Everything was so perfect and there were so many rules. You couldn't hang washing outside in your garden. You couldn't change the colour of your front door without permission from the Committee. You had to park your car in your allocated parking space, NOT outside your front door and it seems children were supposed to be seen and not heard. Really!

The play area for the children had been moved a little closer to our block of 8 mews houses because of water collecting near the swings. Would you believe there were then complaints to the Committee about the children making too much noise? I couldn't believe it. I loved to hear the kids play, it made the place feel more normal.

Moreover, the house was a new build and was decorated with cream and white throughout. Not ideal when I moved in with 4 tri-coloured collies and 2 black and white cats. It was a constant battle to keep on top of the black animal hairs and my poor cats, who up to that point had been yard cats, had to live in the guest room because Cal hated cats. They did have an en-suite though! No, I was not settling into my new home at all.

Things weren't much better at the yard. I was upset at the way the other horses were being treated. It took me 3 hours every day just to muck out my own stables and for the first time in 10 years I was completely responsible for my own horses with no one to help with their routine.

Actually, at this point I believed that the horses needed a routine. I had to be at the yard for 8am; they had to be in their stables before dark and during the winter months I would be back at 10pm to give them their evening feed and check their water. In years to come I would relax the routine, which I found out was better for me and my horses, but at that time I thought I was doing my best for them. It was tough to go through this routine every day, 7 days a week. I loved my horses but it was exhausting. I was spending more time with alcoholic Jim than I was with Cal, and Cal was constantly irritated by that.

Cal didn't make my transition any easier. He hated it when I was at the yard and if he was home, would keep phoning me to see if I was nearly finished. His calls used to irritate me so much.

"If you'd just stop calling I could get finished quicker." I would tell him.

Only then when I did rush home for lunch, I would wonder why he had made such a fuss. Would I get an enthusiastic welcome? No. Often he just wanted me to make lunch and then he would play his guitar or play on his laptop all the time we were at the table eating.

Then there was dinner, every night I had to make dinner. I wasn't used to that! Cal was working, but he was working on Harry Potter so he was home for dinner every night. It was a shock to my system. When you're on your own a pot of hummus and some carrots would often suffice, but I couldn't offer that to Cal after a full day's work.

When I eventually got to exploding point, Cal questioned me in a very sarcastic voice,

"Well, what can you possibly be missing?" I rattled off a list;

"My home, my own yard, my sister, my friends, my clients, my staff, knowing where I am, my farrier, my feed supplier, I even miss Tesco's!"

By the time I got to Tesco's, what I had meant to say was that a visit to my local Tesco's was a pleasure for me in Cheshire. Many people knew me through the riding school and I would always bump into a friendly face, also the people on the tills were much chattier in Cheshire. Cal replied.

"Well, I can program Tesco's into your sat nav if you like?"

WHAT? I'd just bared my soul. I'd just listed everyone and everything that I missed from Cheshire and he tells me how to get to my nearest Tesco's. I was furious. and he was confused. Having done so much more work on human relationships since that day I now understand what happened here; Cal was trying to find a way of helping me. Each time I stated something, he would decide if he could do anything about it or not. Until I got to Tesco's on my list, he couldn't help. When he heard my problem with Tesco's he thought he could fix it for me and that is what he tried to do.

At the time, I thought he was being cold and thoughtless. What I know now, but didn't know then, was that he was trying to show me he loved me by fixing one of my problems. I didn't understand that, and his attempt at supporting me had only made matters worse. We were not understanding each other at all.

> ***"The single biggest problem in communication is the illusion that it has taken place"***
>
> *George Bernard Shaw*

It wasn't a great first few months, until I was at the yard one afternoon just before Christmas and was bringing the horses in from the field. I used to lead all of them in with lead ropes except for Nicky who'd got into a habit of standing at the gate waiting for me. He didn't like all the pushing and shoving that started as I brought everyone in, so that meant that he was usually last. However, if he was at the gate when I arrived, he would push passed me as I opened the gate and trot back to his stable. Once I realised this was what he was doing, I started to leave his stable door open and allow him to take himself back to his stable.

One day as I was walking back to the yard with Colin and Marcus, I could hear alcoholic Jim in the tea room saying to someone who I couldn't see,

"You don't have to worry about that little'en. He learned his way back to his stable from the field in the first week that he came here. He won't bother you. He just wants his hay."

It made me smile as I heard Jim refer to Nicky. It also made me think Nicky had settled in quickly. Bless this little pony. I had turned his world upside down but he wasn't looking backwards. His check list must have been something like this;

- A warm stable to sleep in? Check.
- Someone I know caring for me and looking after me? Check.
- Same food? Check.
- A field to go out in every day? Check.
- Lots of my mates to hang out with? Check.
- Okay, no problem then!

He was just getting on with life. He'd worked out how to get to the field and back to his stable and everything else was as normal.

I felt that there was a lesson to be learned here; maybe the contrast in my life was a little more severe but my growing depression was not coming from my change of circumstances, but from my constant comparison to where I had been and what I had lost.

My thoughts were causing my growing depression

I was constantly thinking about what I was missing, instead of looking forward to a new chapter in my life with Cal.

Maybe, just maybe, it was time to start looking forwards. I decided that afternoon that I would make a New Year's Resolution to stop looking back and start looking forward. The minute I made that choice it seemed that Nicky's job was done, or at least that is how it felt. Christmas came and went and on New Year's Eve I quietly made my resolution to look forwards not backwards.

On January 3rd 2004, Nicky looked very lame as he ambled back from the field. He wasn't his usual sprightly self. The following day he took a turn for the worse. I called the vet but he wasn't sure what was wrong. He gave Nicky some pain relief and anti-inflammatories and took some blood. That night I stayed with Nicky. I had a bad feeling starting to stir inside me. As the night progressed his legs became so weak that he was leaning against the wall of the stable to stay upright. He clearly didn't want to lie down.

About 11.30pm, Cal surprised me by arriving at the yard with a flask of coffee and some nibbles. I told him I couldn't leave and Cal chose to stay too. As I'm telling you about this caring side of Cal, there are tears rolling down my face. This was the man I fell in love with; the man who loved animals like me, the man who was prepared to spend a night in a cold stable to support me and Nicky. I don't know where that man went. He's not the man I think of now as I picture Cal in my mind, but that night he was my loving, caring husband and for all the difficult times we'd had, I still adored him.

By 4am I had made the decision that it was Nicky's time to go. He was old and I couldn't put him through another night like this one. The vet came first thing and, with me by his side, my wise little pony passed peacefully onto the next stage of his life.

Nicky, you will always have a very special place in my heart. You taught me to let go of the past and get on with the present. You taught me to be grateful for what is, not wistful for what has gone. You showed me that it was not my circumstances that were making me miserable but my thoughts. God Bless you Nicky.

Let go of the past
Be grateful for the present
And create the future

Chapter 14: Vale Farm

After Nicky's passing I took an unemotional look at my current situation; we were living in a house I didn't like and my 4 horses and pony were on a yard I didn't like, but the truth was this was only a temporary situation. Cal and I still had most of our belongings in storage, so what I needed to do was stop feeling sorry for myself and start looking for a house I did want to live in. A house where all my animals including the horses would be at home with me. The search began.

I stopped feeling sorry for myself and started to take action to change my situation

As I write this, I am beginning to realise that Cal and I had agreed on very little, and the new house was no exception. I wanted a 3 or 4-bedroom farmhouse with about 5–10 acres for my horses. Cal wanted a country manor, something that would say he was a successful man.

The houses I wanted to look at cost just over a million but Cal wasn't interested unless they were over 2 million. The problem was he was working on film sets with actors who were earning 20 million for a film and consequently 2 million didn't sound like much to him!

I however was thinking about the mortgage for a house of that price and had panic attacks at the very thought. As you can imagine, we saw a lot of houses and couldn't agree on any of them.

On the day we found Vale Farm I'd wanted to go and see a smaller house. I thought if I could find a house in the area that Cal might like to see I could, perhaps, persuade him to look at the one I wanted to go look at.

The day started with everything going to my plan except, as you can probably guess, Cal didn't like the first house I took him to. We then went to see Vale Farm.

His face lit up as we drove through the gates. The house was impressive. It had a short drive way leading up to the house and there were 3 young but beautiful weeping willow trees down the left-hand side. The drive way circled around an island of shrubs in front of the house which was in the Edwardian style complete with large sash windows, a green door and rendered walls that were painted cream. The house lay in 30 acres of its own land.

We were met by the estate agent and taken into a large and impressive entrance hall. I won't describe every room in the house as there were 16 altogether, without counting the en-suites. There was also a one bed cottage in the grounds, lots of outbuildings and 8 beautiful monarch stables. If you're not horsey, the monarch stables won't mean much to you, but to me they were the Rolls Royce of stables. The stables were open so that the horses could see each other and there was a bonus that I could see them from the kitchen.

The kitchen was another plus. It was huge and had not one but two central islands and a four oven Aga. Another tick. There was also a breakfast room, small lounge and orangery on this side of the house and all the rooms were interconnecting.

There were some lovely details such as the fireplace in the small lounge also opened into the orangery and as the orangery faced west you could sit in the evenings and watch the sun set. I've seen some amazing sunsets from this house, but sadly not very romantic as most of these times I was on my own. The rest of the house was okay, but didn't grab my imagination.

The main lounge was huge, and had curtains that trailed on the floor and huge tie backs. I've never quite understood why people have curtains that are too long but I know it is a common practice. So, the parts of the house that I really liked were those four interconnecting rooms and the stables outside.

While we were viewing the house, we got to meet the current owners, Phil and Celia. They were very welcoming and we all got on incredibly well. So much so that we let the estate agent leave and Cal and I stayed for a cup of tea.

As we drove out of Vale Farm Cal turned to me and said rather sarcastically,

"I suppose that one doesn't feel right either!" My answer made him slam the breaks on, emergency stop style, and bring his van to an abrupt holt. Yes, we'd gone to see this country home worth over 2 million pounds in his VW van! The words I said to Cal were,

"I think I can see myself living there." Cal wanted to put an offer in on the house there and then, but I said no. We needed to see the house another time at a different time of day and we also needed to do some number crunching; not Cal's forte! As you have probably guessed, we did buy Vale Farm, but what you would not have guessed was that we became good friends with Phil and Celia on the way.

In September of 2004 we moved into our new dream home to make a fresh start. Cal and I never did anything by the book and moving in was no exception.

We arranged to move the horses the day before all our belongings came out of storage. It was only an hour and a half from Surrey to Buckinghamshire so it was possible to move all 3 horses and my little pony Magic on the same day. It was a hectic day but we got them all settled into their new 5-star accommodation.

The only problem then was that our 5-star accommodation at the main house was empty, so off we set to find somewhere nice to have dinner and pass a few hours until bedtime.

We found The Woolpack in Stoke Mandeville. Neither the name or the area suggested just how lovely this gastro pub would turn out to be. To this day it is one of my favourite places to go. The décor is old and features different types of wood, the staff are young and enthusiastic and the food is gorgeous. It was perfect.

Not so perfect was the nights' sleep we then tried to get, all wrapped up in duvets but lying on the floor. As valiant as our attempt was, no bed and no mattress meant no sleep. It was a long night but the discomfort was alleviated a little by the thoughts of all our furniture and belongings, that we hadn't seen for a year, arriving the next day.

The following day, after I had fed and watered the dogs, cats and horses, I was walking down the drive to see if the removal company were approaching when my phone rang. It was my psychic friend Christine. She started to ask about the house.

"Does it have 3 willow trees along the drive?" she asked.

"Yes," I said.

"Does it have some arched windows." She wanted to know.

"Not really," I replied, but then as I walked further away from the house and looked back at the orangery I realised we did have some windows that looked arched. "Oh, hold on a minute, yes I can see arched windows now."

"Does the house sit in the middle of its land?"

"Not perfectly central, but yes sort of." I agreed.

"Can you see the stables from the kitchen?" she continued.

"Yes," I replied, "but what is with the 20 questions? Do you want me to just describe it to you?"

Her reply took me a back. "No, Darling, just enjoy your time as lady of the manor because you won't be there long."

I was only just moving in. This was the second time we'd moved in 12 months. The furniture hadn't arrived yet. What did she mean I wouldn't be there long?

My heart sank as Christine told me she thought I wouldn't live at Vale Farm any longer than 3 years.

"But don't worry about that," she said, "enjoy it while you can." This wasn't the best news I'd heard. Why on earth would we want to move again so soon I thought. I guess I could have disregarded her prophecy but I trusted Christine. She had been right on everything she'd said to me so far. Oh, all except one thing.

Christine had painted a picture of me sat on my own in front of the Aga with my feet warming against it. I was wearing a black polo neck jumper and was reading a newspaper. At my feet were my 4 dogs. She had suggested this would be after Cal had left me. I always assumed the scene was at Holly Tree and although we had come close to divorce, it never happened, so I thought Cal and I had affected what Christine had predicted.

Besides which, I never believed for one moment that Cal would leave me. I always thought that if my marriage ended it would be me who made the decision. I felt an uneasiness in my stomach. There was an Aga in this new house. Had this scene in my life not been played out yet? My friend Anna had said to me before I left Cheshire,

"Don't let him put you in a gilded cage." The words rang in my ears. Could this be my gilded cage? Would Cal really leave me? Suddenly the removal van was attempting to get in through the gate. I let my thoughts go and focused on the arrival of my furniture and my new life.

The first few months at Vale Farm were chaotic. The furniture had arrived over 2 days. On day one our mattress arrived so we slept a little better and on day 2 the bed arrived. What a luxury it was to sleep in our lovely oak framed bed again. It was like greeting old friends seeing all our furniture being lifted off the back of the removal van. Eventually the grandfather clock arrived and was set up in pride of place in the entrance hall. Hearing that familiar tick of the clock was like giving our new home a heartbeat.

If the furniture gave me a warm glow, the boxes did not. It felt like there were hundreds of them spread all over the house. I swear that when I went to bed at night they multiplied. As Cal went back to work the day after the furniture had been delivered, I started unpacking boxes. I had 3 months to get the house ship shape and ready for all the family and friends who'd booked to visit us over Christmas and New Year. My days were spent looking after the animals, I still had 4 stables to muck out every day, and unpacking boxes. I wanted Cal to be able to see a difference every day when he came home. I took care of the horses but I didn't start to ride again because I didn't want Cal thinking that I was playing. I wanted to get the house sorted first.

The house started to take shape. It never truly felt like ours because we didn't redecorate or change the curtains but with our furniture, ornaments and pictures it started to feel more homely. The energy of Vale Farm felt odd. It wasn't good and it wasn't bad. It sat like a void waiting to be filled. I couldn't quite put my finger on it.

When Cal was at work and I was home alone I hardly ever saw anyone. The gardener, a very amiable, hardworking young lad, came once a week and the farrier visited every 6 weeks. Interestingly all the tradesmen who had worked for the previous owners were available for us too, except for the farrier. Although Celia had taken her horses with her and therefore her farrier should have had room for more, he insisted to me that he couldn't take on any more work.

I therefore asked a neighbour who recommended Daniel to me. I liked Daniel from the day he arrived. He'd been very warm and friendly on the phone when I had first talked to him, but as I got to know him I grew to love his sense of humour and his amazing way of thinking out of the box. The first day he met the horses he surprised me.

My horse Ella had been badly treated before she found her way to me. She'd arrived on the yard at Holly Tree during a period when I was down south with Cal, and

Rebecca was in charge. I had arrived back from my trip to find 2 new horse and 2 new ponies. I had agreed with one of my clients that when her daughter found a horse it could come to Holly Tree on working livery. This all happened while I was away, but at least I knew about that one. Ella and the other 2 ponies were a complete shock when I got back.

Rebecca sold the idea of Ella to me as a horse that would be good for more advanced riders. I did point out that we didn't really have too many advanced riders. That was not the level I was aiming for since I hadn't achieved any dizzy height of horse riding myself.

My vision for Holly Tree was always to give our clients a good foundation in riding and a respect and love for their horse. Rebecca suggested quite strongly that we should have one or two horses to take our better riders forward. She did have a point as the teenagers who had been helping on the yard, some of whom had been riding with me for 7 years, were getting very good.

As it turned out, Ella did not really fill this void. Bless her, she was a very pretty mare but in those early days I couldn't see it. She reminded me a little of my first horse, Rosie, who was beautiful but Ella never quite matched up to Rosie. Maybe the biggest reason I didn't see her beauty was because her eyes were dead; they were dull and lifeless, like there was a veil over them that you couldn't see through.

This was a horse who had retreated inside herself to avoid her pain. She would be a challenge but also another teacher for me.

As expected, Ella was not good in the school. Very few of my clients could cope with her. She was frightened of the indoor school walls and so insisted on being as far away from them as possible. She hated being touched, even if we simply tried to stroke her she would tense up, and if you stood between her head and withers you had a very good chance of getting bitten, which happened to me on a couple of occasions.

It wasn't long before Ella went lame, badly lame. Her whole back end looked like a board. The vet was called but couldn't find anything wrong. The owners were called and swore it had never happened before. Then suddenly the owners wanted to sell her and they were 'willing' to give me first refusal. How kind! They were offering me a bad-tempered horse who wasn't great in the school and who at this current moment in time was very lame. Hardly a bargain! My answer was 'no'. I felt sorry for the horse but I tried to be a business women first and an animal lover second.

That didn't last very long! Ida, who at that time was still helping on the yard, and Dan her partner, suddenly decided that they wanted to buy Ella, and Ida's new best friend, Rebecca, encouraged her to do just that.

This was a disaster waiting to happen for all of them. Ida and Dan had never had a horse before and were already looking at local competitions that they could take

Ella to. Ella needed lots of TLC just to get her to trust a human being, let alone be happy about them riding her.

I voiced my fears to Cal. His reply shocked me. I'm sure he had an alternative motive but this is what he said,

"Why don't you buy her?"

I was shocked to hear him suggest we should add another horse to our menagerie, after all he'd made his thoughts about the riding school very clear.

However, he made me think. I hadn't had a horse of my own since Rosie died. I did miss her but I had lots of riding school horses to choose from when I wanted to ride. Did I really want to take on this horse? I decided to ride her and see.

I waited until her lameness had eased and then quietly took her into the school when no one else was around. She let me climb on board, but she was testing me. She was feisty and challenged my requests but for some reason she didn't scare me. Her attitude reminded me of Rosie and her challenges made me smile. In a way, she was allowing me in, allowing me to see a little of her personality and my heart opened.

How could I not save this horse? I put her back in her stable, went back to Cal and told him I wanted to buy her. He told me to make a silly low offer to the owners and make it clear that the offer was only open for 24 hours. If the answer was 'yes' we would pay them in cash the following day, if not, then we expected them to take back full financial responsibility for her with immediate effect. I will be honest, I had to have a small glass of port before I made the call. This was well out of my comfort zone and my knees were shaking at the thought. However, I made the call and the owners agreed.

Suddenly I was the proud owner of a lame, bad tempered mare with quite a pretty face. I needed a plan.

My knowledge of horses had grown through experience in the seven years since I had arrived at Holly Tree, but on this occasion I didn't know what to do. My intuition however said that my horse's lameness was something to do with her fear and mistrust of human beings.

My first goal was to solve her lameness problem so that I had a sound horse to ride. One of the teenagers on the yard, Emma, had also fallen in love with this mare and wanted to help me. We decided to ask nothing of Ella except to be in our company once a day while we groomed her. As it turned out she didn't even like being touched with a brush so we started by stroking her with our hands and each day venturing a little more into the danger area where she had a habit of biting us. Something she did on several occasions. The strange thing was that she started to look a little apologetic when she got us. It was like her biting was an automatic response. Other than that, she was fed, watered and allowed to go out in the field to graze each day.

I'll be honest, Ella was never an easy horse to own. We had good days and bad days. We took 3 steps forward and 2 back, but she taught me a lot and slowly the veil over her eyes started to lift. As the shine returned to her deep dark eyes, I started to see how beautiful she was and wondered why I couldn't see it before. After 9 months of gently handling Ella, and free schooling her, we got our miracle.

Emma came running out of the indoor school shouting my name.

"KAREN, KAREN, COME AND SEE THIS." Unsure of what I would find, I ran back after her to the indoor school. Ella was resting inside. I smiled to see how relaxed she had become in the indoor school.

"Watch," said Emma, and she encouraged Ella to walk around the school. After a while she asked her to trot and suddenly I was watching a sound horse happily trotting and following the track around the school. I held my breath as the tears formed in my eyes.

"Turn her to the other rein Emma," I said, asking Emma to get Ella to trot the other way around the school. As she turned and trotted in the other direction it became clear that she was completely sound.

Emma looked over to me with tears rolling down her face.

"We did it," she said. I couldn't speak. The words wouldn't come, only the tears. Tears of absolute joy. My theory was right. No matter what had happened to this little horse before she came to us, it was fear that she held in her back end, fear that had made her lame.

Fear has a physical effect on our bodies

It took 9 months of TLC and persistence for this lovely horse to trust us enough to let go of her fear and relax. Even now, words cannot express the joy in my heart that day as I watched Ella trot around the school. When Emma asked her to stop, Ella walked back up to her and nuzzled into her shoulder. Trust and Love, such a powerful combination. It was an honour to be a part of her journey and the process gave Ella, Emma and I a bond that would never break.

The solution was love and trust

When Daniel the farrier arrived at Vale Farm that first day, I never told him of Ella's past. Normally, I would warn a vet or farrier about Ella's before they first worked with her, especially if they were male. I would always suggest that they take ten to fifteen minutes to get to know her first. If they did this, she was fine, but she got very nervous if she was rushed.

For some reason I never warned Daniel and yet, as he went along the line of my horses, all of which were tied up ready for his arrival, he spent 5 minutes saying hello to each one until he got to Ella. With Ella he instinctively took longer, he gave her time to sniff him and work out if she could trust him. It was another special moment.

I knew in that moment, that the universe had sent me an intuitive farrier with an open heart. He would never have described himself that way, far from it. But I saw with my own eyes and thanked God that I had a found a new farrier who I trusted like Ella.

Chapter 15: The Next Affair

That first Christmas at Vale Farm was lovely. I pushed the boat out and had not one, but two Christmas Trees.

Dressing the Christmas Tree was one of my most favourite bits of Christmas. I put the main tree in the small lounge, I call it small because it was small in relation to the main lounge, but it was still a sizeable room and had very high ceilings. The tree for this lounge was the tallest I had ever bought.

I'm very particular about Christmas trees, they must be bushy and they must have that isosceles triangle look. I then cover them in a mish-mash of coloured lights, baubles and tinsel. The way the tree sparkles when I put the lights on makes my heart sing. Of course, the glass of wine or port that I enjoy whilst doing this may also contribute to my joy.

This year I had the joy of a second tree. The hall to Vale Farm was so big it was crying out for a tree. I knew Cal wouldn't be too impressed if I spent a lot on a second tree, so I bought a smaller tree and limited the decorations. I chose a colour scheme of red and gold and amazingly, although it only took a fraction of the time to dress as my main tree, it still looked beautiful. The staircase was also crying out for decoration so I bought 2 chunky lengths of tinsel to dress it. By the time I'd finished it looked like something from a film and I felt very pleased with myself.

Our first visitor to our new home arrived on the 18th of December. My sister did a flying visit without her husband just to come and see the house and exchange gifts. My sister has always been amazing, she and her husband never had anywhere near the kind of money that Cal and I had, but she was happy for me that Cal and I could buy such an impressive home.

To be honest from where we had come from, it felt a bit surreal for me and Julie to be sitting and drinking wine in this huge house that was my new home. We had a lovely 24 hours together with lots of talking and lots of laughter, and yes lots of wine. Her visit was over all too soon and I suddenly found myself waving her off on a train journey back up north.

All the anticipation of her visit, all the joy of spending time with her was over. I've always felt sad, and still do to this day, saying goodbye to her even though I know she is always at the other end of a phone. My heart was heavy as I drove back to Vale Farm, but once there I started to prepare for our next visitors.

Cal's family were coming to Vale Farm to spend Christmas with us as up until now we had always spent Christmas with them. As an Italian Mother, Cal's Mum was the matriarch of the family and she never seemed very comfortable in someone else's house.

This year however, she had shocked us all by agreeing to come to us. I wanted the house to be beautiful and ship-shape; all the bedrooms to be ready with fresh bed linen and, except for the turkey, which Cal's Mum was bringing, I needed to buy all the food for Christmas dinner and the rest of their stay.

The food was my biggest concern. As a vegetarian, I ate very differently from the rest of the family and I wanted them to feel at home. I needn't have worried. Mam was amazing that year; she arrived at the house with her 2 other sons, Cal's younger brothers, and took her coat off and made herself at home the minute she arrived, she'd even brought her slippers with her! The atmosphere in the house was warm and loving.

There was a buzz in the air that Vale Farm cried out for and somehow the house came alive with more people in it. On Christmas day Mam started to prepare the dinner while I was mucking out the horses. Every now and again she would come out to ask me where something was, but apart from that she was happy. Once I'd finished the horses I joined her in the kitchen to prepare the vegetables and finish the trifle, we never had Christmas Pudding, it was always trifle for dessert.

As we sat watching the traditional Christmas film later in the day with the Panettone, tangerines and nuts laid out on the coffee table in front of us, and 4 sleepy dogs stretched out at different points in the lounge, my heart sang. I felt like I had finally found a place where I belonged. This was my family, in my home, and it felt good. Sadly, my joy was not to last.

Christmas was soon over and Cal's family left.

The house was quiet for a couple of days before our friends Jan and Chris arrived with their young family for New Year, and I loved having more visitors in the house. Cal and I are Godparents to Jan and Chris's son, so we were very close to all the family. The house once again became alive and although we stayed home on New Year's Eve, we had lots of fun.

I thought the visit had gone well. There was only one occasion that I can remember when Cal made things a little awkward. We'd decided to go for a walk and everyone, except Cal, assumed this would be with the dogs, in fact the children wanted the dogs to come. Cal insisted that if we were going to drive, there wouldn't be room for the dogs, so despite us travelling in two separate cars, the dogs were left behind. It all felt a little uncomfortable at the time. Cal had been quite short tempered when he'd said the dogs couldn't come, and although I attempted to quietly change his mind, I eventually gave in because I didn't want to cause a scene in front of our guests.

Do you always have a good reason for not speaking your truth?

We went over to Wendover woods that day which was full of families walking their dogs! Apart from this one uncomfortable occasion, it was lovely having Jan, Chris and their family with us for a few days. They left on January the 4th, and Cal left for Czech on January 8th. He had 3 weeks work out there on some film version of a computer game.

Once everyone had gone, the house felt empty again and I missed everyone incredibly. I got on with taking care of my animals and bringing the book keeping for Cal's business up-to-date, but I couldn't settle. I felt anxious and weepy. It was January, the days were short and the weather was gloomy. My S.A.D symptoms were kicking in and I felt very down.

When Cal came back from Prague he was not as pleased to see me, as I was to see him, something had changed. He was snappy and critical and no matter what I did it wasn't good enough. He complained about the horses, the dogs and the house and I was accused of being lazy. He would happily eat with me at home and even talk while we ate, but if I ever suggested that we went out for lunch or dinner he would make an excuse. He started doing things without me. He got himself in a band, he was and is a great guitar player and was either out rehearsing with them, or they would come to Vale Farm and rehearse at the cottage.

He started seeing his mate Pete more often and would go away with him, supposedly windsurfing. Cal was making a life for himself without me and naively I didn't know why. One day I approached him about the subject. He sat on the wicker couch at the end of the kitchen and I sat opposite him on a pine chair. I started to share my concerns expecting him to say I was imagining it, expecting him to do his usual 'don't worry, we'll be alright.' Instead, as I continued to desperately reconnect with him, he first crossed his legs and then folded his arms across his body. I knew I was in trouble.

"Cal, if we don't sort this out, if you're not already having an affair, you soon will be." The words were out of my mouth.

Deep down I intuitively already knew the truth, I just didn't want to admit it. I desperately didn't want to know, not now; not after I'd walked out of my previous life to commit to our marriage. Not after I'd closed the riding school, left my home, my sister and my friends. Not now I was living in a huge house in 30 acres of land where I knew no one. No not now. He wouldn't do that to me. Not when I'd asked for a divorce and he'd begged me not to go. He promised he would be faithful. Not now.

The fears bubbled up and I pushed them back down. Up, down, up, down I was fighting with myself.

Cal mumbled something about me not being so stupid and he got up and walked out. I later saw him in the garden talking to someone on the phone. I refused to accept that day what I knew deep down in my heart, but what I did accept was that I was in trouble.

Cal went back to Prague in March supposedly for 10 days' work, but I've no idea if that was the truth or not. I still didn't know he was having an affair. I still didn't know he had met the woman who would become his next wife. Life with him was up and down. We slept together in the same bed, but there was no physical contact. It wasn't all bad. In fact we were probably living more like brother and sister than man and wife. We could rub along okay, but something was missing.

I felt lost and alone. I tried naively to do things that I thought would please him, but most of the time he didn't even notice. It was the beginning of a tough few years. At some point between him coming home from Prague in March and returning in June, he told me he'd met someone. It shocks me now that I cannot remember that day or that conversation. Was it such bad news that I blocked it out?

I do remember that I didn't know about Nikita when Cal came home from Prague in March, but that before he returned in June I did. In fact, his entire reason for going and spending time with Nikita in June was to see which one of us he wanted to be with! How arrogant is that? I cannot believe I allowed him to have that choice. I'm clearly a much stronger person now than I was then.

To add insult to injury he then asked me to help him book his flight to Prague, which I did. Ever the skin flint he chose to fly Easy Jet from Gatwick. When Cal travelled around the world for work he always travelled business class, but when he had to pay himself - this man who lived in a house that was worth over 2 million pounds - he chose the cheapest option. The problem with booking from Gatwick was the question of how would he get there? Yes, you're ahead of me again. When he asked me to take him, I agreed. The journey should have taken an hour at the most, but the traffic was bad and it seemed more like two hours. I dropped him off, he kissed my cheek and set off towards the departures entrance, his small case in one hand and a guitar in the other.

Did I tell you that when we booked Cal's ticket it was only one way? He said he didn't know how long he would stay, but he'd let me know when he was coming back. Of course he would, he needed a lift home. He stayed for 2 full weeks and my life went on hold while he decided what he wanted.

I dropped further into my own depression but my animals kept me going. No matter what happened I had to get up, I had to go out, I had 4 dogs, 3 horses, 2 cats and a pony who were relying on me.

It was a long two weeks made worse by a text that arrived on the 20th of June. Cal and I had first gone out together on the 20th of June. and although we'd got married on November 2nd, we always celebrated June 20th because we were together for 10 years before we got married. It was June 20th that I got a text. It said,

"I am having the time of my life.
I should have done this years ago"

The text went on to tell me that he was mucking out the cows and going for long walks with Nikita and her dog. Could this man I loved, the man I'd known for 30 years and been married to for nearly 20, really be so cruel? No doubt about it, his text was cruel. It hit me right in the heart.

I fell dramatically to my knees as I read it and sobbed from a place deep inside myself that I'd never found before. Not only was he telling me he was choosing her, he had done it on our anniversary, and to add insult to injury, he told me he was doing things with her that he wouldn't do with me. I wanted him to walk the dogs but he wasn't interested. I wanted him to help with the horses but he wasn't interested. My world as I knew it folded on the 20th June 2005.

I did think about not picking him up from the airport but I was too nice. How would he get home if I didn't? If he got a taxi it would be expensive and it would be our money he was spending. No, it was best to pick him up. When he arrived, he had the suitcase but no guitar. I asked where it was. He muttered something about leaving it there for next time. There were very few words in the car going home. What could be said? He'd made his choice. Where would we go from here? I was hurt and angry, depressed and scared all rolled into one. I'd spent most of my life since I was 14 with Cal. Now what?

Life became a bit of a blur. Cal still expected me to make the meals and look after the house and the washing etc. He would happily sit and eat with me but apart from that he lived an even more separate life than before.

I was his housekeeper, PA and bookkeeper. There were constant phone calls and text messages which lit him up. He was indifferent to me but happy with himself that he had a new relationship. I would find out the hard way how indifferent and cruel this man could be, but it took a long time before I could see through his manipulation.

At that point I still loved him, and although I had to admit she existed, I couldn't believe he really would not care if he hurt me. He'd loved me for so long he must still care about me, mustn't he?

We muddled through the next few weeks, although neither of us started divorce proceedings, we hadn't really even had that conversation.

One day when he was rehearsing with the band in the cottage I decided to move him out of our bedroom. While the music of the band thudded outside I took action. There were 2 other bedrooms at Vale farm with en-suites but one was a little girly. It was down the far end of the house and would have been preferable, but I decided against it. No, I cleaned the bedroom and bathroom that used to belong to one of the previous owner's sons; Cal could sleep in there, then I moved all his clothes in. There was a built-in wardrobe in the room so there was plenty of storage space for his stuff.

When the music eventually stopped and he came back in I told him what I had done. He didn't have a problem with us sleeping in different rooms but was surprised that I had moved his stuff and not mine! Really? However, he didn't put up a fight. We now had separate bedrooms. We were living in the same house but I guess officially we were separated.

August soon arrived and with it the football season started up again. Cal was a film cameraman but specialised in a thing called Steadicam so he could also be seen running up and down the side lines of a football pitch.

When Sky had approached him with this idea we'd thought that it was crazy as the Steadicam and camera are heavy and the footballers are incredibly fit. However, Cal agreed to try it out and surprisingly it worked incredibly well. He'd worked for Sky ever since.

The first match of the season was the Charity Shield. Now I'm not a dedicated fan of football, but I do enjoy watching a match and with Cal working on it and wanting to watch what he'd done when he got home, I soon started watching quite a few matches.

Although Cal had grown up living near Manchester City's ground they had not been doing so well, so he'd become a Manchester United supporter. I followed his lead and my Dad supported United so it seemed a good choice. United weren't playing in the Charity Shield, it was a match between Chelsea and Arsenal, so I wasn't that bothered about watching.

I forgot about the match and went outside to muck out my horses. As the time passed I kept getting a strong feeling that I should watch the match. Time and time again I dismissed it, but each time the feeling came back stronger. I finished the stables and decided it wouldn't hurt to make a coffee and then see how Chelsea and Arsenal were playing this season. When I settled in front of the television, the second half was just beginning. It was 1-0 to Chelsea, no surprise there then. I happily sat and watched as Chelsea soon scored a second goal followed by the first from Arsenal. The match finished at 2-1 to Chelsea. I was just about to turn the television off when the director cut to a shot from a Steadicam on the pitch. I'd forgotten there was a charity Shield Cup to be presented. All the players were still on the pitch plus lots of behind the scenes people. It was a bit chaotic. Cal and his brother, who was also a Steadicam operator, were on the field. I continued to watch.

After a few minutes, I saw Cal's brother in the back of Cal's shot. The director soon cut to his brother's camera and Cal unknowingly walked through the shot with a female assistant in tow. Now I need to explain to you that when the camera is on the Steadicam the operator can't touch the camera. Have I explained what a Steadicam is? Well, in case I haven't, In layman's terms, the Steadicam is a piece of equipment that is worn by the operator. The camera is attached to the Steadicam and a skilled operator can then move without any camera shake. It can be used for a lot more than just getting rid of camera shake once the operator gets creative. However, all you need to know is that Cal would always have an assistant, called a focus puller, because the assistant would remotely focus the camera.

My heart sank as I watched Cal in the back of shot. I paid all our assistants and we only had one female assistant at the time and that was Lou, my friend who used to work at the riding school. This was not Lou. This girl had long blond hair tied up in a ponytail. Three times I saw Cal and his assistant on the pitch that day. I was horrified. Not only was Cal having an affair. Not only was he choosing to be with someone else after all these years, he was flaunting her on national television.

How could he do this to me? I texted my friend Alex, who was an avid Chelsea supporter and would be at the game. Had she seen Cal? Did she see his assistant? Had he introduced her? My mind was racing. Alex had seen Cal, but only to wave to from a distance, and at the first game of the season she really hadn't taken much notice of his assistant.

She was shocked when I shared my fears. My thoughts then switched to my brother-in-law. He must also know, he must have met this girl. How many people had Cal introduced her to while I was locked in my gilded cage? I remembered Anna's comment and I felt sick.

How unfair was this? He was making a fool of me. I had loved and supported him all these years, I'd helped him get where he was success wise and now he was dumping me for a younger model and wasn't even embarrassed by what he was doing. He was arrogant and proud to have a younger girlfriend in tow. I was hurt. I was angry. I was embarrassed. I felt stupid. I felt ashamed. I couldn't believe he would do this to me. Who was this man?

Cal didn't come home until the following day, by which time I'd regained my composure and so we talked about mundane things. We avoided the divorce word and I kept quiet about what I'd seen. I could have launched into him when he got back, but I wanted to catch him off guard. The following day we started to talk about his work. This was my chance.

"Which assistants did you have at the football on Sunday?" I asked.

"Tony and Sam" he replied.

"Who did you have working with you?" I asked as innocently as possible.

"Tony." His reply came back instantaneously.

"Are we paying him?" I asked.

Cal stopped what he was doing and looked up at me. Suddenly a glimmer of a thought that I could know passed over his face.

"Er... why wouldn't we?"

My moment had come. "Because he wasn't there, was he? You had a female assistant and it wasn't Lou so who was she?"

He ignored my question. Ignored the fact that I had caught him out. His only concern was who had told me.

"It was Alex, wasn't it? I knew she wouldn't keep her mouth shut."

My heart missed a beat. Had my good friend lied to me or was he just diverting my attention?

"No, it wasn't Alex. I saw you. I saw you and her on the television."

My heart started to race. As hard as I tried not to the volume of my voice started to increase.

"YOU PARADED HER ACROSS NATIONAL TELEVISION FOR EVERYONE TO SEE. HOW COULD YOU?"

He became defensive. "It's none of your business what I do, or who I choose to be my assistant and I didn't parade her. We were working."

As you can imagine the heated discussion had just begun. He did confirm that the girl was Nikita but apart from that he stayed in defensive mode. When I realised we were going around in circles and he was getting more verbally aggressive, I stopped and walked away. He would later change that last statement and say he had no choice, he didn't know she would be in the country, she'd just turned up. He had to have her with him and the only way he could do it was for her to be his assistant.

I now know that this is a pattern with him. He always plays the victim and blames someone else. He never wants to be seen as a 'bad' man. At that point I was still hurt, but a bit of me wanted to believe him, wanted to believe that Nikita had arrived without invitation. I wanted to believe she was a Czech girl doing what Czech girls reputedly do. I know now that my thoughts were both unfair and very far from the truth, but I was in emotional turmoil and not able to think rationally. It would get worse.

Chapter 16: Meeting Nikita

In the following few weeks Cal spent a lot of his time away from Vale Farm.

On the day of my first meeting with Nikita, Cal had been home but told me he was leaving to pick up his friend Pete from Heathrow airport. He said he would probably stay with Pete that night. I knew deep inside of me that he was not telling me the truth. I had no proof but my intuition told me he was lying. As his car left the drive I wondered if I should follow him.

Did I really need to see them together? Did I really need to put myself through that sort of pain? Did I need to prove he could and would lie to me more easily than ever before? I couldn't decide, so I phoned a friend.

"Of course you need to catch him," came her reply, shocked that I was even questioning the need to find them. "Put the phone down and go now. Karen Go Now. JUST GO."

I got the message and jumped into my car. Cal was well ahead of me so I couldn't follow him now. I didn't even know where to drive to. I decided to use my intuition. Every time I got to a roundabout or road junction I chose to go the way that 'felt right'. I don't know who was guiding me but as I continued the journey the direction decisions were getting easier and easier. I found myself on the M40 and then the M25. The Heathrow turn off was approaching. Had I got this wrong? Had Cal gone to Heathrow after all?

I strangely had no desire to take the Heathrow exit, so I continued. When we got to junction 12 my inner guide told me to exit the motorway. I suddenly knew where I was going; we were heading back to Virginia Water. Cal and I still owned the house at Virginia Water, we'd tried to sell it without any success so we'd rented it out for a year.

The new tenants were in the house and so had most of the keys, but Cal had held back a key to the swimming pool complex. I drove through the gates as the security man recognised me and parked my car in our old guest parking space. It was hidden out of sight there. I then walked towards the pool building with my heart pounding in my chest. As I approached the swimming pool I could see Cal's VW van in the parking area. They were here. I ran back to my car and stayed out of sight, what am I doing? I wasn't doing anything wrong.

It suddenly struck me that I had no reason to hide, so I turned the key and started the car up. I made sure I parked outside the swimming pool and opposite Cal's van.

Then I waited. I didn't really know what I was doing, didn't really know what I would say to them, but I was fed up with waiting while my life fell apart around me. I had to do something to take some control back. I waited for about 20 minutes and there they were.

Clearly they'd been for a swim. Cal didn't have hair but her long hair was very wet. They skipped hand in hand down the steps outside the pool building.

I got out of the car and walked towards them.

"You Bastard." I said.

He looked up and smiled at me "I knew you would find us," he said smartly, as if somehow knowing made it all acceptable.

My voice got louder. I was angry and hurt all rolled into one. This man just didn't give a s**t about me. He had that proud look of a man having a midlife crisis who mistakenly thinks everyone is admiring him for having a girl 18 years younger than him on his arm. Nikita's face remained expressionless while Cal tried to calm me down.

People started to turn their heads; this sort of thing didn't happen at Virginia Park. Amazingly there were more people out and about that day than I had ever seen in the year I'd lived there. I didn't care. My life was unfolding around me and I was in a fog where I could only see the two of them standing in front of me, not caring that their happiness was turning my life upside down.

"Let's go to the pub and talk about this," Cal said, and as ludicrous as this sounds, that is what I did.

As I got back into my car, every cell in my body was shaking. How dare he do this to me? So many questions had run through my head since that day Cal had sat in front of me with his arms and legs crossed. So many questions every day and as yet, I didn't seem to have any answers.

The pub was just down the road from the house. There were wooden tables with benches attached outside and it was a nice day so it seemed sensible to sit outside. Sensible? Was any of this really sensible? There I go again, another damn question.

"I take it we are sitting outside?" I said, as I looked over to Cal.

"Yes," he replied. "I'll go and get some drinks. Do you want the usual?"

I nodded yes and turned to walk over to one of the benches expecting Nikita to go into the pub with Cal. As I sat on the bench I was startled out of my thoughts as she sat next to me. Not opposite me, next to me.

"I've been telling him he is being cruel to you," she said.

What did she mean, 'she' was telling him he was being cruel to me? 'She' had only known him 6 months and for most of that time they had been in different countries; I had known him 31 years. How could she possibly know what was right or fair for me? I was lost.

I hadn't expected her to follow me. She was brave and direct I would give her that, but it felt like she had invaded my space. At this point I was trying hard not to blame her for the hell that was now my life, but as she sat so close I felt anger rising inside that was aimed solely at her. I swallowed that anger, I didn't want to react emotionally, that was not who I was.

Sometimes I frustrate myself, this situation was not of my making. I accept that I had to be partly to blame for Cal and I growing apart, for the breakdown of our marriage but if it had been up to me, Cal and I would have talked and sorted this out without me having to 'catch them together' so to speak. This bit was cruel and she wasn't helping. She couldn't put herself on my side of the battle. At this point in time she was a part of the enemy. Surprisingly, one day, she would become my friend, but not at this point.

Cal came back with the drinks. He sat opposite us, the present wife and the future wife. He seemed to enjoy having two women 'fighting' over him. He did all the usual 'I didn't tell you because I didn't want to hurt you' comments. How stupid is that. If he hadn't wanted to hurt me, he wouldn't have slept with someone else. Or even if he had slept with someone else, he would have told me without me having to play detective all the time. Surely after 30 years I deserved that.

Cal had nothing to offer to the situation that day; no solution, no way forward, no apology for hurting me. We talked but we got nowhere and as the second glass of wine started to settle in my empty stomach I started to feel a little hazy.

It was time to go I decided. I made it clear I intended to divorce him. One affair that I knew of was forgivable, but this was beyond forgiveness. This was rubbing my nose in it and he didn't care. I tried to stand up with dignity and walk back to my car.

"Will you be safe to drive home?" Cal asked.

I knew I was over the legal limit but on that day I justified my actions. I knew it was wrong but I needed to go home. What did he care? Me crashing the car and ending my life would be an easy way out for him. My thoughts were not very clear as I got in the car and drove away without looking back.

Drove away from them, away from the hurt, back to my gilded cage and back to the house that would be my sanctuary for another 2 years. And all the time I drove, I cried.

The next day I woke up feeling numb. Did that all really happen yesterday? I had promised to phone my friend the previous evening when I got back to let her know I was okay, but I was too exhausted to tell anyone else.

I muddled through my morning jobs. The animals are great when you feel down. They cannot look after themselves so you have to get up and start the day, but most importantly they accept you as you are.

Animals see you and accept you as you are

I didn't have to put on a brave face and smile. I didn't have to pretend to be anything other than what I was; numb, detached and maybe just a little relieved. Yes, even a little relieved. I had fought to try and make my marriage work for so long I could stop fighting now. I could stop making all that effort and concentrate on my divorce.

I was scared too, but the numbness took the edge off that. I couldn't think about what next, I could only focus on today, on now and right now my 'save my marriage' battle was over. I idled the morning away with my dogs and horses. My 4 dogs stayed close to me, they tried to protect me from whatever it was that was making me so unhappy.

Afterwards I sat quietly in the kitchen nursing a cup of coffee as lunchtime came and went. As the time approached for Daniel the farrier to arrive, I wandered back outside and brought the horses in from the field. Soon enough I heard his van turning into the drive. I pushed the hair off my face and forced a smile ready to great him. I was just tying my 17hh Irish draught gentle giant, Jim, outside his stable as Daniel reversed his van onto the yard.

Daniel wasn't very tall, he had longish floppy hair, some of which he tied in a ponytail when he was working with the horses, and the most beautiful blue eyes. I had been struck by those eyes the first day I met him. He reminded me of Brian Adams in a good looking sort of way.

Daniel cheerfully jumped out of his van and opened the back to get access to his kiln. We exchanged pleasantries and once he'd started work on Jim, I went inside to make the usual 2 cups of coffee. When I returned, I placed his coffee at the back of his van and I perched on the telegraph sleepers that surrounded the lawn. I spent many an hour sat like this chatting with

Daniel over the next couple of years. That day Daniel could tell I was not my usual happy self and asked me 'what's up?'. I took a deep breath and related the goings on from the day before starting at Cal's lie that he was picking up Pete, and finishing with my exit from the pub. Once I'd started I couldn't stop and Daniel showed enough interest for me to keep going without thinking I was boring him.

As I finished my account of the previous day, Daniel said,

"I don't know how you remained so calm, I would have hit him."

Somehow that comment made me laugh. My giggles would continue as I then said to Daniel,

"What I don't understand is why he couldn't tell me. After all these years together I deserved that, I deserved to be treated with more respect, not just led a trail of bread crumbs to follow."

Daniels reply completely disarmed me, "No man is that brave!" he said.

The giggles turned into more belly laughs and suddenly the day after my life had taken a nose dive, I was laughing uncontrollably with a man I didn't know very well and it felt good.

The conversation lifted, my mood lifted and Daniel and I giggled our way through the rest of the afternoon. I was grateful that day that Daniel always made his appointments with me at the end of the day so he never had to dash off. That day I really appreciated his company and his sense of humour. As Daniel left I walked back into the house, with 4 dogs at my feet, feeling tired but much happier. My happiness wasn't likely to last, but I could wrap myself up in it for one more evening and hopefully then get a good nights' sleep.

It wasn't long after Daniel had left that I heard my phone ping to say I'd received a text message. The message made me smile. It said,

"If what is good for the goose is good for the gander, please put my name at the top of the list before all the good-looking men who will show up when they know you are free."

Again, I laughed and felt flattered. It had never dawned on me that Daniel may have seen me that way. To be honest it never dawned on me that any man could see me that way and at that moment my self-confidence was on the floor.

His timing was perfect. I didn't believe that what was good for the goose was good for the gander. At this point in my life I had been on two sides of the affair triangle and it was painful on both sides. I had cheated on Cal with my holiday fling in San Lucia and look how that had turned out. I had also just found Cal with another woman; that had hurt like hell. It had also hurt when I'd found out about Cal's previous affair only 5 years before. I thought we had grown through that experience and that the affair had saved our marriage, but it seemed not. The last thing I wanted to do was to complete the triangle and see what it felt like to be the ‘other woman’. I couldn’t help myself though, I text back.

“I’m not sure that what is good for the goose is good for the gander, but I have put your name at the top of the list just in case!”

Daniel kept me entertained that evening as the jokey text messages flew back and forth. I sat on the couch with my feet up, a glass of white wine on the coffee table and my phone in my hand.

The day had not gone how I’d planned, but I felt better for sharing what had happened and the flirty texts had picked me up off the floor of numb despair. I still had a feeling that the worst was yet to come, but for that night I could stop worrying about it all.

In fact, as Cal came and went over the next few weeks Daniel kept my spirits up with his texts, not every day, but often enough for me to start to look forward to them. Eventually he asked if he could take me out to dinner. The questions in my head started up again. Would that be crossing a line? Can I go to dinner without being committed to anything else? Would it be a stupid idea at this point in my life? Would I be breaking any vows? Would it matter if I did? What would I wear? As the what would I wear question came into my head I realised I had made the decision.

I text Daniel back and asked, “When?”

“Tomorrow? “he replied, “I can pick you up at 8.”

"Great, see you tomorrow." I put the phone down and took a deep breath. Oh my God! What had I done? I had a date the following evening. It was years since anyone but Cal had taken me out. I was nervous. What would we talk about? I have no idea why I would worry what we would talk about. Each time Daniel came to shoe the horses we talked for hours. We never had any problem when we were sat outside, or when we had a coffee after the horses were done. I felt like I couldn't breathe. My throat seemed to have tightened and my stomach was doing somersaults.

The next day I took ages to get ready for my date. It was a long time since I had pampered myself so much and it felt good. Daniel had never seen me dressed up. Whenever he saw me I was wearing jodhpurs, had no make-up on and usually had my hair tied up in a ponytail.

I wanted to look my best; I decided smart casual. I felt at home in my jeans but I could dress them up with a nice jacket, top and scarf. Oh, and I was wearing beautiful Ellie Macpherson lingerie. Daniel would never know, not tonight for goodness sake but it made me feel good to be wearing beautiful underwear. My hair was loose and freshly washed, as always it had a bit of a mind of its own but I quite liked that. I put on some make-up, you know the look. You spend ages putting the make-up on to make it look like you aren't wearing any! And finally, a touch of my favourite perfume Chanel Mademoiselle.

I was ready to go and just about as nervous as a person could feel. This was crazy. I felt like a teenager not a woman of 44. Daniel arrived spot on time and was also spruced up. As he opened the door of his car for me to get in I could feel his nerves too! This was going to be an interesting evening. We chose a local Indian restaurant which was empty when we walked in. It was a bit early for the regulars but they did start arriving after us. The manager had seen me in there with Cal. He greeted us respectfully but I imagined he was looking at me with a raised eyebrow, or maybe that was just my imagination. I was so nervous my hands were shaking and I had to lift my glass of tiger beer with both hands. At some point during the evening we both admitted how nervous we were and that released the tension.

It was a lovely evening that was over far too soon. After a couple of hours we were heading home. I questioned if I should invite him in, knowing what trouble that had got me into in St Lucia, but also aware of the fact that my home was also Cal's house, even if Cal wasn't there. I bravely decide to offer Daniel a coffee but he declined.

"I'd better not," he said, a little disappointed. I got out of his car. He kissed me on the cheek, thanked me for a wonderful evening and drove away.

As I entered the house my disappointment grew. It had probably taken me as long to get ready for this date as the time I'd spent with Daniel! It had been a long time since anyone had held me or kissed me and I guess I was hoping for more. But no sooner had the thought entered my head as the relief took over. All I had done tonight was go out for dinner with a friend. I hadn't broken any rules, hadn't broken any vows. As I kicked my boots off my phone pinged and the smile on my face grew as I read,

"It took every ounce of my determination to walk away from you tonight. I so wanted to come in for coffee but that is so not what you need right now, right now you just need a friend."

Chapter 17: Cal Goes Crazy

It took a few weeks before Daniel asked me out for another meal.

Cal was pretty much living away from Vale Farm although he popped back now and again. His latest visit was to get the Ferrari and take it for a spin. Cal had Italian blood running through his veins and had always wanted a Ferrari; I had always threatened to divorce him if he bought one as I thought it was an expensive waste of money!

Cal took the opportunity to order his Ferrari in1999 after we'd had an argument. He didn't choose the classic red colour, but opted for a silver grey called grigio allio. We'd been in it a handful of times. It growled beautifully, but it was like driving in a goldfish bowl as everyone always looked round when they heard it coming. With depreciation and the lack of times he had driven it, I reckon it cost us £1000 every time he took it out. Not only that but even though Cal had waited three years for his dream car, within a month he was looking at the catalogue for the next model.

Whilst Cal was working on Harry Potter, he had talked Ferrari's with Michael Gambon who was doing up an older Ferrari in his spare time; I reckon Michael Gambon got far more enjoyment out of his car than Cal ever did out of his.

The day he took Nikita for her first ride in the Ferrari, I couldn't help but think people would look at him and think: mid-life crisis. The roof was down on the Ferrari and Cal wore a t-shirt with 'long' shorts, he lived in shorts no matter what the weather. Nikita wore a skimpy vest top, very short denim skirt, flip flops and had her long hair loose. It may have been me feeling a touch jealous, but in my head I was thinking I would have always dressed up a bit before I went out in the Ferrari. Maybe that was just my grandma speaking, she always used to make us look 'presentable' before we left the house no matter where we were going. Mind you she always used to say 'toilets and hands washed' before we left too, and now I can't leave the house without going to the toilet!

Happiness is a state of mind

Cal never did seem to understand that happiness is a state of mind, it's not about the things you can buy.

I used to say I would have a t-shirt made for him that said, "Cal will be happy if..." because that 'if' always seemed to be changing.

To be fair he was not the only one chasing happiness. It seems we are trained from an early age to believe that we'll find happiness in a good job, in the right partner, the right car, in being able to buy our own home, in having children, in getting a better job to earn more money, in buying a bigger house and going on more holidays, in giving the children all the latest gadgets and keeping up with technology.

In short, we're led to believe that our happiness depends on the people in our lives and what we own. It seems all human kind is chasing happiness and only a few have ever stood still long enough to realise happiness is a state of mind, and not only that but it is a feeling that comes and goes, and that is just as it should be. Sorry I digress. I have searched for happiness too, and it took a long time for me to understand that happiness is very much a personal choice.

Happiness is a choice

At this point in my life 'happiness' was the carrot in front of the donkey. It was there in front of me but I could never quite reach it. I was living in an impossible situation; trying not to feel angry, trying to take responsibility for my own life, trying to face my fears and trying to lift my own mood. Daniel helped but I was far enough along my own journey to know I couldn't depend on another person for my happiness. So not surprisingly, my mood was up and down.

In November Cal arrived home unexpectedly and announced that he would be staying for a week. I hated that he thought he could do this, just to walk back into my life whenever he wanted to, but the truth was his name was on the mortgage, so he could come and go as he pleased. If I changed the locks, I would be breaking the law.

Having him home was stressful.

We'd decided that we wanted to remain friends once our divorce was through, because we'd known each other for so long. Thinking about it now, that clearly was going to work better for Cal than me but we had agreed. This meant that I would often hold back when I felt angry, and it meant I wouldn't say what I was thinking.

Cal shocked me when he came home. For him it was like putting on a comfy pair of slippers. He had a separate bedroom but apart from that, life went on as normal pre-Nikita. He expected me to make the meals and was even happy to sit down and eat them with me. We talked as if nothing was wrong, as if we weren't getting divorced. We even laughed together at times. It felt surreal and I found it very difficult. Why were we getting divorced if we got on so well? Oh yes, I remember, he wants to be with someone else.

At the beginning of the week Daniel had text me and asked if I would like to go out for dinner again? Damn, I thought. How typical that Daniel would ask me out when Cal was here. In fact, this started to happen a lot. I would be out with Daniel and Cal would text or phone or, as in this case, Cal would turn up and Daniel would ask to see me. Was this more than just coincidence?

I decided that I had every right to see Daniel, so I agreed to dinner but I had to tell him to meet me at the restaurant. I didn't want Cal to spoil anything that I had with Daniel, so I told Cal that I was meeting Celia, the lady who used to own Vale Farm. Thankfully, he seemed to believe me. The texts that week from Daniel kept my spirits up and on the Thursday evening we met at the restaurant and had a lovely meal.

We were a lot less nervous this time and I did share with Daniel why I couldn't let him pick me up. The evening was only spoiled by knowing Cal was at home. Somehow knowing that Cal was at Vale Farm made me feel guilty about what I was doing. How crazy was that? Cal was sleeping with someone else, he had made his choice. Why should I feel guilty? I was proud of myself for not allowing Cal to change my plans, but with hindsight I may have enjoyed the evening more if Cal had not been so close by.

The following morning, I went for a run with my 4 dogs. Running was keeping me sane and the dogs loved it. It was Cal's last day and he had to pick Nikita up from the airport later.

Did I tell you that Nikita had gone back to Prague? Sorry that slipped my mind. Yes, Nikita had gone back to Prague for a week. It seemed she went home because she was having a miscarriage. I didn't know that was the reason at the time, but when I did find out, it only added ammunition to my theory that she had planned to trap him.

Anyway, while Nikita was away, Cal thought it was quite acceptable to move back into Vale Farm and play happy families with me! It had been a long week but I'd survived and he would be gone very soon. I had a bottle of wine chilling in the fridge, and some strawberry cheesecake ice cream in the freezer, all ready for me to celebrate with once he'd gone. I bounced into the kitchen after my run and was met with an atmosphere you could cut with a knife. I'm sure you know what I mean. Nothing had changed, but something was very wrong. My heckles went up. What was I walking into?

Cal and I had rubbed along quite nicely for a week but now something was badly wrong.

"How often does a farrier need to shoe a horse?" Cal asked

It was such a random question. I knew I was in trouble but I didn't know why.

"Every 6 weeks," I replied honestly.

"And how often does Daniel come here?"

As far as I was concerned Cal had no right to know that Daniel had popped in for the odd cup of coffee when he was not working so, again I answered, but not quite so honestly.

"Well, usually every 6 weeks but Magic has been poorly recently so he has been here a little more often. Why?"

"Has he ever come into the house?" Cal continued.

I was cautious but starting to get annoyed with the whole line of questioning. What right did Cal have to grill me like this? He had chosen someone else. He had left me. How dare he?

"No," I replied dishonestly, "what's all this about?"

"DON'T LIE TO ME!" Cal shouted back at me. "I know what you've been up to, I know what you two have been doing in my house...."

Cal was up and running and there was no holding him back. He was angry and I was getting it full barrels. He shouted. He moved into my space. I felt his anger in every cell of my body. I was shaking but I worked hard to look calm.

I tried to defend myself; to tell him I had no idea what he was talking about, but the more I denied it the angrier he got. I started to get frightened. I hadn't seen him this angry before and then the penny dropped. When I'd gone running I'd left my phone at home. Cal must have read my text messages only he hadn't read them correctly.

At that point in our relationship I had kissed Daniel just twice; once the previous evening and once as he was leaving Vale Farm. Neither kiss had led to anything else. However, it seems we had been far more adventurous in Daniel's dreams than we ever had in real life. Cal had read the text about the dream. If he had read to the end of the text he would have known it was a dream and no more, but he didn't. Cal's mind had gone into overdrive. He accused me of having sex with Daniel in the most ridiculous of places and all in Vale Farm. By the time his rant was nearing its end, he was convinced that Daniel had moved into the house and Cal was paying for our food, for the wine we were drinking and for the upkeep of Vale Farm; all so that Daniel and I could live together.

"WHAT?" I screamed, all sense of decorum lost.

Cal was acting like a crazy jealous man. He had worked himself up into a frenzy and was making no sense.

If I had done a fraction of what he had suggested, it was still technically none of his business as he had left me for a younger model. Fortunately for me he had to leave to meet Nikita; I was so relieved that she had chosen an earlier flight.

By the time he left I was shell shocked. I didn't know this man. I didn't understand this man. How could he get so angry with me when he'd chosen to leave me? He had chosen someone else. He had chosen to end our marriage. It was midday but I poured a glass of wine and sank into the comfort of the kitchen sofa. With my legs tucked underneath me, I put my head on my knees and cried. This was all getting too hard.

Christmas approached and for the first time I faced Christmas on my own. I knew that my sister and other friends would be more than happy for me to join them on Christmas day, but none of them lived close to me now.

I had a menagerie of animals to look after and so the decision was easy; I would have to stay home alone. I decided that I would still decorate the house and I would do it all for me. What's more, I would still make myself a Christmas dinner. I prepared myself mentally for a Christmas alone but it didn't happen, not that year anyway.

My sister did her usual pre-Christmas visit, and I couldn't help but notice how my life had changed since she'd visited the previous year. As usual we opened a bottle of wine or two and by the early hours we were a little worse for drink, but both very happy in our drunken state. There was lots of laughter, there usually was when my sister and I got together.

So, in the early hours, we decided a coffee was in order. I need to explain where we were sat for you to understand what happened next. The kitchen had two central islands and one of those islands was in front of the Aga. We sat on high stools at this island and I had my back to the Aga with Julie sitting opposite me.

I filled the kettle with water and placed it on the Aga hot plate and then sat down to wait for it to boil. Julie and I carried on chatting until she suddenly said,

"Should there be smoke coming from the Aga?" I looked round and there was horrible black smoke rising from the bottom of the kettle.

Suddenly reality struck, I had put an electric kettle on the Aga! The smoke was coming from the rubber bottom of the kettle that was now melting all over the Aga hot plate. I lifted the kettle up quickly and then stood with it in my hand looking at Jules.

There was a moment of horror rapidly followed by tears of laughter. Once we started laughing we couldn't stop. We realised that the Aga needed rescuing, so I put down the kettle on a wooden chopping board and with wooden spoons we set about scraping the melted rubber off the hot plate. What a mess and it took us ages and all the time the tears of laughter rolled down our faces.

To be honest, my laughter didn't stop until I walked into John Lewis the following day and realised just how much a Dualit kettle cost! I couldn't buy a cheaper kettle, I had to replace the one we had before Cal found out what I'd done and didn't see the funny side of it.

I paid nearly £200 for a new kettle and returned to my car a little more subdued. As it turned out I needn't have replaced the kettle like-for-like, as Cal had gone out and bought an even more expensive kettle for him and Nikita in the same week. I had to admit though that the Dualit kettle was a beautiful kettle and now it was my beautiful kettle. Jules and I giggle to this day at the sight of that electric kettle on the Aga. Was it stress or the wine that caused me to do such a stupid thing? I will never know but it isn't a mistake I will ever make again.

So, Julie came and went in her usual Christmas trip style and then my lovely friend Lou gave up her family Christmas Dinner to come and spend Christmas with me. I am so lucky. I've got some amazing friends who have seen me through thick and thin. Lou is one such friend and together with Abi and Toni, they are the daughters I never had.

Against all the odds, I had a memorable Christmas for all the right reasons. Lou helped me to look after the animals and on Christmas day we treated ourselves to dinner. We ate when we wanted, we drank when we wanted, and we watched whatever rubbish we wanted on the TV. It was relaxed, fun and I will always be grateful to Lou for choosing to be a good friend to me and spend Christmas with me.

It was the end of a horrid year. The trauma wasn't over but hostilities had been stopped for Christmas. I couldn't help but think that Nikita would be sitting in my chair at the Delmonte family Christmas dinner this year and receiving my presents. It felt like she'd taken my place in the family, a place I'd held for 30 years, but not anymore.

I felt like I had been excommunicated. This feeling became stronger when I sent presents for all of Cal's family with Cal up to Manchester. It never dawned on me that I wouldn't get any in return but, with the exception of Cal's youngest brother, who sent me a present direct to Vale Farm, I didn't receive any presents in return. The facts were harsh, but I was no longer a member of the Delmonte family.

Now before I end this chapter, I must tell you that my perception of the truth was not the actual truth.

Cal's Mum never stopped loving me and never stopped caring for me, but as a good Italian Mother she stood strongly by her son. Without my knowledge, when Cal had first started to take Nikita up to Manchester, his Mum wouldn't let them sleep in her house. Eventually she did give in, but behind the scenes she'd let Cal know she did not approve; behind the scenes she'd made a stand for me, I just never knew it.

Cal's Mum was living in Cal and my first house, so I knew her neighbours very well. When a neighbour phoned me the following year she suggested I phoned Mam. She said Mam missed me and spoke about me a lot, that she was lonely and would love to hear from me.

My pride had been hurt but I'm so glad I rose above it because when I finally phoned Mam, she was overjoyed to hear from me. We were on the phone for hours. This lady had been a mother figure to me for more years than anyone else. We'd had our differences along the way, but I loved her dearly and my heart swelled to know she still loved me.

That phone call was a huge lesson that 'my' truth is not always 'the' truth. A huge lesson that we all contribute our own facts to make up the whole story, but not always the true one.

It wasn't long after this conversation that I came upon Byron Katie's book; 'Love What Is'. In this book she gives you a process for changing your perception that she calls the Work. The first two questions of the Work are: -

Is that true?

Do you absolutely know 100% that it is true?

Did Nikita take my place in the heart of the Delmonte family that Christmas? My first answer would always be yes, but if I had stopped to think about that, I had no hard evidence.

I did not know 100%, so I was making the breakdown of my marriage even more painful.

These two questions are powerful in themselves. We have a tendency to create the facts, create the thoughts in someone else's head, create the situations when we do not know.

We try to fill the void, but we can often fill it with something that is simply not true, and then sadly we act on the story we've made up and not the facts.

Try it and see what you think. I have introduced this question to so many teenagers that many of them would tell me something and then say

"I know, I know, Is that true?"

It makes my heart smile every time!

Chapter 18: Reasons for Divorce

As 2006 started, I wrote a list of five things that I needed to do to get through in this horrible stage in my life.

- Divorce Cal.
- Sort out the finances.
- Buy a new car.
- Sell Vale Farm.
- Find somewhere for me and the animals to live.

Vale Farm went up for sale. I tried to make it feel like a happy home by smudging away the bad energy from the divorce that was swirling through the house.

By this time, I'd had heard through Cal that Celia and Phil, the couple who had owned Vale farm before us, were also getting divorced. They had sold Vale Farm to buy a smaller property, with the intention of splitting their time between England and a house they owned in South Africa.

They found a house and were having some building work done on it while they were away in South Africa.

I didn't quite understand their plan as they had sold a big house, bought a smaller house and then got permission to double the size of the little one! Anyway, that is what they did and Phil came back from South Africa before Celia to oversee the building work.

It seems that while Celia was in South Africa alone she met and fell in love with a younger man. When I eventually met Luke I could see the attraction. He was extremely good looking, had a mop of dark curly hair, was toned as a surfer would be, but was a truly free spirit which was very attractive. Celia and Luke were like chalk and cheese but somehow they'd fallen for each other.

According to Cal, Celia had text Phil to say she wanted a divorce, she'd said she was staying in South Africa because she'd met someone else. Not quite the way I would have done it and at that point, I felt quite sorry for Phil. Like me his partner wanted out of their marriage because she'd met a younger man.

As time went on I would come to understand why Celia had asked for a divorce in this way, but when Cal first told me I was shocked. I was even more shocked when a neighbour who also knew Celia and Phil were getting divorced, said to me,

"Do you know that you and Cal will be the 7th consecutive couple who have owned Vale Farm and ended up divorced?" The seventh consecutive couple! It seems the neighbour thought Phil and Celia had broken the 'curse of Vale Farm' but now they too were also getting divorced.

I don't believe in coincidences, and so it seemed just as Christine had predicted, the universe had pointed Cal and I towards Vale Farm to help us along the path of divorce. I know you may think I am crazy at this point, but I strongly believe that our thoughts and our energy influence the lives that we live, and I had been thinking about divorce on and off for the last five years. Could I have manifested what I'd been thinking about, what I had been worrying about? It certainly seemed a possibility.

To get Vale Farm ready for sale, and much against Cal's better judgement I arranged for the outside of the house to be painted. I also engaged a family solicitor to get the divorce underway. To be exact I engaged Rebecca's brother, Tony. I know now that this was not one of my better ideas, but he'd been recommended to me in the first place by a client from Holly Tree, so I turned to someone I thought I knew, someone who had guessed that Cal had cheated on me before I cheated on him.

Cal wanted to divorce me, so he also found a solicitor to act for him. Of course, he then had to come up with some reasons that my behaviour was *so unreasonable* that he couldn't be expected to remain married to me. It took him some time to do this, but eventually he had his list. One day when he was at Vale Farm he offered to show me the list that he'd come up with.

There and then he forwarded to me the email he had sent to his solicitor. It began,

Dear Mike

Here is the list of reasons for me to divorce Karen. Please will you remember that we want to remain friends when this is over.

I then read his first criticism,

1.We do not have children because Karen prefers animals to children.

WHAT? How could he say this? Where was he when I did years of infertility treatments? Where was he when I was going through three rounds of IVF? Where was he? Where was he? How could he have forgotten all that? How could he do this to me? What would he have said if he hadn't wanted to remain friends with me?

As I read the words, it felt like he'd stuck a knife in my back and turned it. All I had ever wanted since I was a little girl was a family of my own. I hadn't had some great career plan; I'd just wanted to be a Mum.

I had wanted to provide the safe and loving home for my children that I'd never had for myself. I wanted to love and nurture them; I ached to have children. I had felt like a failure for years, in every month and with every failed IVF cycle. I ached for something that seemed out of reach. Everyone else could have children and it was the one thing I was supposed to be able to do as a woman and yet it wouldn't happen for me. IVF had seemed to be the solution, but it wasn't. It had been a long process where the medical world had played with my hormones, taken away my dignity, raised my hopes and then sent me home when my body rejected the foetus. It had been gruelling and soul destroying, and after three attempts I had been on my knees.

Around this time, I had met a stuntman on a film set who had given me some advice. He was a big, solid man, ex- marine and strong, and he had tried an alternative route to conceive his daughter. This man and his wife had their hair analysed by a Harley Street Doctor and after the analysis, they had been put on a special diet with supplements to rebalance their mineral levels. Within six months they had conceived naturally and he was so proud of his daughter.

Normally Cal wouldn't be interested in such things, but this man was someone Cal respected and he was a man's man, if you know what I mean; nothing airy-fairy about him. The stuntman gave me the name of the his Harley Street Doctor and I shared what I had learned with Cal. I wouldn't say Cal was jumping up and down with excitement like me, but he did seem open to trying the procedure, so I sent off for the hair analysis pack. We had to cut a couple of inches of hair from each of us and then send it to be analysed. After a couple of anxious weeks waiting we had an appointment to see the Doctor and discuss the results and the way forward.

On the day of the appointment Cal had landed a job that he couldn't say no to! It was a Director he really liked and missing this one day could have meant he missed out on the whole film. Cal reassured me that it would be okay; he had arranged with the Director that one of the drivers could take me into London for the appointment and then take me back to the film set! He didn't seem to understand why I was so upset, but the travelling arrangements had been made and I found myself heading up to Harley Street on my own.

When I got to the waiting room it was full of apprehensive couples. I felt very self-conscious being by myself but I sat down and waited. After a short time our names were called out. I stood up, apologised that it was only me and then followed the Doctor into a small consulting room. The Doctor immediately questioned Cal's absence, questioned his commitment and as I had done many times before I made excuses for him and as always, his job in the film industry was sufficiently impressive for him to be forgiven.

The results were in. It seemed we both had various vitamin and mineral deficiencies which could be dealt with quickly with the application of supplements. The Doctor also suggested that we both went on an elimination. It consisted of no sugar, no alcohol, no convenience foods or take outs, no condiments or sauces and no wheat. Nowadays this would not be a problem for me, but in those days it felt like no life. I felt a little challenged, but was so excited about having a child I was committed to do it. I paid for the appointment and all the supplements that we both needed and then returned to the film set with hope in my heart. Cal was not overly enthusiastic but I knew he desperately wanted children too, so I assumed he would commit. How wrong could I be?

When the tablets arrived the following week, I was a bit shocked. It was a lot of tablets to take every day and I was not great at taking tablets at the best of times. The diet was also challenging us; our go- to meal was pasta and salad, wine and ice-cream, most of which was now on the banned list of foods. After a couple of days on the rebalancing diet Cal left for Virginia Water taking all his tablets with him. I continued taking the tablets and following the diet for the next few weeks.

Eventually I made an unusual visit to the house in Virginia Water only to find all Cal's tablets stuffed in the bottom of his wardrobe. Clearly, he hadn't taken one supplement tablet since he'd arrived. My heart sunk. There was no point me doing this on my own, it would only work if we were both committed. We had a very heated discussion about the matter afterwards but even as we were arguing, I knew it was hopeless if Cal wasn't interested.

Disillusioned and depressed I turned to my own Doctor when I got back to Holly Tree. He empathised with my pain and asked if Cal would consider adopting? It turned out that my Doctor was on the board of the Manchester Adoption Agency and could put in a good word for us if we wanted to go ahead.

Feeling hopeful again, I returned home to Cal with a spring in my step. It didn't matter to me if I gave birth to the child or not, I just wanted to love and nurture a child. I approached the subject with Cal and again my heart sunk. No, it seems he couldn't adopt because he wanted his children to look like him! Although my head berated him for being so shallow, this wasn't something I could force him to do. I had to honour his decision but I was devastated. Where did I go from here?

So, returning to Cal's list of my *unreasonable behaviour*, I hope you can now understand how unfair and hurtful his first comment felt to me. Before I broke down completely, I scanned the next couple of reasons.

2. Karen will not give up her personal beliefs even though she knows they are offensive to my family.

Another stupid reason. Yes, I believe in a life after death. Yes, I believe I can talk to 'dead' people but this isn't something I choose to believe, this is something I just know. I cannot unknow it. I cannot stop believing what is a fundamental belief for me. I could hide my beliefs, which to be honest I did a lot of the time. I could respect his family's catholic beliefs; despite my not agreeing that any beautiful new born baby can possibly be born in sin, despite my not agreeing that a gay relationship is wrong, despite my not approving of a priest who galloped through the service on Christmas eve in what can only be described as a drunken state! No I did not agree with a lot of things about their catholic faith, but I respected their right to believe and I didn't ever criticise their beliefs. Besides which, he was more anti-Catholic than me. He was the one who refused to get married in a church, now he was using his religion and my spiritual beliefs against me. He was hitting me where it would hurt the most. Did he really want to remain friends?

3. Karen allows the cats in the house even though she knows I do not like cats.

Now the reasons were getting ridiculous. My cats had started life as yard cats. They were born on the yard at Holly Tree and had positions of Chief Mouse Catchers. They'd only been allowed into the house when as kittens they had caught cat flu and it had been a bit hit and miss whether they would survive. Like me they were made of strong stuff and successfully got through the cat flu virus.

The cats had then remained on the yard until we moved. At Virginia Water they had spent a year in the house, but as soon as we got to Vale Farm they had to go back outside again. This hadn't been a great hardship for them as the outbuilding that contained the boiler for the cottage already had a cat flap in the door, so I put some cosy cat beds in there and my cats then had somewhere dry and warm to go when the weather was bad. The cats were more than happy to have their freedom and loved snuggling up on the hay when the weather allowed. They had the best of both worlds and they were happy.

One day however when Cal had left, Sam, who looked a bit like the Felix cat, was sitting on the kitchen window ledge meowing at me. I'd been sitting on a stool at the central island, taking 5 minutes for a coffee and a quick read of the newspaper. I opened the sash window in front of the kitchen sink and Sam hopped across the sink and then leapt onto the central island. Bless him, he landed on the newspaper which, propelled by his weight, slid with him easily across the marble work surface and off the other side! I so wish I had filmed him coming in, it was so funny.

The tears rolled down my face as I laughed at his antics. The look on his face as he brushed himself off and tried to work out what had just happened was priceless. By this time Minstrel, Sam's Dad, was also at the window ledge. Before Minstrel did the same thing, I lifted him over the sink and placed him on the floor. Both cats went off together to investigate. I smiled as I watched them both. I could feel the warmth and joy in my heart grow as I watched them gaining their trust and starting to play.

It suddenly struck me that, if Cal was not choosing to be in the house, then there was no reason why I had to live by his rule that said the cats had to stay outside. He hated cats so much that when he was living in the house it was better for the cats to be out, but now he had gone I could make decisions for me, do what I wanted to do, and I loved my cats. The decision was made, the cats were allowed in if they wanted to be inside.

Why live by someone else's rules?

Cal was not impressed. I understand now it was not about the cats, it was about me making a decision for myself which showed him that he was losing his hold over me.

The cats knew he didn't want them in the house. Sam had remained afraid of Cal and always hid when he saw him coming. Minstrel however had other ideas, it wasn't long before he realised Cal could no longer throw him out. Once he was sure of that, he would deliberately parade in front of Cal with his tail held high as if to say

"So, what you gonna do about it, mate?" Cal would frown, but I stood strong and it made me smile every time Minstrel challenged him.

So, in truth, the cats being in the house was not a genuine reason for our divorce. Even as I write this it sounds ridiculous that he would even use this as a valid reason. The thing is, when Cal was home the cats did not live in the house, they lived outside.

There were 3 more reasons, but I can't remember them. By the time I got to the cats I'd lost the plot. I had been more hurt by reason one than I could ever explain to you. He had put a knife in my heart and twisted it and I was furious; every ounce of anger I had repressed in my past came rushing up to the surface. I was taken over by a cauldron of boiling energy and I wanted to hurt him back.

Oh God, peaceful me, the me that saw the good in everyone, the me that hated confrontation, abandoned to this boiling anger. The divorce list reasons 2 and 3 just added to it, reason 2 was just plain unfair. He was expecting me to do something that was not possible to do. Either I believed or I didn't. I couldn't just say 'okay Cal, from this minute I will stop holding onto my beliefs because you don't like them, because you are shallow, because you are scared by my beliefs, okay that's perfectly understandable. No It F****** isn't. I don't usually swear.

I hate the 'F' word but I used it that day so you can get some idea of just how furious I was feeling. I was out of control beyond my own reasoning. I could no longer stand in Cal's shoes and see it from his point of view; a skill I usually had but not today, not when I read his list. As for reason 3, it was just ludicrous. Could you really divorce someone because they allowed 2 small cats into the house??

I screamed and shouted like I had never done before, or since. He became defensive, of course he did, he'd never seen me like that before. Mind you, I'd never seen me like this before I even kicked his laptop along the kitchen floor. It was in its case but it didn't survive my anger unscathed.

It took a long time before the tears arrived. My tears were my release and meant I was starting to calm down. I looked at him and said,

"You're not using these reasons. I may have been stupid at times in the way I have treated you. For example, picking you up from the airport when you came back from staying with your girlfriend in Prague, and then sending me that cruel message on our anniversary. Yes, I may have been stupid, but my behaviour has **never** been unreasonable."

In my mind, I heard the words of a good friend who had questioned if I could live with whatever reasons Cal came up with for divorcing me. She had pointed out that I should be divorcing him on the grounds of adultery. She also pointed out that I had to live with his reasons not just for today and tomorrow, not even just for this horrid year, but for the rest of my life. For the first time, I knew I had to protect me.

I need to look after me and do what is right for me

I had to do what was right for me, and allowing him to divorce me and make up a whole load of lies just to make a judge think my behaviour was too unreasonable to expect Cal to stay married to me, was not going to be good for me.

I told Cal I was going to divorce him on the grounds of adultery and if he agreed to it, I would not name Nikita. Now it was his turn to be angry, but I didn't care.

"But my Mum is Catholic, you can't use adultery to divorce me."

"Well, you should have thought of that before you slept with Nikita, and Amy for that matter, and Irish Rose and anyone else you have slept with."

He left the house with his tail between his legs and a broken laptop.

I was drained and exhausted. How could a man I had loved me for so long be so cruel? It is a question I would ask myself many times over the next 10 years. Eventually I would see the truth, but sadly, I was a slow learner.

I loved him for many more years after this incident but on that day, once he had gone, it all felt a bit surreal. My life was unravelling around me every day and it seemed I had no power to stop it.

Chapter 19: Give Him an Inch

I consider myself to be an intelligent woman, but sometimes there are aspects of my life that I do not understand.

For example, I have always felt a strong sanctity for life that many others do not seem to feel. It extends beyond human beings to animals, trees, plants, even wasps. I mention wasps because one day when I was at Holly Tree with my friend Christine, there was a wasp buzzing irritatingly around the kitchen table where we were eating. Suddenly and without warning, Christine picked up my huge pepper pot which was on the table and promptly killed the wasp. I was shocked; as someone who connected with Spirit, I really thought she would respect all life.

"I can't believe you've just done that. Don't you believe in the sanctity of life?" I asked.

"Yes, " she said, "it just doesn't apply to wasps!"

She did make me giggle when she said that, but for me the sanctity of life applies to everything and there must be a good reason to take it away. The poor wasp wasn't really doing anything wrong, so I didn't understand her behaviour.

At this point in my life the thing that confused me most was the law. Cal had left Vale Farm but was still coming and going as he pleased. He never gave any warning, he just simply showed up and when he wasn't at

Vale Farm, I had no idea where he was or what he was doing.

It wasn't that I wanted to know everything that he was doing, it was just that it irritated me that he could have his own life and then walk in and out of mine as he pleased. I asked my solicitor if I could stop him from doing this, but other than ask him, I evidently had no rights to stop him.

I was hoping I could change the locks to the house, but as Cal's name was on the mortgage if I changed the locks and I didn't give him a key, I would be breaking the law.

It came as a bit of a surprise then, that I got a letter from the court summonsing me to a hearing with a Judge to confirm that Cal was not living at Vale Farm, even though he was using it as his correspondence address.

Since Cal and I had both chosen solicitors from Manchester I had to travel 3 hours up the M40 and M6 to tell the Judge that Cal was not living with me when legally, I had no right to stop him from coming back. How crazy was that?

Around this same time, Cal had suggested to me that it wasn't fair that he couldn't bring Nikita to Vale Farm when it was still his house. Now I can hear you screaming

"WHAT, is this man for real?" and I would feel the same way today.

In fact, as I write this I can see and feel how outrageous that comment was. However, at the time I thought he had a point!

Desperately wanting to do the 'right' thing, I told Cal about my having to go and see the Judge to confirm that he was not living with me. I suggested that as I would be away for the day then he and Nikita could spend the day at the house, if he would like to.

I had some conditions of my own, because I didn't want to see them together, but Cal jumped at the chance. He agreed not to arrive until after I'd left and to leave again before I got home. I agreed to text him when I left the house in the morning so that he would know that I'd left and also to text on my way home when I got off the M40, so that he could leave before I got back.

On the day of my trip all went to plan. I was a little nervous about appearing in front of the Judge, so my mind was more focused on that than Cal as I left, but I did remember to text him. As it turned out confirming my living situation to the judge was easy, my solicitor and I saw her in a small room, it almost looked like a small classroom. The Judge was female and she put me at ease. and in no time at all the whole 'ordeal' was over.

I used the trip to Manchester to have a late lunch with my friend Anna, and then I returned home. I text Cal as I left the M40 and sure enough he and Nikita had left by the time I arrived back home. It had been a long day and I was very tired when I arrived, but I was greeted enthusiastically by 8 gorgeous brown eyes and 4 waggy tails; a sight which always lifted my heart.

I walked into the kitchen and on the small table at the far end, I could see a used cafetiere with just the ground coffee left in the bottom. Beside it were 2 blue Denon cups and saucers and 2 small matching plates covered in crumbs; I was not impressed.

Then, as I walked into the orangery, I found an empty wine bottle and two dirty glasses. Can you believe it?

Out of the goodness of my heart, I had told him I would be away that day, and agreed he could spend the day at Vale Farm. What had he done in return? He had treated me like a maid, expecting me to clean up after them. Nothing new there then but, as far as I was concerned, it was no longer in my job description to clean up after him. It may have been all those years ago when as an innocent teenager I had loved taking care of him, but not now. How little did I know then the rod that I was making for my own back. The situation would get worse.

A few weeks later the gardener said he had something he wanted to share with me, but he didn't want me to get upset. It seemed not only had Cal and Nikita used the house like a hotel while I was out, but Cal had allowed Nikita to ride Jim, one of my horses, bareback in the field.

I had originally bought Jim for Cal because I wanted him to feel a part of Holly Tree. After our near divorce in 2000, I could understand how Cal felt a bit 'left out' in his own home. I thought if he had his own horse he would come out onto the yard more and people would get to see him and know him. I hoped he would integrate but that hadn't happened.

In fact, despite choosing Jim, Cal took little interest in him except on the odd occasion when he wanted to ride, or when he wanted to impress someone by claiming ownership of the most impressive horse on the yard.

At that particular point in our relationship, he was using the horses and the dogs as a bargaining tool. He threatened to take Jim and 2 of the dogs as part of the divorce, I was very upset on both accounts. Cal had never looked after any of them. He played with the dogs when it fit into his schedule, but ignored them the rest of the time and as for feeding, walking or nursing them when they were sick; that all came under my job description.

Similarly with Jim, he had no idea how to look after him, he didn't even know what he ate or what size rugs he wore, he never mucked out his stable, and had no idea when he was shod or wormed. He knew none of that and yet he was threatening to take Jim, just because Jim was his.

I did threaten to challenge his ownership, to tell the judge that he'd given Jim back to me, then he would have to prove how much he knew about his own horse which, as I have just made clear, was very little.

Doing that would have involved lying to the Judge, and I am not sure I would have really carried that out as I have a strong sense of honesty but, if it had meant saving Jim, maybe I would.

Back to that fateful day, he had added insult to injury by allowing Nikita to ride my beautiful horse. I had tried to remain calm in front of the gardener when he related the events of that day to me, but once again I was angry. Once again Cal had taken advantage of my good nature.

Many years later I would see a photograph which had clearly been taken on that day, it was of Nikita cuddling my smallest collie, Willa, and it would bring tears to my eyes, the look on Willa's face had said it all. She was never comfortable with Cal when he was at Vale Farm; she would run into a stable and curl up in a corner to hide rather than go and greet him when he arrived unexpectedly. Sometimes she would look up at me as if to say, 'don't tell him I am here.' I never did, I never gave her away.

Willa was Cal's favourite dog but now even she didn't trust him, but I trusted her judgment.

Feeling angry with Cal was becoming a more regular occurrence and I didn't like the feeling, not one little bit. In 2006, I had started to do some 'work' on me. I wanted to do something productive with the time I had whilst I was living through this difficult period. My solicitor had advised me, wrongly as it turned out, that it would affect my divorce settlement with Cal if I got a job, so he recommended I didn't do that until the finances had been settled. I was still looking after all my menagerie and ironically doing the book keeping for Cal's company, but I needed to feel I was doing something positive. Everything about getting divorced is soul destroying and I wanted to find some hope, to do something for me that you would get me through my divorce without ending up bitter and resentful.

I bought Louise Hays book You Can Heal Your Life and started working through the chapters.

Wow, this book was a revelation to me. It teaches you to take a hard look at yourself, to question the reasons why problems show up in your life, to face the underlying beliefs that hold you back and to work out where those beliefs come from. It guides you to change those beliefs so that you can move forwards. It helps you to heal relationship and money problems so that you can move forwards free of your past.

The book was, and is, life changing and it opened up a whole new world to me.

Don't get me wrong, it was tough going at times. The only way to really make use of this book is to honestly work through each exercise as it comes up, and much of the initial work looks at your past. It brings up feelings that you have buried and carried for many years. It's not an easy process, but it is an essential one if you want to live life to the full. At this point I was starting to understand the importance of taking responsibility for me, for my emotions and feelings, and for my situation.

Nikita was a catalyst for the end of my marriage, not the reason for it

I could see that Nikita was simply a catalyst for the end of my marriage and not the reason for it.

I was far from happy with Cal's behaviour but I was coming to learn that Cal always did what was right for him. In 2000 when he wanted our marriage to continue he begged me not to leave him. Literally with his hands around my ankles he knelt on the floor and begged me not to go.

Now only 5 years later he wanted out. He was done. He had moved on and I was an inconvenience. It didn't feel good, but I was learning that I needed to do the same for me.

I needed to learn to be honest with me and do what was right for me

The only problem was I no longer knew what I wanted. That day, as I sat there yet again in anger, I decided to take action. I had learned that the body cannot differentiate between action and visualisation. I felt like I wanted to hit Cal, and Nikita for that matter, but that was not something I could physically do. However, I could visualise doing it.

The body cannot differentiate between action and visualisation

I'm not sure where I came across this visualisation but it worked for me.

I sat down and closed my eyes. I took some deep breaths and relaxed my body, then I imagined myself standing in a circle, a bit like a plastic hula hoop lying on the ground. I visualised a second hoop attached to the first and placed Cal and Nikita in the second hoop. I then used a pair of scissors to cut the link between the hoops. I watched Cal and Nikita float off in their hoop, getting smaller and smaller until they had disappeared.

I tried this visualisation 2 or 3 more times and I felt a little better, but the anger was still bubbling. On the fourth attempt, I threw rocks at them as they floated off. Wow, that was much better but not quite clearing the depths of my anger. I then tried shooting them with a bow and arrow; I know a gun may have been easier, and it was only a visualisation technique, but I have a strong dislike of guns in any situation. So, I'd avoided the guns and chosen a bow and arrow. Eventually I found the key to clearing my anger; I would set the arrows on fire and then I'd shoot them. I cannot tell you how much relief I got from doing this. I feel a little embarrassed now that somewhere inside of me, I really enjoyed pelting them with burning arrows, maybe this came from a past life, I don't know, but I do know that it worked well.

When I came out of the visualisation my anger had left me and I felt a little guilty, but very calm. The truth was, I had not actually hurt either of Cal or Nikita. I had also not blamed Nikita for the situation I'd found myself in, which was very unusual for a woman in my position. I did not even have a desire for revenge on Cal. At the end of the day, my visualisation seemed like a win-win situation for all of us.

That evening I curled up on the settee in the little lounge with a large glass of wine. To be honest this was getting to be a habit, but I could easily justify the wine because it had been a very long day. I guess Susan Pierce Thompson (of Bright Line Eating) would say that was my saboteur speaking!

The lounge was softly lit by 2 table lamps and there was a flicker of light from the candles dotted around the room. The television was on but I wasn't paying much attention to it and my 4 dogs were scattered around the room quietly sleeping.

I could hear Riff's gentle snore as he breathed in and out, when my eyes caught the photograph of Cal and I on the shelf above the fire place. All the other photographs on the shelf were of our animals, some had died but some were still very much alive. There were 6 small photographs in all, positioned at a slight angle along the shelf. Cal and I were smiling in the photograph of us; it was a rare photo of us both as usually Cal was in his favourite place behind the camera.

On the chimney breast above the little photographs was a painting that Cal and I had brought back from Italy. It was a beautiful oil painting of a little town called Portofino and both the painting and the handmade frame were gorgeous. The picture reminded me of our only visit to Cal's Parent's home village in Italy. We had gone to celebrate his Gran's 90th birthday.

Suddenly, as I was looking at the picture, it flew off the wall all by itself. I promise I am telling you exactly what happened. As it fell to the floor it managed to knock the photograph of Cal and I onto the floor with it. The glass from the picture smashed into thousands of pieces as it hit the floor face down and the photograph of Cal and I landed face upwards on top of the picture.

I jumped out of my skin. My heart was racing. There was no good reason for this to have happened, no one had touched the picture. How did it only knock the photo of Cal and I off? Panicking, I scanned the dogs. There was glass everywhere but amazingly, there seemed to be a safe space around each animal.

Not one of the dogs had moved, they didn't even lift their heads!! None of them had been affected by the sudden drop of the picture and they were all safe.

But it had happened, the evidence was lying on the floor right in front of me. Nothing like this had ever happened to me before, was there a spirit in the house that was angry with me? I felt a bit unnerved.

I firmly told the dogs to 'stay' which they all did. I guess I should have cleaned up the glass there and then but my first instinct was to phone Christine.

"Christine, you will never believe what just happened," I said, as she answered her phone. As I recalled the story she laughed.

"Well if that doesn't say ditch the Italian I don't know what does," she said, still laughing at my predicament.

Her response was disarming and made me laugh too. Her interpretation of the message seemed obvious as I looked at the mess in front of me. Clearly someone had wanted me to see this.

The picture had flown off the wall spontaneously and I had seen it happen. It was amazing that it had only clipped the photo of Cal and I and even more amazing that the photo had landed right way up on top of the picture. But the real miracle was the area of safety that was very clearly etched around each dog; despite glass going everywhere, none of the dogs were hurt.

Having spoken to Christine I felt reassured that my Guides and Spirit Family were trying to guide me and were letting me know that they were supporting me. I understand that you may find this recollection a little too far-fetched to believe, or maybe you do believe me, but find the whole thing a little scary. I hope however, that like me you are now smiling at how resourceful our Spirit Guides can be. I felt somehow reassured to know my Guides were with me and I was not alone at this point in my life.

It seemed to me that when my head was too full of thoughts and I couldn't hear the whispers from my Guides, then they would take more dramatic ways to get my attention! They sure got my attention on this particular evening.

Chapter 20: The Universe Reveals a Truth

Since Nikita had arrived in the UK and Cal was spending so much more time with her, I had begun to wonder how long it would be before their problem of living accommodation came up.

From Cal's point of view, he was paying £8,000 a month for the mortgage on a property, Vale Farm, that he wasn't living in. Worse than that, I was enjoying the luxury of living at Vale Farm by myself, or depending on what mood Cal was in, with Daniel.

Cal first tried to resolve this problem by suggesting that he and Nikita move into the cottage. On paper that seemed like a reasonable solution, in a left-brain sort of way. It would mean we wouldn't have to pay out for the rental of another property and already we had 3 of us living out of the same bank account.

I know it all sounds crazy, doesn't it? Well it was crazy. Cal and I had always shared a joint account; we had pooled pocket money and my Saturday job wage since we were teenagers. In all the years we'd been together we'd never had individual bank accounts, everything was joint.

Now it seemed, Cal had handed over to Nikita his debit card for our joint bank account. She clearly knew his pin number and so no one had felt a need to challenge her. When I looked at our bank account statements I could see which parts of the UK they were staying in, simply by the places that Nikita had shopped at. Now in her defence she didn't go to expensive designer shops, she was more likely to be found in TK Maxx, and the bank statements showed purchases from TK Maxx's stores from all around the country.

Cal clearly was still working, although like all wealthy people going through a divorce, he suddenly was not earning as much as before we had started our divorce proceedings!! Whether he was taking more time off to be with Nikita or hiding the money I will never know. I did hire a private detective for a while to see if anything untoward was taking place, but he didn't come up with anything concrete.

So, Cal and Nikita living in the cottage would have been a sensible left brain decision, but my heart and right brain could not agree.

You see the cottage was very close to the house. When you came out of the back door of the house there were several buildings on the right hand side. First there was the room with the oil tank, then the boiler room and after the boiler room was the cottage. Every time I went out to the horses I would have had to pass the cottage and the windows looked out over the lawn and the stables. If Cal and Nikita had lived there, they would have been watching my every move. That just felt too creepy. Whatever the saving in money, I couldn't have them living so close. My answer was an emphatic 'NO'.

At this time I had already started looking for a new home for me and the animals. It wasn't easy with 4 horses and a limited amount of money. I did find a cute little house called Rose Cottage, it was tiny but it came with some land. I tried hard to persuade myself that I could be happy in this cottage but it needed lots of work, it didn't have any stables and it was seriously very small.

Cal's second plan also involved the little cottage I had viewed. He suggested that we could get a second mortgage so that I could buy this cottage that I had fallen in love with! I had not fallen in love with this tiny house and I don't think Cal had suddenly taken up NLP or any other mode of psychological techniques that would tell him how to manipulate my actions.

No, looking back manipulation came easily and instinctively to Cal. Of course, my moving out of Vale Farm would mean that Cal and Nikita could move in... just until it sold of course! Even if I had fallen in love with Rose Cottage, I wasn't stupid enough to agree to this plan. Once Cal was back at home in Vale Farm it would have been impossible to him get out. Again I said 'NO'.

This was a new experience for me to say 'no'. I think for most of my marriage I had always said yes and let Cal have the final say on most things. Learning to say 'no' was a new beginning for me. It was all part of the process of me learning what I wanted and that it was okay to stand up for myself. This didn't happen overnight but even as I write my answers to each of Cal's suggestions, I can see with hindsight how the process of change was taking place.

Cal finally came up with Plan C. He and Nikita had found a house near Brill. Cal had done a deal with the owner to get this house for a mere £2,000 per month, but it had to be in cash! Can you smell a rat? It all sounded very dodgy to me and Cal would not tell me exactly where the house was. I tried to say 'no' again but this time it didn't work. It seemed the deal was already struck and Cal and Nikita had a date for moving in.

Strangely Cal didn't want to take any of the furniture but did start to take cd's, his guitars, and some kitchen implements. All these things he started to take out of Vale Farm in dribs and drabs and of course what he took I never saw again and interestingly, they didn't seem to count when we were finally splitting up our belongings. This is not surprising as Cal's view was that everything was already his because he had earned the money that bought it.

Anyway the £2,000 started to go out of our joint account each month and for the first time in a long-time money was getting tight. Cal didn't care about the Inland Revenue or VAT, all he cared about was that he had earned it, so he had the right to spend it.

That July when I had to pay a large tax bill for the first time, I had to cash in a couple of our ISA's to raise the funds. Life was starting to get a bit scary. At this rate, there wouldn't be any money in the pot to share when our divorce finally came through. Was that Cal's plan? I was starting to get sleepless nights worrying, but Cal had his head in the sand and was living on the crest of his mid-life crisis wave.

Now the Universe, or God, which ever you believe, moves in mysterious ways and what happened next I believe was the Universe helping me out. While Cal and I were struggling through our divorce Celia had come back from South Africa with Luke and now needed somewhere to live. By this time, I had started to understand why Celia had asked Phil for a divorce by text. Initially it looked like Phil had been the victim in this life plot, but after his initial shock he found his inner bulldog. It probably started out as an inner bulldog but ended up an inner Rottweiler, my apologies to both breeds of dog.

I can remember the day when Phil stood in my kitchen and told me that he didn't care if he spent all their money on court costs and that he would deliberately keep Celia in the court system for as long as possible. Only when there was nothing financially left would he quit. He felt sure he could earn the money all over again but was equally sure Celia never would. He was determined to leave her with absolutely nothing. I was shocked. He was brutally venomous towards Celia. It was no wonder she was too frightened to ask for a divorce directly to his face. It just goes to show that sometimes we can make wrong assumptions about people when we don't know all the facts. What a great life lesson that was.

We often make wrong assumptions when we do not know all the facts

I started to feel sorry for Celia. Divorcing Cal was tough but he could never be as venomous as Phil, or could he? I would find out later, much later, that he could be but right now I believed Cal was a much kinder man than Phil.

Celia and Phil owned four houses all together; their dream home in South Africa which was now up for sale, their home in Buckinghamshire and two other rental properties also in Buckinghamshire. When Celia came back from South Africa, she asked Phil if she could live in one of the rental properties; Phil said no. Apparently both houses had tenants. Celia was surprised, but unlike me, Celia was not involved in Phil's business, so she had no idea if he was telling her the truth or not. As far as their finances were concerned she was in the dark. Up until now she had been happily in the dark, but now she was getting divorced she felt ignorant and small.

In the past, she would use her husband's debit and credit cards to take care of her family. Sadly, her family were now all grown and her lack of knowledge put her at a severe disadvantage; even paying a household bill was new to her. It was a huge shock and wake-up call as she tried to move her life forward.

Phil would deliberately freeze certain accounts and limit the money she could access. He really was a b*****d as far as dealing with Celia was concerned. Undeterred, Celia found a small house to rent and managed quite well for about 6 months. However, the same courts that Phil thought would protect him forced him to put the rental properties up for sale.

This is Celia and Phil's story really, but it does show how the universe can help you if only you ask. In Phil's

Form E, the form you have to fill in all about your finances when you get divorced; he had written that he was not working. By implication that meant he was not earning anything.

One day Celia was in WH Smiths looking for a magazine to read and her eye kept catching a magazine on Franchising. Celia had absolutely no interest in franchising but this magazine seemed to be lit up for her, not literally. Celia tentatively picked up the magazine and flicked through its pages. Imagine her surprise when she came across a double page spread, complete with photographs on Phil's current adventure into franchising! In his arrogance, he hadn't believed she would find out. Needless to say, she played that ace card much later in the proceeds, but it did prove he would lie in court.

Back to Cal's living arrangements. Since the Judge had forced Phil to put his rental properties up for sale, Celia discovered there was an open house viewing for their property in Stadhampton and she'd decided to go and view it without warning anyone.

When she got to the house the front door was open. and she stepped in. As she walked in she could hear voices in the kitchen and there was a smell of chicken coming from the kitchen. She followed the smell and the noise. As she walked into the kitchen the estate agent looked over.

"Hello," she said, "I'm Celia Brown. I own this house with my husband Phil. How is the open house going?" The estate agent was shocked, he clearly had not expected Celia to show up.

Celia looked around to see two more shocked faces. The tenants of this property were none other than Cal and Nikita, they had guilt written all over their faces. Cal knew he had been caught and if Celia now knew where he was living, it wouldn't be long before I did too. Celia revelled in the moment.

"Hello Cal, I didn't expect to see you here," turning to his companion, "and you must be Nikita?" Celia stretched out her hand to shake Nikita's.

The game was up.

Within 5 minutes of leaving two very uncomfortable people in the house, Celia was on the phone to me. I was out shopping at the time and our mobile connection wasn't great but I heard her say,

"I've found out where Cal and Nikita are living. Are you at... home?"

"No, not at the moment but I can be there in 15 mins."

"Great, I'll get some wine and meet you at Vale Farm."

True to her word, Celia arrived back at Vale Farm only moments behind me. I should have been angry with Cal that day, but we were celebrating Celia's detective work and laughing at the thought of Cal's face.

"Has he rung you yet?" Celia asked.

"Yes, not long after you, but I didn't answer. I'm going to let him stew for a while," I replied with a big smile on my face.

There hadn't been many laughs during our divorce journey, but we laughed that day. I was so grateful that Celia and I had become friends, that we were supporting each other and that we had found out Cal and Phil's secret.

Would Phil really charge Cal £2000? Maybe, but that wasn't much of a deal for Cal. The rental on the house in Stadhampton would genuinely only be around that amount.

Celia and I decided Phil was charging Cal £1000, which Cal gave him in cash, so Phil got £1000 that he could hide away from Celia. Cal was then telling me he needed £2000 per month so he could give Phil £1000 and have another £1000 to hide away from me. They were partners in crime but I don't really know if they were both pocketing £1000 per month.

As Byron Katie would say "Is this true?" In all honesty I don't know if that money arrangement was true.

However, I do know 100% that Cal was lying about where he and Nikita were living. In case you don't know the Buckinghamshire / Oxfordshire border(s), Stadhampton is nowhere near Brill!

Again and again, Cal would show me just how dishonest he could be, and time and again he would accuse me of doing the same. Actually, whenever Cal accused me of something outrageous or unfair, I realised that what he was really doing was telling me that he was the one committing the crime, so to speak. He may have been dishonest but his subconscious kept giving him away.

I let Cal stew all day and by the time I spoke to him that evening, he had his cover story fully worked out. He and Nikita were just helping Phil out by making the house feel warm and welcoming to anyone who was viewing; they were only staying there for a couple of days. Right, did he really think I was that stupid? Well it certainly seemed so.

It amazes me that when you are kind and blonde, and to be honest I am not naturally blonde but when you are, people think it also means you are gullible and stupid. I do have a maths degree to my name, even if I don't mention it often, and I also score very highly on the scale of emotional intelligence. After many years with Cal I'd had to regularly remind myself of this!

During our divorce, my solicitor had suggested that we get a forensic accountant to look at the value of Cal's company. Now this was a tricky situation because while I was a director of this company, with the same number of shares as Cal, it was not a company that we could sell without Cal.

The company had originally been formed because our accountant suggested it would be safer for Cal to work as a Ltd company than as self-employed. At the time the accountant questioned our decision to have equal shares.

And even mentioned the divorce word, but Cal and I couldn't imagine that we would ever get divorced. Here we were only 15 years later in the painful process of getting divorced.

I agreed to the forensic accountant but we didn't go to town. The accountant produced the simplest report he could with the intention of demonstrating what would be a fair value for Cal to pay for my shares.

Of course, Cal's solicitor was not going to accept our figures so he commissioned a much more detailed report and when I saw their report my heart sank. I didn't understand the language and the report made a complete mockery of our forensic statement. There was lots of forensic terminology and lots of mathematics.

Initially, although I was overwhelmed by the report, I decided to sit down and go through it one step at a time. After all, as I reminded myself, *I'm an intelligent woman*. I smile as I write this now, because since then I have repeated this phrase so often, in an affirmative way, that I now actually believe it, but at that point in my divorce I was desperately trying to convince myself that it was true.

I looked up the forensic accountancy phrases that I didn't understand and then I followed the mathematics through, one step at a time, making sure I understood each step before I looked at the next.

It took me a whole afternoon, but once I got to grips with it there was one thing that kept bugging me. Why had this forensic accountant used an 8-month period to analyse the account? It seemed a very odd number to use. I had expected 12 months or even 6 months at a push, but why 8 months?

I decided to follow his mathematical procedure using firstly a 12-month period and then a 6-month period. Surprise, surprise then, when I used either of these periods the business looked far more profitable. Feeling incredibly pleased with myself I typed up my analysis and my results and sent them back to my solicitor.

They couldn't pull the wool over my eyes. It was an expensive process to challenge their report as it brought us back to stalemate and eventually neither set of figures were ever used in our financial settlement.

However, it was a great exercise for my self-esteem which was struggling to raise its tired head.

Divorce is a messy and painful process but it is also an opportunity for huge self-empowerment

Divorce is a messy, painful process. I was shocked at how difficult the whole thing was. When we began I'd assumed it would be challenging, but I had absolutely no idea how draining and depressing it could be. For months or even years the process hangs over your head like a little black cloud that faithfully goes everywhere with you. Even on the sunniest day, that black cloud is always present and regularly sends a shower or a downpour just to remind you it's there. You cannot get away from it.

I know this is a contentious thought but I believe that losing a partner to death is easier. When a partner dies, there is a painful process of grief that you go through but that process has a beginning, a middle and an end. Yes, you miss the person who has died but they didn't choose to leave you, well, not on a conscious level. You don't have to split all your belongings up and argue about who keeps what. You don't have to work out why someone who once loved you so much, could now hurt you and be so mean and cruel. You don't have to see the person you love with someone else. You don't have to see someone else fill your shoes, no matter how badly they are doing it.

The divorce process may have a beginning and a middle, but the negative effects of divorce only end when you decide to let go of the hurt, let go of the blame, stop being a victim and start being a survivor.

They say the top 3 most stressful situations in life are;

- death
- moving to a new house
- divorce

I believe that divorce should be at the top of that list and I say this with an absolute respect to anyone who is currently learning to live with the heartbreak of grieving the death of a partner, or any other loved one for that matter.

I guess for me death is sad, but I truly believe that the person who has died is in a much better place. I don't believe in hell; I believe we all go back to where we came from which is a place without judgment. I believe that in death we go home and this means I do not fear death. It also means that I know the person who has died is in a better place than those of us left in the earth plane. This belief, or faith therefore, means that the grief I feel when someone dies is my sadness for me that I will no longer be able to physically see the person who has passed. I do believe however, that I can still communicate with that person and that one day we will be reunited in spirit. I imagine that if someone does not have these beliefs to hold onto, it would make accepting death a much more difficult process to endure.

Death is not the end

I realised recently that I have not been to the funeral of any of my relatives. It was not by choice I hasten to add, but for various reasons I had never been given the option. For years I felt that I missed out, especially by not being taken to my Mum's funeral, but yesterday I gained a new perspective on this situation; I didn't need to say goodbye to my Mum because she has been with me all my life, not in a physical sense, but as a voice in my head, as a gentle breeze on my skin and as a delicate smell of perfume dancing around me.

Would I ever have developed my senses sufficiently to know when she was with me if I had said goodbye? I think not. Not going to the funeral caused me so much pain, for many years. It made me distrusting of adults who kept me in the dark and weren't honest with me. But then I realised, whoever had made the decision that I should not go had given me a gift. They gave me the gift of keeping my Mum alive in my heart, in my life and in a strange way, I've got to know her more in the years since her continuation day. I love that phrase. Neale Donald Walsh uses it all the time and it seems so much nicer than saying someone has died or passed away.

If you are curious about what happens after death I would highly recommend you read Neale's book At Home with God, it is one of the books in The Conversation with God series.

Take ownership of your life
Do not be a victim

Just one final word about divorce at this point. If you are in the middle of a divorce now, try not to blame the other person no matter how hurt you feel. Blaming someone else for your lack of happiness makes you a victim and means you cannot make life better for yourself. Instead accept your current situation, stop looking at what you are losing and allow yourself to focus on what you want to do with the rest of your life.

Don't be practical, dream big, because it is only in dreaming big that you can start to step into being the magnificent person that you truly are.

Chapter 21: Nikita is Pregnant

Our legal divorce finally came through on June 14th 2006, almost 31 years since our first date, and more years than Nikita had been alive.

I didn't know how to feel when I opened the envelope with the Decree Absolute inside. We were nowhere near finished in sorting out the finances and we still didn't have a buyer for Vale Farm, but I could finally tick something off my list of '5 things I needed to do to get through my divorce'. At least that was something. One experience down, only four to go. Other than having a piece of paper in my hand that said I was divorced, nothing else seemed to change. It wasn't one of my better ideas to get legally divorced before we had completed the financial agreements, but I wouldn't realise that until the following year.

The next real challenge of 2006 came in October. Cal arrived at Vale Farm looking very pleased with himself. As he said the words,

"I have got something to tell you," I had a feeling I knew what that 'something' was going to be. My heart sank and my world ripped apart. Not only was I losing Cal, my place in his family but, as I was about to find out, Cal was adding to that family.

"Nikita is pregnant. I am going to be a Dad." I knew the words were coming; I had dreaded them for a long time. I felt a sharp pain in my heart, a physical pain that hurt like hell and tears started to form in my eyes.

Somehow I found the words to thank Cal for telling me himself, because I hadn't wanted to hear it from anyone else, and also to congratulate him. From the minute he'd met Nikita this day was on the cards.

I wanted to be alone with my grief; I was sad for the family I'd never had, sad for the dream that was long gone of Cal and I having children. I started to sob. I told him I was happy for him, but sad for me. I tried to own my grief, my tears, to not blame him for my current feelings but why was I trying to make it easier for him? I wanted to be alone but he wouldn't leave me.

"I couldn't possibly leave you like this, " he said. Was he really concerned about me, or was he enjoying the moment? I was struggling to control my emotions. I wanted him to go. I wanted to allow myself to sob and I didn't want an audience.

Again, I asked Cal to leave, but he insisted on staying. All the time he made out he was thinking of me but the more he stayed the more I couldn't help but think he was enjoying seeing me so distraught. In a way, it felt like he was saying 'see, there is nothing wrong with me, it was you that was to blame'. He didn't say it but it seemed to be written all over his face.

Cal and I not being able to have children was one thing, it was something I had come to terms with, but it had never dawned on me that he would have children with someone else. It had never occurred to me that he would get himself out of the 'no kids' club.

I moved from the kitchen to the orangery, I wanted to get away from him, I wanted to curl up on the settee and wallow in my grief. Again, he followed me. This was now starting to make me angry. Why wouldn't he leave alone?

"For God sake leave me alone," I begged him angrily through sniffles and tears.

"I can't. I don't know what you'll do."

What on earth was he suggesting? I wasn't having some sort of break down I was justifiably upset about his news. The more I shouted at him to leave, the more he insisted on staying.

He was clearly enjoying the moment, enjoying seeing me in so much pain. He was proud that he was going to be a Dad and rightly so, but he was rubbing it into every cell in my body. I was shocked at his behaviour, shocked that now he had a baby on the way how quickly he had forgotten the intensity of pain from being childless. I was shocked at the smug look on his face as he kept telling me he was only staying because he was worried about me.

All these years later I know this is part of his manipulation tactics. I didn't want to believe he was enjoying my grief but my intuition was screaming at me that this was the case. His words were voicing concern but his eyes told a different story.

He seemed to stay forever but of course when he was ready to leave, he suddenly got up and left me. Life seemed so unfair. All I had ever wanted was a family of my own. I had spent my life trying to be helpful and kind and where had it got me? All the support I had given to Cal to help him get where he was counted for nothing in his mind. He had achieved, he was the one that was successful, and now even our lack of children was my fault too.

Cal in contrast was not nice to people, he put himself before everyone else. He moaned if I gave money to charity or the homeless people on the street. He only helped someone if there was something in it for him and yet now, he was being rewarded with a child of his own. If what you put out into the universe is what comes back, why was he getting everything he wanted while my life was crumbling? I would eventually learn the answers to these questions, but at this moment life seemed very unfair.

Amongst my grief came waves of anger. He had taken any chance of me being a Mum away from me. He hadn't taken the minerals and vitamins. He had refused to adopt. He had begged me to stay when I wanted to divorce him 5 years before, and now that I was too old to have children with anyone else, he'd traded me in for someone who could have children. How cruel was that?

I sat in my righteous indignation for some time and ignored any part I'd had to play. I ignored the decision that said, 'I love you enough to stay with you without us having children'. I ignored my own desire for a divorce in 2000, and my subsequent decision to stay because he begged me to. I'd had my chances but I hadn't taken them, and now I sat in my anger and my sadness and blamed him. Life did not seem very fair. I still had a lot to learn

My relationship with Cal got worse over the coming weeks. The house was up for sale and the estate agents kept sending the wrong kind of people to view it. If you are a horsey person, then being able to see your horses in their stables from the kitchen window is absolute bliss. If you are not horsey, it is a real disadvantage. So why did they keep sending people with no interest in horses?

Eventually a couple came who showed an interest. They offered the full asking price, but there was a catch, they wanted me out by Christmas. Since Christmas was about 6 weeks away I told the estate agent that was not possible. She challenged my decision and recommended that I rent somewhere short term. To be honest, that was never going to be easy with 4 dogs, 3 horses, 2 cats and a pony. She thought she could find somewhere for us to rent, so I stayed open minded until her I saw what she was suggesting.

The only house she could find had no garden, no central heating and there were no stables locally for the horses; I was insulted. Clearly, she had just wanted her money, money that personally I didn't think she had earned. I refused her suggested rental property and said no to the sale of Vale Farm.

The following day Cal rang me. He was furious about my saying 'no' to the sale. He went on and on about me not wanting to move and about how I was sponging off him. He screamed and shouted down the phone until I hung up on him. Not long afterwards I heard his van screaming down the driveway. Idiot I thought. I went out to meet him but as he got out of his van I knew I was in trouble. He hadn't come to talk, he had come to shout at me. I'd never seen him so angry, so aggressive. I suddenly felt afraid of him, afraid of a man I had known for over 30 years. I ran back to the house with the dogs at my feet. As we got through the door I locked it behind me.

"LET ME IN!" he screamed through the back door.

"No, not until you calm down," I replied.

He started to walk to the front door, so I raced through the house and got to the door before him and put the inside lock on the door so his key wouldn't work.

My actions were making him angrier but I didn't know what else to do. As he went back round the house I ran back to the kitchen only to realise I'd left the sash window over the sink open. To my absolute horror, Cal was climbing through the window. He was struggling to get over the sink, it wasn't easy or graceful, but he was getting through. The cats were nowhere to be seen and the dogs had hidden in the lounge. Great, so much for protection!

I stood my ground but on the opposite side of the central island to Cal. When he moved, I moved. I stayed quiet at first hoping he would calm down as he let all his rage out in my direction, but that wasn't happening. It seemed the estate agent had rung him and told him she didn't think I wanted to leave and that I had refused the opportunity of renting a property that she had found for me. She even made out that she had pulled in a few favours to get me first refusal. She had no idea what danger she'd put me in that day. and now Cal was getting angrier and angrier; I was terrified of what he might do.

He jumped onto the subject of Daniel. Now I will admit that I'd had an on/off relationship with Daniel for many years. I will be honest and tell you that I'd loved Daniel in a way I had never experienced before, but I didn't think we were intended to be together, not in this life time. We saw each other from time to time and yes, by this point I'd even slept with him, but it was not the relationship Cal was making out.

Cal started to focus on the amount of wine I was drinking. He was convinced that Daniel was spending a lot of time with me because of the number of empty wine bottles that were in the recycling box. It is true that the one glass a night, because I was getting divorced, had easily turned into 2 glasses each evening. When those 2 glasses started slipping down rather quickly it seemed silly to stop at 3 glasses, because it doesn't leave much in the bottle. I was drinking much more than was good for me at the time, and the events of this day would make me change that, but right now Cal was barking up the wrong tree.

Just as I thought things couldn't get any worse Cal picked up the first empty bottle and threw it to the floor. It smashed at my feet, not close enough to hurt me but close enough to threaten me. Speaking very slowly and very deliberately he shouted at me as if I were a child and all the time he was smashing empty glass bottles in my direction. One then another, and another and another. He continued to throw the bottles at my feet and I was regretting having built up so many empty bottles in the recycling. Miraculously none of the glass was hitting me, but I was shocked and scared. He continued until every wine bottle was smashed on the kitchen floor and the floor was covered in broken glass.

I phoned my sister and through my tears and sobbing I begged her to confirm to Cal that I did not have Daniel living with me at Vale Farm. Confused, but ever supportive, when I passed the phone to Cal, she started to do just that. Somehow Julie knew what to say to Cal and she started to calm him down in a way that I couldn't. I don't know what she said to him, although I did hear all his complaints about me, some of which were hitting home a little too hard.

I was drinking a lot of wine. I didn't think I had a problem, but in truth I couldn't remember the last wine free day I'd had. I decided there and then to give it up for a month just to check that I could. He also called me lazy and moaned to Julie that I was just sponging off him. I felt a bit uncomfortable, I shouldn't have done, but I did. I wasn't working as such but I was still his company secretary and doing all the book keeping for the business.

Also, I was keeping the house presentable for all the viewings. I know there was only me living in it, but I had to keep all the rooms feeling fresh and dust free and a full clean from top to bottom took me three days! I often felt like a chamber maid as I prepared for a viewing, rather than Lady of the Manor as Christine had put it. I wasn't being lazy; I was taking care of the house, the animals, the paperwork for his business, and my self-growth.

I had even given Cal all the information that he had needed to fill in his Form E. It was an intimidating form but I took one section at a time and, as I did mine, I sat with a small black notebook next to me and put all the equivalent details for Cal in it as I went along. When I'd finished mine, I then handed over the little book for Cal to do his. He trusted me, he took that black book and used it because he knew I wouldn't rip him off, knew I wouldn't give him false information. I laughed years later when he had to do the same for his divorce with Nikita, but didn't know where to start. Of course he didn't, he hadn't done it the first time around.

So, my actual crime was not earning any money, and in Cal's eyes that meant I was being lazy. The reason I wasn't earning any money was that I had given up my work when I'd moved 200 miles down south to be with Cal. It had always been my intention to start another business once we'd got settled but I hadn't felt settled since we left Cheshire, and of course there was the fact my solicitor had told me not to earn any money yet. Cal had always accused me of being lazy, of stitching him up by not getting things done. The truth was, it had never actually been physically possible to do all the things he had expected me to do, but heroically I'd kept trying.

Every day I started a fresh and tried to get everything done, and every day I had failed. This process alone had eroded my self-worth, fed my belief that I was a failure and added to my fear of being abandoned.

I had struggled with bouts of depression, always believing it was my failings that made me feel so worthless. Yet somehow, each time I'd found my inner strength and hoisted myself back up to start the cycle all over again. I never let Cal know or see my struggles, I'd never shared how bad I felt, I'd just hidden it and pushed forward so many times that it had become a way of life. Incidentally, Cal never gained any true understanding of how much work I did for the business until he had to do it himself! Only then when he missed a VAT return did he acknowledge how difficult it was to keep on top of it all, but I would have to wait another 2 years for that admission!!

Julie had taken the edge off Cal's anger sufficiently for me to cope with him when he came off the phone. He didn't leave straight away but I felt safe again. He was still angry but calmer. He was still accusing me of all sorts but the venom had gone out of his words. I did try to talk to him, to reassure him that Daniel was not living at Vale Farm but Cal's reaction was to make threats towards Daniel if he ever found him there, and his final parting gift was;

"He won't want to have anything to do with you when he knows you do all that woo-woo stuff. He'll drop you like a tonne of bricks then." And with that parting blow, Cal was gone.

We should never have to hide who we are in order for someone else to love and accept us

When he left I was shaking. All sorts of thoughts went through my head. Now, I must admit that Daniel was married. In my defence, I hadn't realised that when I became involved with him, although I did know he had a girlfriend. The day I realised I was so shocked I never said anything to him. That was a pattern of mine, there was a lot that went on in my head that no one ever knew about.

I had to do some deep soul searching to decide if I wanted to stay in yet another love triangle. For someone who had stood on a soap box and said she would never have an affair I was now on the third side of the love triangle having already experienced both of the other two sides and as I now know, it is painful on all three sides.

Much to my surprise I found a way to justify my choice; I was free to be with Daniel, he was the one who was in another relationship, not me. He was the one who was breaking the rules, not me. And if his wife turned up, I would just have to accept any angry words that she threw at me.

Since I had chosen not to blame Nikita for the break-up of my marriage, it wasn't too big a step to justify my choice to remain in a relationship with Daniel. Besides which, Daniel wasn't happy in his marriage! Oh ladies, don't we all use that justification when we want to 'save' someone and make their life better. Of course, if I could do that for Daniel, I would be doing it for me too.

My judgement was clouded; I was head over heels in love with this man and not ready to give him up. There was a connection with Daniel that I'd never felt before. A pull that kept bringing me back to him time and time again. I did end the relationship quite regularly, at least once a year, and my reason was always *I do not want to be someone's mistress.* Daniel would respect that, but I guess it wasn't long before he started to know that I never stuck to my decision. Be it a week, or a month, or 3 months I always got back in touch with him. I liked who I was when I was with him; we talked and drank coffee, he made me laugh and whenever I was with him, I honestly just wanted to rip his clothes off!

I'd never had these sort of feelings before, I thought that stuff only happened in films, but here I was experiencing it. There was always long gaps between us communicating or seeing each other, but it felt like there was a rubber band holding us together. The further apart we were, the longer the time since we had connected, the stronger the pull to be together and yet, this relationship could sometimes be harder than my divorce. It seemed we weren't meant to be together but we couldn't be apart.

I now believe Daniel is my twin flame. Being with him is amazing but he also holds up a mirror to every part of me that I still need to heal and that is hard. Accepting that he is out there, that we love each other but will never be together in this life time, was my first experience of unconditional love for another human being. I love him, but I expect absolutely nothing of him.

Love is only unconditional when we have absolutely no expectations of the other.
Then we love them for being who they are not who we think they should become

At this point in my story however, I was worried that Cal would somehow scare Daniel off, just like he had scared Messenger off all those years earlier. What should I do? I had touched on my beliefs with Daniel but had I told him I was a Healer, had I told him I talked to dead people? I couldn't honestly answer yes. Somewhere in the back of my mind, like Cal, I believed Daniel would walk away once he found out. Also, I needed to warn him about the situation with Cal and give him the chance to walk away from my drama. Tentatively, when Daniel contacted me later that night, I gave him some of the details about Cal and asked if I could talk to him. Bless him, he came around after work the following day. I was so nervous of the conversation but I needn't have been. When I related Cal's threats towards him Daniel smiled and said,

"Don't worry, I've got myself out of much worse situations than this!" He was so relaxed and nonplussed by the whole situation.

He was also completely unfazed by my admission of using Reiki to heal people and of talking to the so-called dead. It seemed either Daniel 'just knew' or I'd shared more of myself than I had realised. Daniel couldn't stay too long that evening but when he left I felt amazing for two reasons; I'd been brave and completely open with him and he had chosen to accept me just as I was, and for the first time in my life I had a man who was choosing to stand in my corner.

It is a joyful feeling to be accepted exactly as you are

Chapter 22: Cal and Nikita are Married

Christmas 2006 was my first experience of Christmas on my own. As usual I had invitations to join different friends for Christmas dinner, but yet again they were all in the wrong part of the country and I needed to stay home to look after the animals.

As with the previous year I decorated the house and the trees just for me. As I awoke on Christmas day I felt a little sad, I liked my own company and I'd spent many days on my own, but somehow Christmas Day was different. I couldn't help but feel sorry for myself but I got dressed and wandered downstairs to be greeted by my 4 collie dogs all of whom were very happy to see me. How lucky I was to have such a menagerie of animals. I made the decision there and then to have a happy day.

Happiness is a state of mind

I ran back upstairs to find my flashing Snowman Earrings and a bit of tinsel for the ponytail in my hair. Feeling more Christmassy, I made a mug of coffee and headed outside to feed the horses. Four heads appeared over the stable door and a chorus of whinnies wished me a horsey Happy Christmas. I know they probably just wanted breakfast but I felt better thinking their whinnies were Christmas greetings.

I put the radio on loud, fed the horses and checked that the frost had lifted from the field. I then rugged up each horse and turned them all out for some Christmas grazing. As I sang my way through all my stable chores, I didn't notice all the text messages that were coming through to my phone, or the vibration of the missed calls.

My sister had been first, she is always the first to greet me on Christmas Day. No matter how old she gets her inner child wakes her bright and early on Christmas Day, much to the annoyance of her Yorkshire born husband.

When I got back into the house, I made a coffee and phoned her back. It was lovely to hear the vibration of her voice and before long we were laughing and joking on the phone. After my chat with Jules I joyfully opened my presents and then headed to the kitchen. I may be on my own but there was no reason why I couldn't enjoy a Christmas dinner. A vegetarian nut roast is much quicker to cook than a turkey and I was determined that I wasn't missing out on the roasties and seasonal veg.

With my Christmas CD blaring out happy tunes I cooked a full veggie Christmas dinner and while the food was cooking, I made up the fire in the lounge. I did think about eating at the table but that was a bit lonely and it was so lovely in front of a real fire in the lounge. It was also comforting to have the dogs lying around me munching away at their Christmas treats.

As I flicked through the channels on the television I realised I could watch anything I wanted and soon I came across Holiday Inn. I love the old musicals and always cried, in a good way, at the rendition of White Christmas at the end of this film. I went back into the kitchen to get a celebratory glass of wine. I had achieved my 4 weeks without wine and proved to myself that I didn't have an alcohol problem. It had also given me a sense of achievement and a clearer head for making the tough decisions I needed to as I went through my divorce. Bright eyed and bushy tailed was definitely a better way to approach my divorce. I preferred my life with less alcohol, but I wasn't going to miss out on a nice glass of Pinot Grigio to celebrate Christmas Day.

I enjoyed every mouthful of my delicious lunch and then curled up on the settee to watch the rest of the film. It felt decadent to be able to sit and do absolutely nothing although it took all afternoon to get through the film as one after another of my friends rang to check I was okay.

I felt so much love coming in my direction, it was almost overwhelming. How lovely to have so many people be concerned about my wellbeing. As the afternoon went on, it almost became a competition with myself to see if I could get through Christmas Day by myself without feeling sad and lonely.

I am happy to say I could, not only that, but I even started to enjoy it. I had to look after the animals needs but apart from that I could eat when I wanted, drink what I wanted and watch whatever I wanted on the television. I didn't have to keep anyone else happy except myself. I even spent some time tuning in to say 'Hello' to my spirit family. By the time the day was over, I was feeling a sense of achievement that I had turned a day where I could have felt sorry for myself into a day for 'me', a day where I woke up feeling sad but spent most of the day feeling happy and loved. I didn't want to spend the day by myself but when it happened I'd had a very enjoyable day.

I didn't understand that day that I was using the power of my thoughts to create my happy day, but I definitely felt the benefits.

Your thoughts are powerful,
choose them carefully

I started 2007 with 4 items still on my 'what I need to do to get through my divorce' list.

By the beginning of March I could tick off another item; buying a car. The car had been a bone of contention, I was driving a BMW that Cal used to use for work. It was an automatic 540, an amazing car to drive although you had to be careful with the speed. You could seriously get up to 100 miles an hour on the motorway without 'feeling' it. The first time that happened I scared myself.

Oh, I must just tell you a lovely angel story connected with this car. I had been driving back down from Cheshire to Buckinghamshire and I always joined the M6 at the Knutsford junction, junction 19 for those of you who know it. Normally I would wiz down the slip road and relatively quickly join the fast lane on the motorway. On this day, I put my foot down on the accelerator and felt my stomach churn. It was such a strong feeling, I automatically lifted my foot a little. I felt strangely nervous, this was crazy. I'd done this journey many times before. I tried again, but once more again my stomach started to do somersaults. Really, what was wrong with me? It didn't feel good being this nervous and driving on the motorway. I tried a couple more times and each time the same thing happened only the feeling in my stomach got worse each time.

Okay, I reasoned. It probably won't take me that much longer if I stay on in the inside line and drive all the way home at 60mph. As it turned out it would take me hours to get home that day, but I was grateful for every moment.

Five minutes after I had resigned myself to driving at 60mph on the motorway, unheard of for me, one of the tyres on my car blew. Because I was on the inside lane and not going too fast, I was able to easily pull the car over onto the hard shoulder and phone for help.

If my tyre had blown as I was motoring down the fast lane as usual, I dread to think what would have happened. I wasn't consciously talking to my Guardian Angels at that time, but I do believe they saved me that day. I sat in my car and said 'thank you' to God over and over again. It took 2 hours for the recovery truck to get to me and he was amazed at how cheerful I was when he arrived. How could I be anything else, something had just saved my life, 'something' had made me feel so bad that I'd slowed down and was in the best possible position when the tyre blew. Someone was looking after me and I was incredibly grateful.

"There are more things in heaven and earth Horatio than are dreamt of in your philosophy"

William Shakespeare

So back to Cal's BMW, which had been gorgeous in its day, but was now past its best. There was over 200,000 miles on the clock and it needed £1600 worth of work done on it to get it through its next MOT. As the age and mileage meant the car was only worth £2000 in good condition, Cal refused to have the work done. He said I would have to buy my own car!

Now, by this time we'd sold the house in Virginia Water and much to Cal's annoyance I had split the money. Well, truth be told, for the first time in my life I had opened a bank account in my name. When the money from the house came into the joint account, I transferred my half immediately into my new account where Cal couldn't get at it. I happily expected Cal to do the same, but he was furious. Now he was forcing me to use that money to buy my own car.

As you read this, you probably think that was not an unreasonable request and at the time neither did I. I had always wanted a Landrover Freelander, but Cal always said we weren't buying a rubbish British car. For a man who was born in Britain and grew up here, he was very anti-British. His Italian roots came first every time. Granted they do make good food and wine, oh, and clothes, and of course shoes, and then how could I forget the handbags?

Yes, the Italians undoubtedly have a lot going for them, but the reason I got mad was that Cal had never lived in Italy. He was born in Rusholme, for goodness sake, the curry centre of Manchester. He did speak Italian for the first 5 years of his life, but by the time I met him he was too embarrassed to speak it unless he absolutely had to. It was a fake allegiance and I was sick of hearing how the Italians were so much better than the British. You can imagine what life was like when the football World Cup was on. I can only remember one occasion when England got further than Italy and even then it was only one round. I did enjoy it for a few days though!

As I said, Cal disliked British cars but I knew the Freelander would be good for me. It was a small 4x4, there was room for all 4 of my dogs and I could easily carry bedding or feed bags for the horses. It would be a workhorse, but a workhorse that I liked the look of.

I phoned up an old friend who was the MD of a Land Rover show room and asked for some help. He did warn me that the Freelander's were not so reliable, but my heart was set and he soon sent me photographs of a demonstrator car that was now up for sale. It was black, which was not my first choice for colour, but the reg was MM06NUC. All I could see were the words 'mmm, now u can', so feeling empowered I bought the car and today, as I write this ten years after buying the vehicle; I still have it.

There were two reasons I felt a bit cheated about having to pay for my own car. Firstly, once I had bought the Freelander, Cal decided to keep the BMW and had the work done on it, paid for out of our joint account. Secondly, Cal started taking lots of cash out of our joint account, £250 a day. He will deny it to this day, but miraculously Nikita suddenly got a new car which I am sure was paid for out of our account.

Of course she needed a reliable car because she was soon to give birth to Cal's first child, and that was my next nightmare.

Within half an hour of the birth of Angelo, Cal phoned me to tell me his good news. I congratulated him, I asked all the right questions; how much did Angelo weigh? What time was he born? Are Nikita and the baby both okay? Though my heart was breaking, I acted like a good friend.

Of course, my friends were shocked that Cal rang me so soon, or that he rang me at all, but I justified his actions. For me, he simply saw me as a best friend and therefore he wanted to share his good news with me. I didn't want his son, this innocent baby, to get in the way of our future friendship so I stayed strong while I was on the phone, but the minute the call ended and I put the phone down I cried.

It wasn't that I wasn't pleased for Cal, I was just feeling very sorry for me. Also, my life as I had known it was coming to an end. I seemed stuck until the house was sold and the finances were sorted, but Cal was just getting on with his life. This had happened before. When we had moved to Holly Tree, Cal went to work from a different house but my life changed dramatically. When we moved down south, Cal went to work from a different house but my life changed dramatically. Then, when Cal decided he wanted to be with Nikita, he went straight ahead and made a life with her before he had ended the life he'd had with me. This is his pattern but I was stuck and he was moving forwards.

I was struggling with feelings I thought I had dealt with. The pain of not having children, the pain of not having a Mum in physical form and not being a Mum myself. The medical label for our lack of children had been 'Unexplained Infertility'! In other words, there was no good reason. We just didn't work together. Wasn't that just the plain truth? Maybe life was trying to tell me that Cal and I were not meant to be together. If it was, I hadn't listened but I was listening now.

It was so hard to watch Cal live my dream with someone else, and even harder when later in 2007 he would bring Angelo to my new house so I could meet his son, so I could watch him with the child I always thought we would have. I didn't share any of my pain with Cal, I played the game, I bought a card and a small present and sent it to Cal and Nikita. I have no idea what I was doing. I really didn't want to start being involved in the life of this child, but what else would a good friend do? I buried my pain and played the part well. Cal would never guess how hard it was for me, and I could never have guessed at that point how one day I would love and adore this baby boy.

The arrival of Angelo didn't soften Cal when it came to anything to do with our divorce, if anything it made it worse. He now had Nikita and a baby to take care of. I was off his list of dependents. For some time, Cal had been accusing me of being sneaky, of doing things behind his back. I was taking money out of our joint account and squirrelling it away, but I was only matching what he took and he could see what I was doing. When Cal withdrew £100, I withdrew £100. If Cal withdrew £250, then I did the same.

I couldn't understand why he kept accusing me of hiding things from him. Then one day in May, he arrived at Vale farm to talk about splitting all our belongings. As he walked through the door something shiny caught my attention on his left hand. He walked to the end of the kitchen and sat down ready for the battle ahead. I sat opposite him and all my peripheral vision went blurred. It was like a cartoon. Suddenly, all I could see was Cal's left hand and a wedding ring. Yes, a wedding ring. A voice in my head said; 'don't say anything. Don't Say Anything. DON'T SAY ANYTHING.' It didn't matter how loud that voice shouted at me, I heard myself saying to Cal,

"Are you married?"

"Yes."

"And you didn't think to tell me?"

"What's it got to do with you?"

"We haven't sold the house, we haven't sorted the finances, and you decided to get married. You couldn't finish one marriage before you started the next?"

Yet again I could feel the anger bubble up inside me. This man had been accusing me of being sneaky for the last 3 months. Accusing me and yet he was the one that had got married without a word.

"When? When did you get married?"

"February, on Valentine's day."

"February? You said you were never getting married again?"

"Well Nikita didn't want Angelo to be born to parents that weren't married."

"I bet she didn't! And why haven't you worn a ring until now? Why have you been coming here for 3 months knowing you were married and not wearing your ring?"

"It needed resizing."

"Really???"

Did he really expect me to believe that? Yet again he had been accusing me of doing something that he was doing. He'd been lying to me for 3 months. It never actually dawned on me that he would get married again so soon. Now there were two of us called Mrs Delmonte and we were all still working out of the same bank account. How did I let this happen?

I had never realised when I applied for the Decree Absolute that by completing the legal side of the divorce I had given Cal the option to marry Nikita before he had completed everything with me. It was a mess. And yes, it hurt.

I couldn't talk to him that day. I told him to leave and this time he did. As I thought about the new situation I realised I *couldn't* keep the name Delmonte, what's more, I didn't *want* to keep the Delmonte name. For a long time I had been Mrs Delmonte, but now Nikita was Mrs Delmonte.

I couldn't be 'Miss' Delmonte, I didn't feel I could be 'Miss' Anyone. I was too old to be 'Miss'. I didn't like 'Ms', but now I understood why some ladies used it.

Who could I be? It is a strange thought to think about changing your name. You identify yourself with a name. I had been born Karen Lynne Davies but I didn't feel a part of the Davies family, so I couldn't go back to Karen Lynne Davies. I had become Karen Lynne Delmonte and been known as Mrs D at school, as Mrs Cal on a film set, as Karen from Holly Tree. Who was I now as my life with Cal had come to an end? Who did I want to be as I started a new future.

Before the end of the year I would decide to become simply Karen Lynne and change my name by deed poll, but at this moment I was simply asking...

Who Am I? And

Who do I choose to be?

Chapter 23: Midsummer

Did I tell you we had found a buyer for the house? Sorry, I should have mentioned that earlier.

At the beginning of the year I had contacted the estate agents and voiced my concerns about the lady who was handling our sale. I told them that I didn't want to work with her and I also said that unless they started advertising our house in equine publications we would change to another estate agents.

I don't know where this more forceful version of me was coming from, but when I am in a corner I do often come out fighting, much to the surprise of those who believe I am a pushover.

Amazingly the house was advertised in Horse and Hound and suddenly we had 7 viewings booked in 6 days. It was going to be a busy week; I cleaned the house from top to bottom, but on the day of the first viewing a strange thing happened. The front door locked and I couldn't open it. Somehow that little button that stops the door from locking when it is open had pushed in while the door was shut; I couldn't even go to the outside of the door and open it with a key.

I was home alone, tired, stressed and at my wits end to find a way to open the door. It got to 30 minutes before the arrival of the first couple to view, who happened to be a famous television presenter and his wife, and still the door was locked shut. In desperation I shouted at Archangel Michael. Now, I know you maybe thinking I had lost the plot at this point but amongst his many jobs I believe that Archangel Michael helps to fix things. So I shouted, really shouted at the top of my voice,

"HOW AM I SUPPOSED TO SELL THE HOUSE IF I CAN'T EVEN OPEN THE FRONT DOOR?"

I promise I'm not making this up. No sooner had I finished my rant than I heard a click and in front of my own eyes the door opened.

I was taken aback, I can tell you. I believed in Angels but I had never had such an instant response. A little overwhelmed I looked up, I have no idea why I did that, I guess I believed that AA Michael was above me! So I looked up and in a very small voice whispered,

"Thank you."

As it turned out, this television presenter who always comes across as a cheeky chap on the TV was anything but on the day he viewed my house. Either he was having a bad day, or he had been forced by his wife to view a house he didn't want to see. She on the other hand was lovely. They arrived in two cars and he left very quickly after the viewing.

She had their young labradoodle dog in the car and asked me if it was possible to let him stretch his legs. As an animal lover myself, of course I immediately agreed and we had a lovely chat as we wandered around the yard with 5 dogs at our feet. Not surprisingly they didn't put in an offer to buy the house.

The week passed quickly with one viewing after another, until on the final day a couple came to view who genuinely seemed interested in the house. They stayed for a chat and a coffee after the viewing and they were easy to talk to. The next day they put in an offer for the full asking price and, having heard a little of my situation the day before, gave me almost 6 months to find a new home for me and my animals. We agreed on a completion date of July 29th 2007. Cal was not so impressed that the date was months away, but at least he was happy that we now had a buyer.

On the day that we agreed the sale I could feel the anxiety flush through my body. Now I really had to find somewhere to live, and it wasn't going to be easy to find a house with stables in Buckinghamshire on my budget. I could have moved to a new area, but to be honest I was fed up of starting from scratch. If I stayed in the area at least I would know where I was, know where to buy horse feed, be able to use the same vets and farrier (or so I thought). I thought the transition would be a little easier than starting a fresh somewhere new.

As I started to look on line for potential houses my anxiety began to grow. When I filtered stables or land into my house search, the number of potential houses would reduce to single figures. After a week of looking I was feeling constantly sick with anxiety.

I needed a new approach. As I said I already believed in Angels and I decided to ask for their help. I wrote a long list of what my new house had to include for me to be happy, and of course top of my list was an enclosed garden for the dogs to play in and stables for my horses. I then counted 8 weeks back from July 29th which took me to June 3rd. I reckoned the quickest time I could buy a house from viewing to completion was 8 weeks. Therefore, if I hadn't found a house by June 3rd I was in trouble. However, until that date I was not in trouble, so I was not going to worry. The Angels had my order, all I had to do was look on line or in the local papers, at least once a week, so the Angels could draw my attention to my new home. In the meantime, I would start packing up Vale Farm and complete my negotiations with Cal over who would have what.

As you would imagine negotiating with Cal was not easy since he really believed everything was his. I kept my cool. I suggested we should estimate how much each item of furniture cost so that we could split the furniture fairly. At first he questioned my estimates; I tried to explain that it didn't matter if my estimates were good or bad as we weren't selling the furniture, I only had to be consistent for each piece. Eventually he understood and the negotiations began.

Oh my goodness it was hard to stay cool; Cal had an argument as to why he should have all the better pieces of furniture. I decided early on that I didn't care if Cal had more furniture value wise than me, just as long as I could get most of the furniture I wanted. As luck would have it Cal wanted all the modern furniture that we had chosen for Virginia Water, while I preferred the pieces from Holly Tree.

We had huge arguments over the oak bedroom furniture, but eventually I negotiated that Cal should take the pine bedroom furniture and the 2 sleigh double beds, while I got the oak furniture and the original double bed which had seen better days. This was the way the negotiations went.

We were slowly, over a course of many days and weeks, heading to an argument over the grandfather clock. I loved the grandfather clock. It felt like the heartbeat of my home and I didn't want to lose it. As the pieces of furniture were whittled down, I started giving in to Cal so that on paper he had more furniture in value than I did. This meant that it would only be fair for me to keep the clock. My plan worked perfectly and I had to smile when he finally said,

"I suppose that means you should have the clock," I managed to stop my smile from showing as I agreed that I would take it.

There was still a lot of negotiating to be done, as we had a lot of stuff, but I decided that things could only come with me if they fit one of the following categories.

They had to be practical

They had to look beautiful

They had to make me smile

The only thing that I took with me that didn't fit into any of these categories was my university notes. I have since thrown them all away, but at that time I somehow couldn't part with all my notes, so I allowed myself to keep them.

Now another strange thing started to happen as I began to pack. Cal had never really helped me pack when we moved. He always managed to get a day off on moving day but apart from that, his excuse was always that he was working. I started my packing upstairs and as I sorted through each room and labelled up the boxes, some for me and many for Cal, I started to feel a sense of achievement as I put a label on the door to say the room that door led into was finished. I also started to feel energised by the process and almost addicted to this thing I was doing, which was decluttering and packing.

Decluttering is surprisingly an energising process

I cannot remember how many times I wrote on a box, CAL BOX OF BITS! There were various versions of this label such as CAL ANOTHER BOX OF BITS. It made me smile as I realised that all the stuff that we had kept that I didn't want to keep was now going to go with Cal. Poor Nikita, wait until she sees this lot, she's no idea who she has married. Cal hates throwing anything away. I had even hired a skip to throw rubbish into, and now when Cal came to the house his first job was always to check the skip, just to make sure I hadn't thrown anything away that he wanted to keep. Now you may laugh at this, but he did seriously retrieve some stuff from the skip... just in case he needed it! That is such a dangerous phrase. In my opinion, it gives you permission to keep hold of stuff that you really should let go of. I didn't want my new home, when I found it, to have any clutter at all and I was becoming energised just by letting go.

The negotiations with Cal were tricky but we were doing okay. The sale of the house was going through smoothly, but June 3rd was approaching and I was no nearer finding a new home. Every visit Cal would ask me if I had found somewhere, and then question why I wasn't getting worried. As the months passed by, my friends started to do the same thing. 'No I am not worrying until June the 3rd,' I would reply, taking a deep breath.

On June 1st, I started to panic! I was in Princes Risborough thinking I may be in trouble when I suddenly felt a desire to have a coffee. Now we lived so close to Princes Risborough that I would usually go home for coffee but on this day, I chose to follow my instincts.

I sat down in a small coffee shop with my cappuccino and noticed a local newspaper on the table next to me. No sooner had the thought crossed my mind that I should have a look through it, than I found myself flicking through the pages. On one of the larger adverts I came across a house with land. I didn't like the look of the house from the front and it was out of my price range, but it had 3 stables and a field shelter, 11 acres of land and it wasn't too far away. Something told me to take a look. I phoned my friend, Lou, to see if she was free to view the house with me and when she agreed, I phoned the agent and booked a viewing the very next day.

On June 2nd, we drove down a very steep hill towards an incredibly pretty village. It had a pub, a church and a primary school. There were pretty thatched cottages and lots of different types of houses; it was chocolate box perfect.

The house I was viewing, Midsummer, sat in the middle of the village. I still didn't like it from the outside but the very second I stepped into the hallway, I knew this was my house. It wasn't perfect, the staircase leading to the upstairs came off the lounge and there was a separate dining room and kitchen. The kitchen was a little dark, but the rest of the house was light and airy. It was quirky and I loved it.

There was the enclosed garden as I had ordered and it came complete with a fish pond and pretty summer house. The master bedroom had its own en-suite and the window looked out over to the church and a thatched cottage over the road. I could so see myself living there but I wanted Lou to give me a completely unbiased opinion, so I remained impartial.

As it turned out the stables and land were not attached to the house. We had to take a 7-minute walk through the village to view them. My heart sank a little as I viewed the tatty stables, but as we started to walk through the fields it began to lift again. The view around us was of open countryside as far as the eye could see. It was magical, like being on top of the world.

The stabling wasn't what my horses were used to, but if it was a question who was going to rough it, be it them or me, it was better that it was them! Besides which, the horses wouldn't judge the place on the star rating of their stables. I knew they were going from 5* to 2*, but they wouldn't know that.

I thanked the estate agent for showing us around and said I would have a think about it and get back to him. How cool was I? Underneath I was jumping for joy. Lou and I decided to go to a pub in the next village for lunch but as soon as we were out of earshot I asked her what she thought. She instantly beamed and said,

"I love it and can really see you living here."

"Me too, me too," I eagerly replied.

We hugged and replayed the whole viewing, excitedly sharing the details of what we liked about Midsummer. Now I just had to get the sellers to reduce the price!

The next week was hell as I put in a much lower offer, only to have it refused. I upped my offer but said this was as high as I could go. I was telling the truth, so in many ways it was up to them. I held my cool. I never chased the estate agent, I always waited for him to get back to me. I never contacted him. As 'luck' would have it the owners of Midsummer had found a house that they really wanted. They tried to agree to my offer but with less land included in the sale. I calmly said no. Unless all the land was included, I was not interested. After what seemed like forever, they agreed to my offer so that they didn't lose the house that they wanted to buy.

I had done it! I had knocked £95000 off the asking price and bartered my way to buying my first home by myself. The Angels had delivered. I didn't want to put every penny of my divorce settlement into my home, and at that point we hadn't agreed the final numbers, so I managed to get a small mortgage because I still had my job as Director and Company Secretary with Cal's business.

I knew I would soon be resigning, but on paper I was employed and hopefully I would be able to get my own business up and running before I ran out of money. As the deadline approached for us to move out of Vale Farm and the sale of Midsummer continued, I started to wish I had given myself more than 8 weeks to buy a house.

The Angels had delivered; they had guided me to my new home one day before my deadline. If I had thought it through, I could have brought the deadline forward. However, by working with my Angels I had saved myself nearly 6 months of worrying about finding a house

Ask the Angels for help.
Take inspired action and
Have Faith in the outcome

Cal started to move his share of the furniture etc. before our final day at Vale Farm. He did make me laugh; instead of paying for a removal company, he moved things one horsebox load at a time. Yes, he used my horsebox to move his stuff! This wasn't any great surprise to me. Cal earned good money, he loved buying expensive things that he could own, but hated paying for services. He would rather walk than pay for a taxi, so it was no surprise he was using the horsebox. Each time he came to load up the van I helped him. On one occasion I laughed as he said,

"I need to take the furniture today. Nikita will divorce me if she sees one more box of bits."

On another occasion he shocked me. We were loading a large piece of furniture and had paused for a rest before we moved it up the ramp into the horsebox. Suddenly Cal looked at me and said,

"You won't be on your own for long you know. You look great for your age."

Now I know it may have been better if he had left the 'for your age bit' off, but this was a man that had never complimented me, a man who looked at how I was dressed and always commented on something he thought I should change. The wrong shoes, the wrong top, the wrong earrings. Whatever I was wearing he always seemed to criticise. So this compliment was a shock and its timing seemed ironic.

"How come it has taken for us to get divorced before you give me a compliment?" I asked.

He looked confused.

"You know I only choose the best, what makes you think that didn't apply to you?"

The tears filled my eyes. It had never dawned on me that this applied to me. I always thought I was not pretty enough, not slim enough, not interesting enough, not brave enough, not talented enough. I didn't think he found me attractive anymore and let's be honest he had just traded me in for someone nearly 20 years younger.

It was a poignant moment, a sad moment that I had never known what he thought about me, and he had never known how much I worried and devalued myself because of it. No wonder our marriage hadn't worked.

The final weeks leading up to July 29th passed quickly. I had allowed the new owners to start doing some work on the land. Unlike me, they believed in separating the horses. They wanted to split one of the fields up into smaller plots so that each horse would have its own section, its own field shelter and water supply. I had no idea how messy or noisy it would be as they started to work, and I felt sad as they trashed my 10-acre field where my horses had happily grazed and played together.

Vale Farm was no longer my sanctuary. I felt like I was being pushed out even before I had left. As Christine had predicted, my time here had been short.

The 29th finally arrived and my faithful friend, Anna, yet again came down from Cheshire to help me move and to help move the horses. The horses were staying an extra day until the 30th, but the removal van arrived early and all my belongings were loaded during the morning. Cal still had a few bits to pick up so was at the house too. Anna left for the new house ahead of the removal van which followed shortly after. The new owners were around but not in any way pushing us to move any faster. They offered to feed my horses that evening so I didn't have to return until the following morning. Cal and I eventually left together. I followed his van down the drive and as he indicated to go right the symbolism of us turning in different directions out of the gate hit me.

Suddenly he stopped the van and got out. I stepped out of my car to see what was the matter.

"Are you okay?" he asked gently.

"Not really," I replied as the tears rolled down my face.

Cal hugged me. Time paused as we took a moment to acknowledge our journey. I had never imagined that Cal would leave me, never imagined that we were not strong enough to see life through together. My foundations were crumbling. My security was dissolving and my heart was breaking for the loss of my relationship with a man I had loved since I was 14.

The moment ended. No words were said.

Cal got in his van and turned right out of the gates. I followed in my car but turned left. The finances were not sorted yet, but life as I had known it with Cal was well and truly over. Now I was on my own for the first time in 32 years.

Chapter 24: Settling into Midsummer

It was a strange feeling arriving at my new home. It was chaos when I arrived. I found Anna and her son busy in the lounge.

Anna was instructing the removal men where to put the furniture and her son, who was only 13 at the time, was already starting to set up my television.

Celia had also arrived to help. Bless her, she'd offered, but as she made it clear she couldn't lift any boxes, I wasn't sure how much she would be able to do. I laugh now as I think of her contribution. She was ferreting away in the kitchen, emptying the contents of every kitchen box onto the work surface. The kitchen looked like a bomb had hit it. I didn't want to offend her but this wasn't the ordered way I would've done it.

If I'd unpacked, each item would have lovingly been given a specific home as it came out of the box. I would have unpacked in an orderly way, this chaos made me feel physically shaky. I said my hello's but then hid in the dining room and made myself busy unpacking cd's, which was not a job I would normally have done at this point. Bless Celia, her heart was in the right place, but she would never know that I didn't get to bed until 4am the following morning, all because I couldn't sleep until I'd organised the chaos that she'd left in my kitchen.

As the furniture started to take its place in my new house, it was uncanny the way it all seemed to have a clear place. Anna even commented on how it looked like it was bought for the house.

In the bedroom there was a 5”6 alcove which my chunky oak bed needed to fit into. Anna and I laughed that it was either going to ‘just fit’ or ‘just *not* fit’ in. If it was the latter, we were likely to be sleeping on a bed in the middle of the room that night. As the ceiling of the bedroom sloped quite dramatically on one side, and the placement of windows and doors meant the bed couldn’t lean up against any other wall, there was only really one place for it to go. Of course we needn’t have worried; the bed, like all the other furniture fit in perfectly.

The removal men soon had all my belongings unpacked from their van and said their goodbyes. Celia left soon afterwards and a sense of peace fell on the house. I thought I would be in tears for most of the day, but I felt at home here very quickly and surprisingly, my 4 dogs and 2 cats settled in quickly too. The dogs all found their own little spot to curl up in and fall asleep, and the cats sat on the windowsill of my bedroom watching their new world go by. The day passed incredibly quickly.

The following day our priority was to collect the horses. Anna and I headed up to the stables and made up fresh beds for them as best we could. I’d managed to get a farmer to pull the double field shelter onto the yard so in effect we now had 5 stables for 3 horses and one pony.

Once the stables were ready we headed back to Vale Farm. It was a strange feeling turning into the driveway now that Vale Farm was no longer my home. As we jumped out of the horsebox and headed to the stables we were greeted by a chorus of whinnies.

The horsebox would have to make two journeys in order to take all the horses to their new home, but as that was only 10 miles away, it shouldn't take too long. What could be a problem was if the horses would load or not. Bless them, they only seemed to get in a horsebox when they moved to a new house, and while that seemed a bit too often for comfort in my case, it was not often enough to feel normal to the horses.

We decided to take the easiest horses first. Marcus was already in his 20's. He was the elder statesman in the pack, and had done lots of competing with his previous owner before he'd become a riding school horse, so loading was not a problem for him. Then there was little Magic, he loved travelling so much he'd often been taken places during our years at Holly Tree, just to give a nervous horse some company. He was so funny, he may have been little but I had to use all my strength to stop him from loading himself onto the box before we were ready for him.

With Marcus and Magic loaded, we set off on our first journey. Anna was much better at driving the horsebox than me, so she took away my anxiety by being the allocated driver that day.

It wasn't long before Marcus and Magic were happily grazing in their new field and we were heading back for Jim and Ella. On the way back my phone began to ring and much to my surprise it was Cal. I hadn't expected to hear from him so soon. Out of habit I answered and greeted him warmly.

"Is everything okay?" I asked. He shakily replied,

"No, I've had an accident." I could hear the shock in his voice. It seemed Cal was at work; he'd been sitting on the back of a quadbike with his Steadicam when the driver, who obviously didn't understand the physics of the situation, set off a little too fast. As Cal was not attached to the quadbike, he hung in mid-air like a cartoon as the bike disappeared from underneath him, and then landed rather heavily on the ground.

I think he was in shock more than anything else, but had some cuts and felt very bruised. I sympathetically listened to what had happened and tried my best to comfort him. As our conversation ended, I put the phone down and Anna asked if Cal was okay. I relayed the story, this time chuckling as I described how he'd fallen off. I felt a little guilty for finding his mishap funny, but I could just see him hanging there in mid-air as I told Anna what happened. Her next comment surprised me.

"So why did he phone you and not Nikita?" she asked.

It suddenly struck me how old habits die hard. Cal shouldn't have rung me, it should've been Nikita but our years together meant that when he was in trouble and on auto pilot, I was the first person he'd called.

My giggles stopped; Anna's comment had been innocent enough but it was like a slap to my face.

Comforting Cal was no longer my job, he was no longer my responsibility. I may have seen it that day, but it took another 10 years before I would really understand that.

We arrived back at Vale Farm to collect Jim and Ella. Now the last time they'd travelled we'd had to blindfold both of them to get them on the horsebox. I know that seems crazy, it certainly felt crazy to me at the time, but we'd tried everything else when Lou suggested it. Amazingly when we took their sight away they walked straight onto the box! We had blindfolds at the ready but we needn't have worried. Somehow the horses new that the way to their new life was on the horsebox. Without pausing for thought, first Jim and then Ella walked calmly on the box.

Quickly we closed the door behind them, shocked at how easy it had been. We made a final check to make sure we hadn't left anything behind and then left Vale Farm for the last time. Watching Jim and Ella trot out into the field to join Magic and Marcus at the other end of their journey made my heart sing. Horses had taught me much over the years, but that day they taught me the value of friendship. Their surroundings maybe different. Their stables may be only 2* but they were with me, they were with each other and they were now happily grazing in a new field. What more could they need in life?

You can never put a price on the value of friendship

As I watched the horses I became very aware that although my marriage was over, I was lucky to have some really good friends, which included the amazing lady that was standing by my side on that day. Anna has always stood by my side and still does today. She is incredibly calm in a crisis and can put her hand to anything. She is warm and funny and loyal and although she may not be quite on board with all my beliefs, she allows me to be 100% myself when I am with her. I love this lady like a sister and will always consider myself very lucky to have her as my friend.

When Anna and her son left, it felt strange to stand alone in my own house. I'd spent a lot of time on my own, but that had been different. Normally I was on my own because Cal was away, now I was on my own because I was no longer in a marriage with him; our relationship was now friendship or so I thought.

The first few weeks at Midsummer I kept myself busy. I started to freshen up the house by painting most of the rooms. The change wasn't dramatic, but it put my stamp on the house. It shocked me at how neat and tidy I was, for years Cal had convinced me that I was messy, but this house was proof that I wasn't. Every item in the house was either something I liked, or something I needed to use. Everything had a purpose and a place and it felt good, really good.

As the house started to take shape and pictures went up on the walls I would wander around and admire my new home, like an artist who stands back and admires his work. As I drilled holes in the walls to hang the pictures and set up my new broadband by myself, I was beginning to feel more confident in myself. It wouldn't all be plain sailing in this house though, there would be times when I sat and cried at having to do everything on my own, at having to shoulder all the responsibility by myself. There would still be dark days ahead, but I didn't know it at that point.

Cal and I were nearly through our battle, but we still needed to agree the finances. I'd told him I wouldn't accept less than a certain figure and of course his first offer through his solicitor was to that specific amount. Cal had Italian blood in him and I knew that he would expect me to barter a little before we reached a final settlement. What I didn't expect was that my own solicitor would say,

"This is the best offer you can get. I think you should accept it." What? Accept his first offer? Even Cal didn't expect me to accept his first offer. Besides, what Cal was offering didn't seem fair to me. Yes, he was earning the money, but we'd spent our whole lives putting his job first to give both of us security. I'd stood by him, taken care of him, encouraged him, dealt with every difficult situation that came our way. He wouldn't be where he was without me and yet all that didn't seem to matter now, none of it seemed to count. I'd even swapped jobs because of him, was even out of a job now because of him.

Yet it was now that he wanted to cut me loose with very little to secure my future, a future that I'd always worked towards with him. I know in relative terms what Cal was offering me was a lot of money to some people but I was in my forties and starting from scratch. I had to protect me. Shocked at my solicitor's reaction I turned to the friend who'd sold me my car, he was an excellent business man so I asked for his advice. He suggested that my solicitor just wanted to get paid and didn't have my best interests at heart. I would soon find out how true that statement was. He also confirmed my feelings that I shouldn't accept the first offer on the table and then gave me two pieces of excellent advice. First he said,

"You know Cal better than anyone, use that to your advantage," and then he added, "look at what he is offering, decide how much you want, and double the difference between the two. Then ask him for an amount that is his offer, plus double the difference. He'll suggest you meet him halfway and then you will get what you want."

I thought about his advice. You are either with Cal or against him and at this moment in time, as I negotiated my divorce settlement, I was well and truly against him. Somehow, I needed to put us on the same side, it was then I had a light bulb moment, I would make my solicitor the bad guy.

Actually, my solicitor did turn out to be a bad guy, but I didn't fully understand that at this point. I knew Cal didn't want to go to court, so if I told him that my solicitor was pushing for us to go to court, but I thought Cal and I could sort the finances between us, that would hopefully put Cal and I back on the same side of the table. All I needed to do then was convince him why he should pay me what I wanted.

My words worked like a charm, Cal's attitude towards me changed as he now saw me as an ally in his battle. Ironically, he was now trying to convince me that we could do all of this without the solicitor.

We arranged to meet in our favourite pub, The Woolpack, the following week. In the week leading up to our meeting I worked hard calculating the figure I was going to ask for using the formula that my businessman friend had suggested. I then wrote down an analysis in detail of why it was fair for Cal to pay me this amount and printed a copy off for Cal to keep.

We were both nervous when we met. Cal was a little guarded and completely glazed over, just as I knew he would, when I showed him all my sums. He then did exactly what I had been told; he suggested we compromised on the middle value between what I was asking for and what he'd offered. Bingo! I got what I believed was fairly mine. I didn't want to fleece him, I wanted to be fair to both of us, but I had to look after me.

I also had to take into account that I was starting again from scratch and I'd already made some mistakes. For example, I'd always been a named driver on Cal's insurance policy. When I had bought my own car and needed to get my own insurance it was like starting from scratch; I'd driven for over 20 years and never had an accident or made a claim. Now I had to start climbing the 'no claims bonus' ladder again, only since I had absent-mindedly acquired two speeding tickets as I went through my divorce, I now had 6 points on my licence. Life really did seem to be against me at that point. Both tickets were for going too fast through a 30mph speed limit. I accept that at 38mph I deserved the points, but 34mph seemed a bit harsh.

At one point, I thought I wasn't even going to be able to get insurance for my car and when I finally did, it was like being a youngster with no track record; it was expensive and a tough lesson to learn. In hindsight, I should have had my own car insurance in my own name since I'd started driving. In the long run it would have been a better option. So, I wanted to be fair, but I wanted to protect me.

Be fair to others but take care of yourself first

Cal was happy with our agreement and suggested a glass of wine to toast our decision. He returned from the bar with a bottle and 2 glasses. We sat happily in the sunny pub garden pleased with ourselves for what we'd achieved.

It had taken an immense amount of effort on my part to share our belongings, split our finances and remain as friends; effort that Cal would never understand. That afternoon we enjoyed a last couple of hours comfortable in each other's company. Little did I know then that it would take another month for the solicitors to cross the t's and dot the i's before I received my part of the settlement, during which time Cal would not put another penny into our joint account.

If I'd not squirrelled some money away, I wouldn't even have had money for food. I did question him and ask him to put some more money in our joint account, but he refused, he wasn't giving me any more than we had already agreed. If I hadn't taken my friends advice and put money away, I would have been in big trouble. Cal had no idea about my hidden money but he didn't care about me anymore, I was not his responsibility, and as he would say in an argument many years later,

"You have done pretty well out of me." I cannot tell you how much that hurt when he said it. At the time, his behaviour shocked me but another battle was brewing.

Once my solicitor realised there was an agreement in place he sent me a nice email to congratulate me and informed me that he would be taking £9000 + VAT out of my settlement fund before he passed it on to me. £9000 + VAT!!!! His estimate had only been £3000 + VAT. He had not even negotiated my settlement, I had done it all directly with Cal. Yes, he had held my hand in the early days but did that really mount up to another £6000? My heart sank. I asked Cal how much his solicitor was charging him and guess what it was £3000.

It struck me at that point that my solicitor had seen a house worth over 2 million pounds, and a Ferrari, and he'd decided my divorce would be a good little earner for him. I was shocked. I had naively thought that someone who upheld the law, and spent time working within the judicial system, would be honest and honourable.

What followed next demonstrated how little I knew and rocked my already shaky faith in human beings.

Chapter 25: The Battle with My Solicitor

I was bullied as a child, but I don't have many memories of that time. I sadly was the tubby kid in my class at school as my Grandma showed her love for me through food, and as she was constantly trying to make up for the loss of my Mum, there were always lots of treats. I wanted to be skinny like the other girls, but that was not my physique despite the ballet and tap lessons. No, I never was the right shape for ballet, although as I write this, I can feel my enthusiasm and fondness for my tap lessons. Maybe I should try tap again? But I digress.

I can remember one occasion as a youngster, when I was pushed so much that I eventually found myself in a fight. The girl who was bullying me had me doubled over and in a head lock. My only course for release was to bite her in the stomach. It was a bad decision, on my part . I bit her, she released me but then showed the bite mark to a teacher. There were no marks on me so I was sent to the Head, and in those days it was acceptable to hit a child if the crime warranted it.

Evidently taking a chunk out of a bully's stomach warranted punishment, and I literally had my knuckles rapped. What happened to me was wrong, but ironically what I remember the most was that I lost my temper and got into trouble.

From that day, I started to put a lid on my anger, and I did it so well for all of my early years, that I convinced myself I was a person who did not get angry. I know now that burying anger is the worst thing we can do. For our own good we need to feel it and release it without aiming it at anyone else.

Do not bury your anger. Feel it and release it without aiming it at anyone else

The situation with my solicitor was the first time in my life that I felt I was being bullied because I was female. After his email informing me he would take his payment before I'd even been given an invoice, I decided to get some advice from the Law Society. I was advised to email him and tell him that if he took any more than the original quote of £3000 + VAT he was doing so without my permission. Oh my goodness did that rattle my solicitor.

I received the first of many threatening letters, all headed with the words, 'Without Prejudice' , which as far as I was concerned meant I couldn't show them to a Judge. I'd just come out of a 3-year battle with Cal. I was tired, I was battle weary and now I would have another 12 months fighting my divorce solicitor who intended to fight dirty. There was nothing honourable or honest about the way he treated me. There was no respect or kindness. He was going in for the kill. He was incensed that a woman would challenge him. I should have known better, he was Rebecca's brother after all. Why on earth had I thought he would be so much more different to her?

My faith in human beings was starting to collapse. I wanted to believe that people were honest and caring, but that had not been my experience during those years. I cried on the phone to my sister, I didn't think I had any tears left, but there they were. Why me? Why now? Well, the why me soon became apparent. The strange thing was the more this man threatened me, the more I wanted to dig my heels in and not let him get away with it. I wasn't simply defending me, I was standing up for every woman who'd ever been bullied by this man.

At the time my sister was a Cost Draftsman. No, I didn't know what one of those was either until she started doing the job. In a nutshell, she worked for solicitors negotiating the legal costs of their cases. All that mattered for me was that she was familiar with the way solicitors cost their bills, with their legal jargon and the court system.

Luckily for me, my sister could and would stand by my side to fight against my divorce solicitor. Well it took 5 months and a Judge's Court Order before I was even given an itemised bill, and all the time I was being threatened with the escalating costs that this would cost me if I continued on my course of action. When I viewed the itemised bill, it became apparent that my solicitor had made a lot of it up! Seriously, I know that sounds horrific but that is exactly what he did. For example, he documented a one hour meeting with me on February 30th! He also documented meetings and phone calls with me when 'he' was away on holiday. He even documented a meeting at his office on the day when I had gone to court to confirm Cal did not live with me. He also charged his time in blocks of 5 minutes which was very old school, most modern solicitors charge in 6 minute blocks. However, Jules reckoned this might work in my favour so we weren't going to question it.

Fortunately for me, and unfortunately for him, I had kept every email he'd ever sent me and Cal's solicitor sent all the emails between my solicitor and him to Cal, so that Cal could forward them on to me. Staying friends with Cal had worked in my favour at this point. We had my divorce solicitor covered email wise. The only lies I couldn't prove were dates and times of phone calls as I hadn't felt a need to document them. The itemised bill however, had created more questions than it answered; questions we would have asked in court if only he had shown up.

For our next court appearance, he'd hired a solicitor to represent him; a solicitor who pushed for an out of court settlement before we went in front of the Judge, but who once he was standing in the court room looked very exposed.

On the third court appearance, my divorce solicitor was supposed to show documentary evidence of his claim that I owed him so much money. The Judge started to get very angry when the hired solicitor assured him that all the original documents had been sent to the court and, for some reason, the court could not find them! Did my solicitor really expect a Judge to believe this story?

The Judge sent the solicitor to talk to his client, my divorce solicitor. He then turned to my sister and I and said,

"Ladies, you'd better vacate the courtroom before we are accused of having improper communications." Julie smiled as we left.

Outside the courtroom she told me she thought the Judge was on my side. When the documented evidence could not be found, the Judge had to order a continuance but, he suggested that if the evidence could not be found then my solicitor needed to turn up in person.

I am sharing all this with you relatively quickly, but the wheels of justice turn very slowly so I had to wait for weeks, sometimes months, in between court dates. All the time this hung over my head, that little black cloud was back, and my divorce solicitor continued to send threatening, without prejudice, letters to me.

According to him I was going to have to pay the original amount plus all his court costs and a penalty payment. As 2008 was ending, I was getting very weary. My sister and I knew we were in a strong position but there was a growing fear that my divorce solicitor was so arrogant that he would stand up in court and commit perjury and if he did that, where would that leave me?

Part of me wanted to fight, to have my day in court and accuse him of lying, but a bigger part just wanted this all to be over. Jules suggested putting one last offer on the table. She said we would have to increase the original estimate by a small amount but it could be as little as £500. Even this seemed too much for this obnoxious man, but wanting to start 2009 without this hanging over my head, I told her to go ahead.

Julie waited until 2 days before the next court date and then sent him our offer. He jumped at the chance! Of course, he made out he was doing it out of the goodness of his heart, because of my past friendship with his sister, but we all knew the truth. I paid him a total of £3500 + VAT and he paid his own costs. Although he would've believed I paid my own costs, in truth my sister stood by my side for free, so his payment was my only expense.

When the case was finally closed, I was emotionally and physically wiped out, but happy that I didn't let the bully win. I wanted to send him a Christmas card that wished him a Happy Christmas and a Prosperous New Year and I wanted to sign it from Karen Lynne and her sister Mrs J Belt. I wanted him to know that two women, neither of which was a trained solicitor, had stood up to him and won, but Jules didn't think that was such a good idea. She didn't want the solicitors that she worked with to think she could cause them trouble. It was probably the right choice. The important thing was that we had stood up to him.

You need to be strong and stand in your power, when faced with a bully

So, 2008 had been a challenging year with my divorce solicitor, but it had also been a year when I'd learned to talk to Angels. Learning to be an Angel Therapy Practitioner after that was as big a surprise to me as it may be to you as you read my story. Somehow, I had transitioned from a science based Maths teacher, who loved a process and a right or wrong solution, to a person who was connecting with Angelic beings. I was opening up to possibilities I could not prove. I could only feel and know if what was being told to me resonated with me or not. This has often happened in my life, experiences were sent my way when I was ready for them. Let me tell you how I became interested in Angels...

When I was first in a relationship with Daniel, my farrier, I used to feel distraught every time he drove off the premises. It was a strange reaction as I didn't know him well enough to be feeling so upset. I mentioned this to a friend who suggested that Daniel and I had had a past life together.

Now to be honest, I'd been on a spiritual path for some time by 2008, but I'd never really considered reincarnation or past lives. My friend suggested I should have a Past Life Regression session to see if she was right. If I'd known Daniel in a past life it may explain some of my present feelings, so I found a lady locally who did these sessions and I booked one.

I was very nervous as I drove to her house but I needn't have been, it was a bit like a hypnosis session. I was conscious of her questions and my answers throughout the session, although sometimes words came out of my mouth without me seeming to have any control over them. It turned out Daniel and I had had a few previous lives together.

In the most recent one we were married, but he went off to war and never came back. As I experienced his leaving in this hypnotic state all the same feelings surfaced that I felt when he drove away from Vale Farm. Of course, I was distraught, I had loved him very much in this past life and he had never come back from the war. The feelings and the details of my life with him at that time felt very real to me, while I was in this hypnotised state, and I started to welcome the possibility of reincarnation. It certainly made sense of the feelings I was having for Daniel.

During the session, the therapist had also taken me back to when I was in my Mum's womb at the beginning of this lifetime. I could feel the dampness and the warmth of my surroundings and feel my Mum's love for me, I could also hear her playing a piano and singing. It was a magical experience to feel just how much I was loved by her even before I was born. The therapist asked me what my purpose was for this life. Strangely I heard myself replying with these words: -

"I am here To Light The Way, I don't know what that means but I know I am here To Light The Way."

The therapist told me not to worry as she knew what the phrase meant and she would explain it to me after the session. Later, as I came out of the session, I was curious to know what my purpose was.

"What did I mean by light the way?" I asked. In reply the therapist asked if I had heard of a lady called Doreen Virtue, but I didn't know the name. She went on to say that this lady was known for her work with Angels and that I needed to buy a book of hers called 'The Lightworker's Way'. I politely agreed that I would.

Actually, I was curious about it, so I probably would have bought the book anyway, but then the therapist said,

"There is a lady here who says I need to get you to promise to buy the book."

I laughed as I heard her words. There was only one person who would know that if I' promised' then I would be true to my word, and that person was my Grandma; my Mum's mum. I couldn't see her but she was with us. Just as I was thinking about my Grandma, the therapist started to describe her. I stopped her in her tracks and told her I knew exactly who the lady was.

Still smiling I promised to buy the book and when I left the therapist's house, I headed straight to Waterstone's bookshop with a scrap of paper in my hand to remind me of Doreen Virtues name and the title of her book. It wasn't difficult to find. I picked up the book in the Mind, Body and Spirit section and opened it to look inside. On one of the first pages was a list of experiences that a Lightworker may have as he/she goes through life. It listed many things such as;

- you feel called to heal others.
- you want to resolve the worlds social and environmental problems.
- you have endured harsh life experiences that have eroded the knowledge of your divine perfection.
- you feel compelled to write, teach or council about your healing experiences and know that

you are here for a higher purpose, even if you are unsure what it is or how to fulfil it.

- you have had mystical experiences.

The book went on to say that Lightworkers are waking up to an inner calling that can't be ignored, a calling that says it is time to go to work.

Now I know this all sounds very grand and maybe a bit 'woo-woo' to you, but I'd felt for some time that I was here, in this body, at this time, to do something to help heal the world.

For many years I'd suffered and seen others suffer too; I just wanted to make the world a better place, a place where human beings loved each other, a place where we would never dream of hurting or killing each other. I was often overcome with immense sadness about what we were and are doing to each other, to the earth we live on and to the children and animals. I ached to be a part of something that would turn our hate and mistrust into love and respect. It was a feeling that had been growing inside of me, a feeling I had not shared with anyone for fear of being ridiculed. It was a feeling of *Being Called.* I am sure this all sounds a bit grandiose and far-fetched, but in the first pages of this book Doreen Virtue acknowledged the feelings I was having; she ignited my curiosity. I bought the book, went home and started to read.

The Lightworker's Way was a turning point for me. I resonated with much that Doreen said about life and she introduced me to my Guardian Angels and the Archangels.

At that point in my life I hadn't thought much about Angels. My friend Alex always talked to her Angels but I thought that was her equivalent of me talking to my Mum. It turned out I was wrong, and now I was ready to take the next step in my spiritual journey by learning about these wonderful beings of pure love.

I learned that with the exception of Archangel Metatron, none of the Angels have ever lived in a human body. They vibrate at a much higher level than we do, a higher level than even our Spirit Guides, a level of pure love. Now, the exciting thing for me was that I discovered I had two Guardian Angels who had been with me since I was born and who were just waiting for me to ask for their help. I do need to say at this point that these are my beliefs. I am not saying this is *the* truth, I am simply sharing *my* truth with you. If my thoughts resonate with you that is great, please pick them up and take them with you. If my thoughts about Angels do not fit into *your* truth, that is good as well. I simply ask that you read on with an open heart and an open mind.

So, my new understanding was that on earth we've been given free will which means our Angels cannot step in and just make life better for us. No, by all accounts they must wait until we ask for help and asking for help couldn't be easier. We simply talk to our Angels as if we were talking to a friend, always talking with love and respect and honesty and gratitude. Our Angels can see the truth of who we are, so there is no point trying to fool them.

I loved the idea of talking to my Angels and started to use some of the techniques in the book to hear what they were saying to me. I began playing with my Angels, so when I needed a car parking space I would order it before I'd even started my journey.

I know when I bought my Freelander I was a bit worried that I would have difficulty parking it. In fact since the day I started asking my Angels for help, I've always had a parking space that was easy for me to drive in and out of. I will explain more later about these techniques for connecting with and hearing your Angels, but for now all you need to understand was that I was learning to connect to my Angels and to ask them for help. I suddenly had a great sense of never being alone and I loved this new feeling.

As my divorce from Cal had come to an end, my next thought was that I had promised myself a holiday. I needed a break, time to relax and time to recharge my batteries. Early in 2008 I had started to look on the internet for possible destinations. I didn't want to spend all my time on my own, so I looked for a course that I could attend where I would meet like-minded people; somewhere that I would have company during the day, but could have the choice if I wanted to spend some time on my own in the evenings.

An advert for a Doreen Virtue course popped up on my laptop called The Angel Therapy Practitioners Course.

To be honest I didn't pay much attention to the title. What I did notice was that this was a course run by Doreen Virtue and it was being held in Hawaii. How lovely would that be?

I had no idea at the time just how far away America was to Hawaii, and even less idea of the epic journey I was considering, but it sounded lovely so I looked at the details.

The course was in March and I was surprised to find there were still 3 places out of 250 still available. I immediately phoned my house sitter to see if she was available. Because of the number of animals that shared their lives with me, it was easier when I went away to have someone come and live in my house and take care of them all. As luck would have it my house sitter had just had a cancellation and was free the exact week I wanted to go away. I don't believe in luck anymore; I believe that my Angels were helping me to go on this course, they were clearing any obstacles out of my way and making it easy for me to go.

By the time I'd sorted the house sitter, I booked the last place on Doreen's course. I had no idea what I'd signed up for, all I knew was that I was going to Hawaii to learn about Angels with Doreen Virtue.

The journey to Hawaii was a bit of a challenge. Thank goodness the Americans speak the same language as us, otherwise I would really have been in a panic. I enjoyed my Business Class seat from Heathrow to LAX airport in California. There had been a slight delay as we boarded the flight, but that meant I had got to talk to the man in the next 'pod' to me, but he was very lovely and our conversations passed the time away before we were able to take off and that managed to stop me from worrying about why the plane hasn't been ready to fly.

Eventually we were off and my adventure had begun. The air stewardess took great care of me during the flight and for the first time in a very long time I started to relax. My anxiety didn't return until I saw the length of the queue for us non-Americans to get into the country. The time until my connecting flight was only 2 hours and it was taking forever to get through Customs. As it turned out my connecting United Airways flight to Hawaii was delayed. There was no need for me to worry, but I couldn't help it. When I say 'I couldn't help it' I do know that this phrase is not true. I did have a choice and because of my fear of making this journey by myself I chose to worry, a lot.

Eventually I was through and I rushed to get myself to the departure gate only to find a melee of people hanging around the exit; we were delayed for hours! All the chairs were taken and I ended up sitting on the floor. I'd now been awake for over 20 hours and as I sat there propped up against a wall, I could feel my tired eyes closing. I turned to the lady next to me and asked her if she was on my flight, she said that she was, so I asked her if she would wake me up if I nodded off by the time we started boarding. She smiled and agreed, although because she loved my English accent, she then went on to talk to me constantly right up until it was time to board.

Four hours later we were on our way. The plane felt so much smaller after my first trans-Atlantic flight, but my eyes closed as I sat in the seat and I was away with the fairies, or maybe the Angels, before we taxied down the runway. Five hours later I awoke as we landed at Kona International Airport. It was one o'clock in the morning local time.

Even at that time in the morning, the heat and gentle breeze hit us as we exited the plane. There was no fancy terminal and although there were some buildings around us, we didn't seem to need to go through any of them. We were simply guided to a place where we would be reconnected with our bags. There weren't any officials there to greet us and with bags in hand, I wondered where I needed to go to get a taxi. I asked the only person I could find who was wearing a uniform and he pointed to the only road and told me to start queueing at the palm tree. I looked up to see a whole row of palm trees along the side of the road, when I asked which one he meant his reply made me laugh.

"Any palm tree," he said, "you choose. We sent the taxi drivers home when we knew you were going to be late. I have phoned them all to ask them to come in. They will arrive very soon. Please now queue at a palm tree and wait." He was so charming, so smiley, that I smiled back and went and stood next to my chosen palm tree.

As it often happens, I was soon joined by others who asked me if I was waiting for a taxi. The queue got longer and it turned out that many of us were all going to the same hotel because we were attending Doreen Virtues course and, despite the time of day, we chatted our way excitedly to the Sheraton Hotel which would be our home for the next week.

Chapter 26: Angels in Hawaii

By the time I entered the Conference Hall of the Sheraton Hotel some 19 hours later, I'd already found two new friends, Jessica and Faith. These two ladies would accompany me through the week and share my free time in the evenings.

On that first morning as we left the sunshine outside and entered the hall, we were greeted with welcoming smiles by Doreen Virtue's staff, showered in fairy dust, and asked to choose an angel card from the huge bowl of cards at the entrance. Mine said 'Time to Heal'. It was spot on. I was still in the middle of my battle with my divorce solicitor but I needed time to heal from my 30-year relationship with Cal. We took our seats nervously. There was an anxiety in the air that would disappear after that first day. Soon we were up and dancing to live music, a song that would be played before each session, morning and afternoon. On that first morning, we were a little shy but the die-hard Doreen Virtue fans got up, joined hands and danced around the room. By the end of the week we were feeling energised by the track and with carefree abandon we joined hands and danced too. There were people in the room from every continent in the world. It was an angelic version of the United Nations and each day we would feel more and more like a large happy family.

Doreen was a delight. She entertained and she guided us. She didn't put herself on a pedestal but stood shoulder to shoulder with us. As the morning progressed I began to realise I was not just here to learn about Angels, I was here to learn to talk to Angels and learn how to give Angel Readings to other people. When I first realised what being an Angel Therapy Practitioner entailed, I was very nervous I can tell you, but as the week went by I began to love working with the Angels.

On that first morning Doreen gave us a gift of a pack of Angel Cards, with the intention that we would be using these cards during the week. There were 4 different packs being handed out and as I loved horses I really wanted the Unicorn pack. As luck would have it the Unicorn Cards were being handed down one end of my row and the Fairy cards were being handed along from the other end. I was sitting pretty much in the middle of the row and praying to get the Unicorn cards, but instead received Fairy cards! Just as I was wondering if the lady next to me would swap, I heard Doreen say that whichever pack we had received was the right pack so 'no swapping'. Damn I thought; Fairy cards it is then. Now as you know, I started my work life as a Maths Teacher. So, if the pack of cards contained only 4 cards, then the number of possible combinations of 3 cards that you could pull would be calculated as follows.

You would have 4 choices for your first card, 3 choices for your second card, two choices for your third card. Meaning the number of possible permutations is 4x3x2=24 and this is just for choosing 3 cards out of 4.

The packs of cards that Doreen had gifted to us contained not 4 but 44 cards. This means when you are pulling 3 cards to give a reading, for your first card you have a choice of 44 cards, for your second card you have a choice of 43 cards and for your third card you have a choice of 42 cards. This means the total number of permutations are 44x43x42 which comes to a huge 79,464.

I loved tuning into the Angels, but I was a little sceptical to say the least, that pulling 3 cards to answer a question could provide an accurate result. What if you shuffled one more time or one less time? Wouldn't that change the reading? During that week, I developed my own way for choosing cards. I would ask the Angels to make the appropriate card jump out of my pack and once I did that, it was like my pack of cards came alive. I have even asked the same question and pulled the same card from the pack 3 consecutive times.

You may be as sceptical as I was when I started, but I have truly come to trust the cards over the last 10 years and now have an assortment of different packs.

Doreen also taught us there was a lot more involved than simply choosing the card and reading from the book what that card represented. She taught us to lay a hand on the card and share anything we saw, heard or felt with the person we were reading for. I can remember on one of those early practice sessions we were focusing on health. When I touched the card I had pulled for my partner, a Japanese lady who I had not met before, I saw a potato in my mind's eye! Panicking a little, I thanked the Angels for the potato but said I needed more information to share with my partner. They simply showed me a whole field of potatoes!! I laughed nervously as I related what I could see to this Japanese lady. She smiled as I mentioned potatoes. She then explained to me that she had an allergy to something in potatoes and shouldn't really be eating them. However, the chips were so lovely in the hotel she had ordered them for every evening meal since she'd arrived. She knew instantaneously that she was being reminded that this was not good for her. This was a lesson in trusting what I was getting. The potato meant nothing to me but it meant a lot to her!

As the week continued I got more and more excited by these Angel readings, and I started to trust what was coming into my head. I was also fascinated by the hierarchy of Angels from the Seraphim's who rank highest through the Cherubims and Thrones, the Dominions, Virtues and Powers, and finally the Principalities, Archangels and Angels. The latter of which work most closely with us; this was a whole new and exciting world to me. As Doreen Virtue taught us to connect with the different Angels and Archangels I could feel the change of the energy in the room. I find it difficult to describe the blissful feelings of Pure Love that you can feel when you are joined by the Angels, but it is one of pure joy, fulfilment and acceptance. All is well in my world when I am surrounded by Angels, and so I have chosen to work with them ever since this course. I cannot tell you how grateful I am to the person who guided me to have that Past Life Regression, it opened a world that I never knew existed.

Now for anyone who is interested in communicating with their Angels, I would just like to add one or two pieces of advice here. Words are a very ineffectual way for your Angels to speak to you. When you have asked for help, your Angels will often try to guide you in easier ways. They may make you aware of a song, this often happens to me as I love music. If the same song keeps coming into your head look up the lyrics. What relevance could they have for you? What are your Angels trying to say to you? They may guide you to read a certain book which is what I believed happened the day I was guided to read the Lightworker's Way.

This would happen to me with another book, Conversations with God, the following year. At this point however, I was avoiding anything to do with God as the God I'd found in religion, was not my idea of God. Again, I'm not being disrespectful here. I am simply stating my truth as I saw it at that time. I fully accept that many people relate to the God they find in the Christian faith, and if that God resonates with you then I honour your choice. However, for me at that time, I would refer to the Divine Energy Force that I believe in as the Great Spirit or Universal Life Force, but I would like to point out that the name I use has evolved as my understanding has evolved.

Getting back to how you communication with your Angels. Often the Angels will leave a calling card to let you know they are with you. One such calling card is a white feather which you will find in an unexpected place. I have a funny story about a white feather. A few years after I'd started working with the Angels I still hadn't received a white feather of my own.

One day I was talking about Angels to a young boy of 11 who I was working with. This young lad was being bullied and I wanted to introduce him to one of his Guardian Angels so that he didn't feel so alone when he was at school. We did a meditation so that he could 'meet up' with his angel and then we asked the angel to show him a sign. Within 2 hours of doing the meditation this young boy was due to attend his second sea cadets meeting.

This particular evening they were going canoeing on the river. My young client was excited but nervous too. As he queued to get into the boat, he said a prayer to his Guardian Angel and asked her to keep him safe. When he opened his eyes and looked down, lying across his shoe was a white feather. He was so happy. He kept the feather with him and when he got home he asked his Mum to take a photo of him and his feather.

That same evening I received a lovely photo of him holding his feather and absolutely beaming from ear to ear with delight. It made my heart sing. This young boy would never feel alone again and next time he was near his bully, he could ask his Guardian Angels to keep him safe. I do want to point out that I did give him some other tools to combat the bullying that he was experiencing, but they were all based on changing his energy when he was around the bully.

I could never have guessed at that point that he would use these tools so well, that by the end of the school year he'd tell me that he would quite miss the boy who had previously bullied him when they both moved on to new schools. I felt so proud of him.

Now to finish this story about signs. The next morning I was feeling a little hard done by. I had been working with the Angels for some time when this happened and I had never received a feather.

My young client had received his first feather within 3 hours of me introducing him to his Guardian Angel. That morning as I talked to my Angels my inner child voiced her sense of unfairness quite strongly, or should I say *very* strongly if I am being honest. I then put leads on my dogs and we started the morning walk to my stables to feed the horses. It was a beautiful day, the sun was shining, the sky was blue, and the birds were singing; it was a beautiful British Summer's Day.

As we walked to the yard I followed the road around a ninety-degree bend and in front of my eyes I saw the most incredible sight. Above my yard was a huge cloud feather. There wasn't a cloud in the sky other than my feather and it hung there magically above my yard. I know you will think I was imagining this, but I promise you I wasn't. I took a photograph because it was such a special moment and everyone who I have shown the photograph to sees the same feather.

The sight of this massive feather in the sky took my breath away. I thanked my Angels and felt so excited about the possibilities of a world where working with my Angels could create such an amazing sight. It is a day I will never forget.

So, to recap; the Angels can communicate with you through the words of a song, they can show you signs. and they can guide you to a book or an article, as happened to me when I saw Nikita with Cal on national television, they can guide you to put the television or radio on just at the right time to be exposed to a relevant piece of information.

Your Angels can also communicate with you through number sequences. The most popular number to see is 444, which is a sign from your Angels to tell you they are with you and the number 222 is telling you not to worry as everything will work out.

I bought a car once because it had 222 in the registration number. It was a beautiful red BMW Z4 sports car. I'd never had a car like it and I didn't need it, but when I saw it I so wanted it. The reg was M222LET. How could I not buy it? Every day that I saw that little car it reminded me not to worry. There are plenty of these number sequences and if you are interested to find out more, you can look up a small book by Doreen Virtue called Angel Numbers. As a Mathematician I love numbers, so this is a way my Angels often speak to me.

I mustn't end my thoughts on Angels without saying I also believe they can talk to you with words, or in pictures or feelings, depending on which of those senses is most dominant for you. They can even talk to you through automatic writing, which I will come back to later.

For me, my main sense is to feel, but after much practice I do now hear angel words in my head, or sometimes they will show me pictures.

I want you to know, I am not doing anything that you cannot do. Whether you connect to the Angels, to your Higher Self, to God or to a Divine Life Force, in my opinion you are connecting to the Universal Life Force that we are all a part of, and each one of us has the ability to make that connection. Sadly, we often have to relearn this skill, but I want you to know I believe it is a gift that we all have. In fact, when we truly remember who we are it is not only a gift, it is a necessary tool for living a fulfilling life in this physical world.

I felt very sad to leave the safety and joy of Hawaii. While I was cocooned with like-minded people, life was exciting and joyful. I loved my week in Hawaii with Doreen Virtue, her wonderful team and the 250 people who made up the wonderful class of 2008. I believed our daily affirmation that I was a powerful Lightworker and I felt that I belonged, which is not how I felt in my normal life.

Although I arrived home to the on-going saga with my divorce solicitor, I was excited about introducing people to their Angels and sharing the Angels messages with them. I wanted everyone to know about their Angels, to feel the absolute love that I felt when I was connected to them, and to know they are never alone. For me it was an immensely comforting thought to know that my Angels were and are with me every minute of the day. I was filled with enthusiasm and hope.

It didn't dawn on me that not everyone would share my joy.

I wanted to start working and be listed as an Angel Therapy Practitioner (ATP) on Doreen's website, but there were a few more hoops to jump through. First I had to do angel readings for twenty people. I was quite nervous away from the support of Doreen's team, but I was determined to be listed, so I offered to do these readings for free.

Some of the readings were for other trainee ATP's, and these readings were easier to do, as the people I was reading for understood beginners nerves. In return they would do a reading for me which was very lovely and encouraging. I also did readings for some of my friends. I found these much harder because I already knew the people I was reading for. Many a time I would think 'Am I just making this up?' but my friends would react in a positive way and as my confidence grew, so did the depth of my readings. I managed to compete the twenty required readings and the compulsory written questions within 3 months and my name was added to Doreen's website list. I was so happy and so excited but then nothing happened. No enquiries. No calls. No readings. This wasn't quite how I'd imagined this to play out! I was learning then that sometimes life doesn't give you what you ask for, it gives you what you need to grow into what you ask for. I would love to claim ownership of that statement, but it isn't mine. I heard Dr Michael Bernard Beckwith say these words, although he did use the word God instead of the word Life. I think it works either way.

Life doesn't give you what you want,
it gives you what you need
to grow into what you want

Even then, life was trying to show me that I couldn't live my life by hiding behind my front door. I was being guided to get out into the world, but I didn't understand that then.

Instead, I stayed behind my front door and bought a small internet business making natural skin creams off an old school-friend. Initially I loved this business, it was very cathartic making natural skin creams and my house constantly had a wonderful aroma of essential oils wafting through it. I got a real sense of achievement creating the bottles and containers of gorgeous lotions and potions and the orders streamed through the internet. I would make up the products if I didn't have them in stock, and then I took them to the Post Office to despatch to the customer. The business started to put some order back into my life. I took care of the horses in the morning and worked on Nature's Recipe in the afternoon. I wasn't earning a great deal of money, I didn't have much of a social life, but I was starting to pick myself up after my divorce, or so I thought.

I had hoped that my life would take off once I was free from Cal. I had always thought that he'd held me back, always thought his demands on my time and his disapproval of my spiritual interests had stopped me from being who I wanted to be, and doing what I wanted to do.

I must be honest, it came as a bit of a shock to no longer be married to Cal and still not feel that my life was moving forwards. It would take another 8 years to understand why I felt this way, but at that point it was phenomenally disappointing to admit that the only person I could now blame for my life not turning out the way I wanted it to be... was me!!

Be the predominant creative force in your own life

Robert Fritz

Chapter 27: Gabriella

After a year of making creams, I was starting to get a little stir crazy with only my own company and decided that I was not here on earth to hide behind closed doors and avoid people.

I wanted to be a part of the world, I wanted to contribute, I wanted to help people. I wasn't sure how exactly, but I knew that I didn't want to go back to teaching maths.

No sooner had I made this decision than my Angels pointed me towards a new door. I kept seeing an advert for a free foundation training weekend for people who wanted to be life coaches. I hadn't considered being a Life Coach before, but I knew that people always turned to me for support and advice. I often found myself helping complete strangers when they sat next to me and started to tell me their life stories.

I loved the idea of empowering others and helping them to find their way. The irony of seeing that I could do this for others but was struggling to do it for myself is not lost on me, but I didn't see that at the time. So, I signed up for a training weekend with The Coaching Academy.

I was very nervous to say the least, but I was proud of myself for overcoming my own nerves and attending. My confidence was so low after my divorce that even this was an achievement. Usually when I go on courses now, I find it very easy to make new friends, but as I look back at that course I am struck by how isolated I felt as I attended. I was surrounded by 200 other potential coaches and I did talk to people during the breaks and lunchtime, but there wasn't anyone who I clicked with.

The Coaching Academy did its job well and by the end of the second day, I was fired up with the idea of being a Life Coach. This was my way forward and if I signed up there and then I would get a huge discount. Of course I would, I had to spend thousands to get such a great deal but I was hooked and reeled in. I signed up there and then to be a Coaching Academy Protégé. The amount of money it cost scared me, but I felt sure I would earn it all back and more, once I had qualified and this way, I would have the Coaching Academy support for life.

Within a week of signing up I'd received two huge packages with the course paperwork and dvd's for the Personal & Business Coaching Courses. I wasn't really interested in business coaching, but I thought I might learn something about running a business if I completed it. However, it was my intention to complete the personal training course first.

I started the course feeling a little overwhelmed but none the less enthusiastic. As a protégé, I qualified for a monthly coaching session from one of the Academy's qualified instructors. I chose a lovely lady who'd given one of the lectures over the foundation course weekend and who I'd discovered afterwards, when I chatted with her, talked to her own Angels. I thought we would be a great match. I started the course well, I wasn't always sure that I was completing the written work correctly, but

I was getting through the modules and it felt like I was doing well with my practice clients.

I eventually did my first coaching session with a trainer listening in. I was very nervous but I needn't have been. My trainer was very surprised that I hadn't done any form of coaching in the past, and he had only praise for the way I'd facilitated the coaching session. As I progressed, I got better and better at the coaching, but found the analysis and the written work more and more difficult. When I thought about what questions I was using, or whether I was following the GROW model I struggled.

However, when I worked intuitively and trusted that the Angels would guide me through each session, together we were wonderful and I loved it.

Asking the right questions every day is a great way to create the life you want to live

My own personal sessions with my chosen trainer got progressively worse. She was a lovely warm person and yet I found her processes becoming increasingly colder. It felt like she simply fired a load of questions at me at each session and I was beginning to dread them and struggled to think what we should focus on. This all started to worry me.

At the time, I was working with a Law of Attraction Coach. She asked me, another question I know, how would I feel if I knew I could do the work without the qualification? I cannot describe the absolute relief that surged through my body at that moment. I decided to tune in and ask my Angels but they also asked me a question. I'm not saying that asking questions is wrong. In fact, asking the right questions every day is a great way to create the life you want to live. I guess I was always destined to be more teacher than coach.

So as I said, the Angels asked me a question too and their question was,

"Who came up with the first coaching qualification?" The minute they asked me, I realised every qualification is formed in the mind of a human being at some point. It's a human being who says 'this is the way to do it'.

So, with that in mind, I could work in my own way, start using my own methods, draw upon my own knowledge and experiences. I didn't need the Coaching Academy qualification to start helping people, I needed to believe in me. Now although this wisdom hit me between the eyes, it did take a few more weeks of thought before I chose to walk away from the Academy and all the money I'd invested.

I would like to add that, I have since met many good coaches who qualified with the Coaching Academy, so I don't want you to think I would not recommend them. It's simply that for me, they were not the right choice. Life, God, my Angels were all trying to teach me to have faith in me.

Believe in yourself

Setting out on my own was like trying to find my way blindfolded up a dark alley, that had passages leading off on both sides and people shouting words of guidance at me from every junction. I made so many mistakes over the next few years. I trusted people I shouldn't have and I made the biggest mistake of all, I tried to do it all by myself.

I now know that no one succeeds by themselves, they always have a team of people working with them or they work in strategic alliances with others. The original idea may have been mine, but my success depended on working with others, in helping others to shine so that they in turn could help me to shine. The following years were a steep learning curve and many a time I would question whether I was good enough to do what I wanted to do. I did, however, start to attract some amazing clients.

One of the families I worked with early on had a profound effect on my self-belief and the way I worked. This family lived in the same village as me and therefore I had met them initially in a social environment. They had three daughters, Gabriella, Leah and Matilda (Tilly) and they were having serious problems with their oldest girl, Gabriella. You couldn't miss Gabriella, she was incredibly tall for her age and was built in an Amazonian way. If she could ever train her body, she would be a force to reckon with. Even without training she was incredibly strong, especially when she lost her temper, which she seemed to do on a regular basis. She would get angry at her sisters or her parents; she would hit them, throw anything to hand at them and on many occasions locked them out of the house. Even when she wasn't angry she was loud.

People saw her as a badly behaved and unruly teenager. I saw her as an unhappy child who was having a problem finding a way to fit into life. However, deciding whether it was a genetic issue, i.e. the way her brain processed the world, or whether it was bad teenage behaviour was challenging me.

As I said, I first met Gabriella socially. I was able to make a connection with her because she adored horses and I still had my 3 horses and pony at that point. I saw that the horses were going to be the way to open the conversation. Although she became a client, I first started working with her on a very ad-hoc basis as I was just helping a family out in my village. I spoke to her Mum, Pauline, and Dad, Lesley, initially to find out what they were worried about. For them it was a discipline issue, they were worried that they had lost control of their daughter. As I spent more time with Gabriella, I realised that she had some fundamental problems.

Firstly, she was unable to empathise with anyone else. She was obsessed with things not being fair, except when the unfairness gave her the advantage. She wasn't able to see things from someone else's point of view. She would do things to her sisters which, if they did the same back to her she would instantaneously lose her temper over it.

I know some of you maybe thinking this is normal sibling rivalry, but it was much more than that. She struggled to interpret facial expressions and would constantly misinterpret them becoming angry and frustrated when she did. She hated change and struggled to control her temper.

If we measure anger on a scale of 1 to 10, for you and me as we get angry we progress up the scale. Granted sometimes more quickly than others, but a progression never the less. With Gabriella, she went from1 to 4 and then to 10 and she was aware that she had no control when she was at 10.

Gabriella had struggled to make and keep friends, so she was quite lonely. She also struggled to concentrate for any given time, so school was a nightmare for her too. Life was a nightmare for her; the unhappier she became, the more extreme her behaviour which inevitably pushed people away from her, but she didn't understand why and then she became unhappier. It was a vicious circle.

On top of all that, her Mum was at the end of her tether with the situation. Gabriella always said her Mum loved the other two sisters more. At first I disregarded this comment, but as time went on I began to think she was right.

Gabriella's Mum, Pauline, had wanted a child so much but when her first daughter arrived she was a challenge from day one. Pauline wanted to hold and cuddle her baby, but she had a baby that screamed when she was held. All her dreams of doing things with her daughter were dashed within the first few weeks of Gabriella's life. Pauline had never faced her grief for the loss of her dreams. Then to make matters worse, when Leah came along, she did live up to Pauline's dreams. The situation was difficult for all of them; it was nobody's fault but there was a lot of healing that needed to be done here.

Before I continue, I would like to point out that at this stage I didn't know a lot about children with Asperger's, but when I listed my concerns about Gabriella's challenges to her parents, who were both psychologists, they knew. They didn't want Gabriella to be tested, they didn't want to put a label on her but they knew, and they shared their concerns with me.

I was pleasantly surprised that my way of assessing the situation, using only my intuition had come up with a list of symptoms/life challenges that were in alignment with a diagnosis of Asperger's.

I started to work informally with Gabriella and slowly she began to trust me. When she refused to go to school, I was called. I would rush around to the house and talk her out of her bedroom and into the car to go to school. When she locked everyone out and screamed profanities at them through the letter box or the windows, I was called to calm her down.

Bless her, she always let me in. She knew why her parents called me, but she still let me into the house. When I'd calmed her down, she would then let everyone else in. Working with her in short bursts, I taught her about energy, about us being energetic beings and she was fascinated. I helped her to accept that she was different, but that did not make her less than anyone else.

I began to work on her treating her sisters and parents better, but it was a long process. She would frequently get herself into trouble at school; if she thought something was wrong or unfair she couldn't keep her mouth shut. Within seconds of the thought coming into her head, it was leaving through her mouth. She wasn't doing it to be naughty, she simply did not have a switch to stop it from happening. Bless her, everything was a challenge, every day was a challenge, life was exhausting and when she was exhausted, she lost her temper even quicker.

I started to feel bad about continually being the one who could persuade her to go to school, especially as the school she went to had no empathy for her problems.

At one point she'd been suspended for a couple of days and before she was allowed back there was a school meeting of teachers, social workers, psychologists etc. Gabriella and her parents were invited to attend and they cleared it for me to attend too. I sat at Gabriella's side to keep her calm, as losing her temper was not going to do her any favours in this environment.

The Deputy Head (DH) was chairing the meeting and it didn't take long before I thought he was out of his depth. He pontificated about school rules, school standards and how Gabriella's behaviour was not acceptable. He then related his version of the incident that had caused Gabriella to be suspended in the first place. I allowed him to finish and then asked if Gabriella could share her perspective; Gabriella was chomping at the bit by what he'd said. The DH acknowledged me and said he would give Gabriella time to speak later.

I had to badger this DH a further 3 times before he would let her speak, by which time Gabriella was in sulking mode. I held the floor while I worked with her and encouraged her to speak. Just as he was trying to move on, she found her voice. She accepted that physically hurting someone was not an option but in her version of events, the girl she hurt had verbally abused her, calling her names until Gabriella reacted. This girl was then very quick to call a teacher for help. Gabriella was amazingly accepting that she needed to be punished, although to be honest, 3 days at home was not really a punishment for her as she hated school so much, but she thought the other girl should be punished too.

Gabriella's 'fairness scales' as she saw it, said this situation was completely unbalanced, and in my opinion it was. The DH didn't care. He listened to expert after expert who added different perspectives all saying the same thing; that the difficulties Gabriella had were genetic not behavioural, and had to be taken into consideration. The DH disagreed and made it clear that all pupils in the school would be treated in the same way. How little he had understood of what had been said to him. My heart sank.

On the day that Gabriella returned to school after her suspension, the DH made the situation worse. I cannot believe that anyone who understands children would have done what he did, but his ignorance caused another battle.

On the morning of Gabriella's return she had to go through a procedural re-entry, which meant she was not in assembly. The DH decided to point out to all the children in Gabriella's year that she would be back that day and to try and avoid any confrontation with her. He then went on to ask all these children not to tell Gabriella what he'd said. I cannot believe that as a Deputy Head he knew so little about kids that he didn't realise he had just loaded the gun. Within an hour of Gabriella being back in school, half a dozen kids told her of the Deputy Head's comments. She marched up to his office, burst in and called him a w****r. Not a word I would use, but definitely a situation that his ignorance caused.

As you can imagine, Gabriella's days at this school were numbered. Her parents were told that if they thought another School would be better suited for their daughter, then that was their decision. The school wouldn't expel her, but they let Pauline and Lesley know that they didn't want this one of their daughters to be a pupil at the school.

In the area, this school was considered to be the best. It had high standards of academic achievement, it did well on the school league tables, but in my opinion it was rubbish when it came to a child that needed to find a way to survive in our world.

Gabriella refused to go back and my heart wouldn't let me try and persuade her. This school didn't understand the challenges she faced, like many people, they only saw bad behaviour and a blot on their achievement statistics. I shared my thoughts with her parents, who unsurprisingly, were not happy with my opinion. However, by this time they were paying me for my professional help and, as I pointed out, I had to be authentic and not simply tell them what they wanted to hear.

I worked with Gabriella and her family for some time. Gabriella's Mum was struggling with her own issues and often her slow progress hampered the progress I made with Gabriella. Dad also caused some problems, I can remember hearing him talking with Gabriella at a village fete. They were going through all the villagers within their eyeline and finding fault with them. I was horrified. I'd worked hard to try and minimise the judgments that Gabriella made of others, and now her Dad was fuelling them. He saw my look, he knew what I was thinking.

"We're only having a bit of fun," he said.

"But it's not helping Gabriella." I replied and walked away.

He did follow me and apologise, but I was getting exhausted trying to help this family. They were relying on me. I was becoming a member of their family, but not in a good way. Whenever there was trouble they would turn to me, even the younger children started to leave their house and knock on my door the minute Gabriella kicked off. This family taught me so much.

They taught me to set my own boundaries when working with families. I must never become part of a family; I needed to empower them by sharing what I knew, not by becoming the person that calmed every difficult situation.

They also showed me first-hand what it was like to live with someone with Asperger's. Children with Asperger's are not easy, but there is an honesty about them that I grew to love. I learned that my energy created a calm environment for children such as Gabriella, a calm space that they felt drawn to. In fact, it soon became apparent just how much effect my energy had on all the children I was working with, and so I started to share these understandings with the parents.

This family's situation highlighted the negative reaction that society has to people with mental issues. This made me feel sad to think that because people cannot see the difficulties these children were having, they would judge first and ask questions later. I started to understand that to help the families I worked with, I had to encourage them not to judge others and to stop making assumptions when they didn't know all the facts.

And finally, they taught me that if I am to make any lasting change in a family, I needed parents to come on the journey too.

To change the behaviour of a child
it is first necessary to alter the
actions of the Parents

This last comment reminds me of the day I worked with this family to create a set of house rules. I believe there should be a set of rules in every house that clearly state the expectations of how one member of the house will treat another. These rules are not about what time the children will go to bed but state expectations like *Be Kind*.

Anyway, it took the best part of 2 hours to get a set of house rules for this family. When I suggested *Be Honest* as one of the rules it was Dad that said,

“Hmm I am not sure, that may be difficult to keep.” I was astonished.

How could he expect his children to be honest, if he couldn’t do it himself? In my opinion parents need to lead by example. The days of ‘do as I say and not as I do’ are well gone, and so they should be. We should not expect a child to behave in any way that we cannot ourselves.

Now, I am not suggesting you should give up on Father Christmas or the Easter Bunny with young children, but I don’t believe it is acceptable to lie to a child to avoid saying the word ‘no’.

You know the type I mean; the ice cream van only plays music when it has run out of ice cream, the tantrum police will take your photograph and put it up on the wall of kids who behave badly, only Grandma has the magic coins for the ride outside the supermarket. I’m sure you can think of some phrases that you’ve used yourself.

My belief is that trust comes with honesty. Discovering that their parents, who they trust above everyone, have lied to them causes a child serious problems, so I encourage you not to do it. If you need to say 'No' then please use the word. You may be challenged the first few times but once they realise you stand by your word, they will respect your decision.

Set house rules that state how members of the family should treat each other.

So back to my story. We had taken nearly 2 hours to decide on the 5 house rules. The children had written them neatly on a piece of card and decorated them.

Dad then decides that they should all sign the card to say they will follow the rules, and that I should also sign as a witness to the signing. I hadn't viewed the rules as a legal document, but if this would make him happy I was happy to comply. 6 Year old Tilly had other ideas, she refused to sign and said,

"I'll do that one, I don't like that one, that one is okay, that one is okay, but I am not doing that one!" As my heart sank everyone started to laugh.

It was funny the way she did it, but I had to wonder if we would have all been laughing in the same way if it had been Gabriella that said those very same words?

Fortunately, since Tilly was only 6, it was relatively easy to persuade her to sign. Ironically Tilly then became my voice in the house. She wrote the rules down in a small pad of paper and carried it everywhere. If any member of the family did anything wrong Tilly would tell them which rule they were breaking.

Bless her, she may have been the youngest but she held them all accountable to the new house rules, even her Mum and Dad.

Please remember the best way to teach a child anything is always by example. Trust me, they will easily follow your lead.

Chapter 28: Dainan

I understand now that one of our main purposes in life is to grow, to understand who we are and to try to become a better version of ourselves every day.

Over the next few years the Universe sent me clients that would help me to understand myself better as I worked to help my clients. I worked with children and teenagers who were feeling anxious, who were being bullied, who were having a hard time because their parents were divorcing or simply because they saw the world differently. The universe was sending me youngsters who would help me to understand me. I empathised with the youngsters that I worked with. I could feel their pain and I wanted to make the world a better place for them.

I came to understand that I am a highly sensitive person, that part of my problem, all of my life, was my sensitivity. I learned that it was a fixed aspect of me like the colour of my eyes. I couldn't change it, I couldn't simply learn to just toughen up; I had to learn to embrace it and once I'd done that, I could learn to value it. I had to learn how to protect my energy, how to control what I did and did not feel, and then how to take responsibility for my own feelings. With every child that I helped, I learned more about me.

I devised my own MEDS; these were simply things that were essential, that I needed to do for me to feel good. They were not luxuries if only time allowed, they were absolutely necessary for me to function in the world. My Meds are as follows: -

MEDITATION – I need time away from others, quiet time to give my mind a rest. This meditation can be in a traditional form where I sit quietly, or it could be a time when I walk in nature with my dogs and focus only on them and the beauty that surrounds me. Whatever form my meditation takes I need to do it every day.

EXERCISE – I need to move. Without exercise I find it hard to function in a world full of such violence and hatred. This is not my way and I find it overwhelming. Exercise releases all the endorphins that help me to stay cheerful, despite all the horrific news stories. Without exercise my black cloud is never far away. My exercise doesn't have to be tough, I simply need to move every day.

DIET – I began to understand that my sensitivity extended to food. I've long since given up eating meat but there are certain foods that I do not feel good after eating. Wheat is one such food, it is like a drug to me and makes me feel very sleepy and lethargic. It doesn't cause me any pain so it's easy to eat, and I do so love fresh bread, but I feel better when I don't eat it.

In recent years I've read that the wheat we use today has been so doctored from the ancient grains that if you throw a handful of wheat seeds into the soil they will not grow!! That seems a very scary thought to me. What are we doing to the food we are eating? More and more I realised that what I put into my body has a direct effect on how I feel and how clearly I can think. Sadly, that does include alcohol and caffeine. No, I didn't give up alcohol. I love sharing a bottle of wine with friends, but I find I drink far less the older I get. As for caffeine, I haven't given up coffee or chocolate either, but I do now drink decaffeinated coffee and I prefer dark chocolate.

The saying *'we are what we eat'* is so true, so if we really want to feel good we need to eat foods that have, as Doreen Virtue would say, a high life force, i.e. we eat best when we cook the food from natural ingredients. I know it all takes time but when we don't take the time, what is the cost to ourselves and our families? And for sensitive people, it's an absolute necessity to eat a healthy and natural diet.

SLEEP – I don't think we truly appreciate how important sleep is. Teenagers, in particular, need an incredible amount of sleep each night, which they very rarely get. Of course, they try and catch up at weekends, but the sleep bank doesn't work quite that way.

Our bodies can only function well when we get enough good quality sleep. Again, this is valid for everyone but especially for sensitive children. These children have a harder time getting through their day because they often experience sensory overload, and that is why they need a good night's sleep. I discovered that one of the kindest things I could do for myself was go to bed at the same time every night and read, rather than watch television for the last hour before I turned the lights out. My good friend Anna has a great saying. She says we should '*Always go to bed on the same day that you get up*'. This makes me smile, but it has been shown that an hour before midnight is more beneficial than an hour after. It has surprised me how many of the sensitive teenagers that I've worked with have seriously taken on board their need for a good night's sleep, and then gone on to take responsibility for their own bed times.

So, these are my Meds for being a functioning highly sensitive person in a world that doesn't seem to yet understand my sensitivity.

Working with sensitive children, I found that they were fascinated by my explanation that they are made up of energy and that they can connect with other peoples energy and feel their emotions as if they were their own. For a sensitive person, understanding that not every emotion they feel is theirs is a huge relief, especially when they realise that simply asking themselves the question '*Is this mine?*' can often dissipate the emotion they are feeling.

I was constantly learning from the children I worked with and adjusting how I lived accordingly, and although I do not consider myself a Master, I do try to be authentic and practice what I preach. As a friend of mine tells her clients '*we have a choice*'. Now I believe our choices simply take us towards or away from our goals and values. If they are towards our goals, they raise our vibration and make us feel better, whilst those that are not in alignment with our values do not make us feel good.

During my intense period of learning, I was gifted a book that made a huge difference to my life. Let me tell you how this book found its way to me; a few years after my divorce, I tentatively started to look at internet dating. To be honest I wasn't enamoured by the idea, but I was networking with women, my friends were all women, and it was the Mums that invited me to work with their children, all in all I was missing a masculine energy in my life.

Being very wary of the whole internet dating thing, I found a dating site for Spiritual People, with some hope of meeting a like-minded soul, I created my online profile and was surprised to get a response from an Australian man called Dainan. I wasn't sure why someone in Australia would want to connect with me but his message was lovely, and so I wrote my first response.

Within a matter of days I was in a routine of replying to Dainan's email at night before I went to bed and his response would be there in my inbox in the morning. I soon found myself jumping out of bed and rushing down stairs to turn my laptop on and read his message. Our emails were getting longer and longer and it wasn't long before Dainan suggested we should talk on the phone. I was very nervous the day I waited for his first call but I needn't have been. It was like we'd known each other for years. We laughed and talked about anything and everything. It was only my pressing need to go to the bathroom that made me realise that 3 hours had passed.

Dainan was the kindest man I had ever known. When it came up in conversation that I'd never received flowers from a man, I arrived home the following day to find the most beautiful bouquet outside my front door. When my horse was sick with colic and I was walking around a field in the dark at 10 o'clock at night, Dainan phoned me from Australia on my mobile, and then when my shower wouldn't work, he got me to point my laptop at the shower so he could see as he told me how to fix it.

I started to get used to him always being there. How crazy is that considering this man was halfway around the world from me? He supported me. He encouraged me in my work and in believing in my connection to the Angels. He believed in me in a way that no other man had ever done.

Dainan was a plumber by trade but was also a wonderful healer, although he didn't have much faith in his healing ability. He wanted to heal the world and got upset if people didn't fully recover from their illnesses after his healing sessions. I tried to explain to him that people could only fully heal if they did some of the work themselves, if they changed their mind set, but he got very frustrated when he couldn't take everyone's pain away for them. He did however help me with a huge issue in my life.

In 2011 two of my friends, Lou and Abi, were due to have babies. I had known them both since they were 13 and 9 respectively and helped at the riding school. I had seen them grow up together with another of the Holly

Tree children, Tonia, and they were like the children I'd never had. I was their friend but also old enough to be their parent.

The girls were both due to have their babies in May and I was excited for them, but worried for me. I didn't want the babies to change my relationship with the girls but since the days of not being able to have children myself. I'd avoided spending time with babies. I hated it when mothers of 'new borns' asked me if I wanted to hold them, I would find myself saying awkward things like "I am ok thank you".

I knew why I didn't want to hold a baby. I was scared that the warmth of the baby would unlock all the buried emotion of not being able to have children of my own. I'd put on a brave face, found all the positive points about not having children and buried my emotions so deeply that I didn't have to deal with them. This solution did require that I avoided babies though.

I told Dainon about my fears and he offered to help me. I loved the healing sessions that I had with Dainon. I know some people will think it crazy that I was in the UK and he was in Australia and he could channel energy to me, but since the energy came from source and we are all connected, it seemed logical to me that it didn't matter where we were. Also without going into too much detail (I am so not the kiss and tell kind), we had played with sexual energy and I was amazed at the way Dainan could make me feel simply by imagining he was lying next to me. It was all a huge lesson and a reminder that we are all energetic beings, that are connected no matter where in the world we live. So, I accepted his offer of healing.

We connected by phone and set an intention for the healing. Dainan then connected to Source and channelled his Golden Healing Light to me. I did cry during the session, but I had learned that tears are a great release so I allowed them to flow. I remember the warmth of the energy in my body, but also the deep feeling of pain that I couldn't be a mother to my own child. I know the session was intense but as I write this for you, the dichotomy of the pain and the warmth are all that come to mind.

When the session finished, Dainan warned me that the energy would continue to process over the coming days and not to be surprised if I felt out of sorts. Well, my reaction to this healing shocked both of us as I was a mess for 3 weeks; I couldn't stop crying and felt like I was sinking into a deep depression I couldn't get out of. Although he was worried about me, Dainan kept telling me I was just processing and it would soon come to an end.

Just as I was beginning to doubt his words, the sadness disappeared as quickly as it came. I woke up feeling energised and happy. All seemed to be well in my world. We were both relieved that I had come through the healing process, but we wouldn't know if anything had changed for me until the babies were born.

A couple of months later I travelled up to Cheshire feeling a bit nervous about whether I had healed. Oh my goodness, it's hard to explain how, for the first time in my life, I felt the absolute joy in holding my friend's newborn son. I couldn't stop smiling and I didn't want to put him down. Dainan had made a huge difference in my life by helping me heal from one of my deepest wounds.

Dainan and I did meet in person and were in a relationship for just less than a year, but it wasn't to be in the long term. To this day, he is still the kindest man I've ever met and as another sensitive soul he is facing his own demons, which I pray he will find a way to heal from.

Dainan taught me many things in our relationship, but my biggest shock was how much I would fight to keep my freedom when I believed he was trying to put me in a cage. When Dainan came to this country I ended up feeling suffocated by him, and I acted towards him in a way that I'm now ashamed to admit. I ended our relationship when he was miles away from home, in a cold country surrounded by strangers. My reasons for ending our relationship were valid, but I cannot say I did it in a kind way and I am not very proud of that. However, as we always talked about everything, once some time had passed, we were able to talk about this too and I did apologise.

Of all the gifts Dainan gave to me, it was the gift of a book that changed my life. I had avoided the Conversations with God books by Neale Donald Walsh because they had the word God in the title. However Dainan loved the books and sent me a really beautiful hard back version of the first three books in the series. The books, if you believe them to be true and I do, are literally a conversation between Neale and God. It was such a beautiful gift I thought I'd better read some of it, but once I started I couldn't put it down.

The God in this book was not the God I'd grown up with in church. This was a God that was not judgmental, he didn't punish people if they did something wrong. In fact, he questioned if wrong even existed. This was a God that was loving and did not require rituals or sacrifices. There was no list of expectations about how we should live. This God wanted to explain who we are and why we are here. This was a God who wanted us to understand the meaning of life so we could be happy and fulfilled, so we could experience love and abundance. This God had a sense of humour, he/she made me laugh out loud as I was reading the book.

Even God's first statement in the book amused me. In the opening page, Neale Donald Walsh is ranting about his life and if you read the book, you will know he had every reason to rant. However, it was God's first comment to Neale asking if 'he wanted an answer or was he just having a rant' that amused me. The author had me hooked, and afterwards I struggled to put the book down; I could see in his reflections the mirror of much that was in my own soul.

There was so much about God in this book, but again, my truth about God does not have to be yours. No matter what advice you are being given, and no matter what source that advice comes from, only take it on board if it resonates with you. What was important about this book for me was that I loved it. I had found my God, a God I could believe in. One who was not a man in the sky with a white beard, but a Universal Life Force that I could communicate with. I had found a home for my faith and what felt true to me; I started to act on the messages it shared.

Suddenly, I found a purpose for life and a desire to share what I'd learned. Of all the messages in these books and there are many, the ones that have become most important to the way I live my life and are what I share with the families that I work with are these: -

- We are energetic beings having a human experience.
- We are connected to each other energetically.
- We communicate with each other energetically all the time.
- We can choose who we want to be.
- We each are responsible for creating our own lives.
- We have been given universal tools to create our lives.
- We each have a gift to share with the world.
- We are here to be the best version of ourselves that we can be.
- We are all having our own unique journey through life.
- When we choose to be the highest version of ourselves we experience a life of abundance.

Chapter 29: Gregory's Farmhouse

Reading the messages from Conversations with God and being inspired by them, and then really understanding how to make them work for me, were two entirely different things.

The book spoke to my heart, to my soul, but it took a while for me to realise that to make the messages practically work for me, I had to focus on my feelings. All this learning took some time, whilst in the interim my life was getting tricky for me again. I had totally immersed myself with the clients I was working with, but to the extent that I felt exhausted a lot of the time. I couldn't work with enough clients at any one time to support myself and my animals and my safety net of money from the divorce was disappearing ; I was rapidly heading towards a crisis.

I started to worry about money. My biggest fear when I got divorced was being homeless and somehow I seemed to be heading towards that situation. The more I focused on running out of money, the more I tried to solve my financial situation, only to find the quicker I seemed to be heading towards the very thing I didn't want.

I had already started to tighten my belt; I was being careful about food bills, putting another jumper on or sitting underneath a blanket instead of turning the heating on, and in my case letting my horses live out instead of stabling them every night. I had even decided that I couldn't afford the medication that my little pony Magic was on. It was a tough call, but I honestly decided if I took him off the medication and he went downhill to the extent that I had to put him to sleep, then that would be acceptable. It would break my heart but he'd had 10 years with me, that he may not have been given with anyone else.

Ironically, my worst fears never materialised here. As Magic's body became clear of the medication that the vets had said was vital for him, he started to have a spring in his step. Rather than go downhill, he looked better than I had seen him for a long time. I never did have to make the decision to put him to sleep because he seemed much better without the drugs. So, the horses were happy but life at home was difficult, and I was starting to use my credit cards to survive.

Eventually I got to a point where I didn't have the money to pay my council tax bill. I sat and cried and felt sorry for myself before I finally turned to my Angels for help. To be honest, it is hard to hear what the Angels are saying when you are wrapped up in your own emotional stuff, but somehow, I got it. I was cash poor but I had put a lot of money into my house. My mortgage was small; what I owed was not very much, although it was too much when you have no money.

On paper, I was worth nearly £250 000 all I needed to do was sell the house and downsize. Feeling relieved that my current situation was temporary, I put the house up for sale.

Dainan was still in my life at the time as a good friend and bless him, he would send me packages of dog or cat food because he knew I would be happier if I could feed my animals, they often contained a box of my favourite chocolates too!

I know you may be asking 'why didn't I find homes for my horses?' I honestly did try, but the economy wasn't great then and the animal shelters were so full that they were only taking the ones that were being abused. I couldn't find homes for them and it would have felt like giving my family away. Throughout all my life, the only stable family I'd had was my animals. As for me, I did try to sign on and get some money from the Council, but it seemed I didn't qualify for much because I still owned my own house and every time I got even one client, I would not qualify for job seekers allowance. Life was getting very dark.

I spoke to the bank and the council to let them know I was selling my house. My credit cards were frozen, but no extra interest was added. The council, who had started bankruptcy proceedings for my council tax, had agreed I could pay them £100 a month until I sold the house. It was early in the year and there was snow on the ground when I ran out of gas. Worse still, they wouldn't deliver any more until I'd paid the previous invoice in full.

The house got cold fast. I can remember thinking that the cold affects us in such strange ways. I knew logically that I should keep moving, but all I wanted to do was sit on the settee under a duvet. The house got so cold that even my Border Collie dog was shivering and I had to allow her onto the settee so we could try and keep each other warm.

I couldn't afford to eat fruits and vegetables anymore so my diet became full of bread and potatoes. Anything that was cheap, but would fill me up. Then on a day in April, my worst nightmare happened. I got a letter through the post to say that I had been made bankrupt. I was shocked, I couldn't understand why. I phoned the solicitor who was acting for the council and she was very off-hand with me.

"We didn't receive your payment," she said.

"But I phoned you and told you when I had transferred the money," I replied, "you told me everything was okay."

She just kept repeating the same phrase. It was my fault. I hadn't sent the money in time and I hadn't turned up in court. Of course I hadn't! I thought the case was adjourned as long as I kept paying the £100.00 a month, after all, I had put my house up for sale. There was nearly £250000 equity in that and I only owed them £1800. I was doing the right thing and yet this situation was ludicrous. She stopped the conversation saying there was nothing she could do.

I slid to the floor and cried; I was cold, I was hungry, I was frightened and now I was bankrupt. I was done and I'd had enough. I would not have taken my own life but I screamed at God; I had tried to be a good person all my life, had tried to be kind and understanding. I had helped anyone I could. I had been kind to people and to animals. I had respected the earth that I lived on. I had tried to be good, why then was my life such a mess? I was fed up of being on my own, fed up of struggling on my own, of having to dig deep and find my own inner strength, of finding a way to stand back up every time life knocked me down. I wanted to die. I wanted to go home back to God, back to my Mum and all my spirit family. I didn't like it here on earth. It was too hard, too violent, too cruel, too cold.

I cried myself to sleep lying on the floor of the lounge with Gypsy my Collie cuddled up against me. That night was my Night of the Soul, my lowest point. I know they say that your night of the soul is a turning point spiritually, but I wouldn't wish it on anyone.

From that moment on the legal system took over. I had to meet with the Official Receiver who sympathised with me. She said the Council had been overzealous in my case, and they were doing the same to other people too. She said it was wrong that I'd been made bankrupt since I had so much equity in my house and she advised that I should get my bankruptcy annulled once it was all over. The key phrase there was 'once it was all over'.

Once you're in the system, you are in it and have to go through it. You can't stop and get yourself out of it. The Official Receiver appoints a trustee and suddenly your life is in someone else's hands. Everyone I talked to kept saying to me, 'this shouldn't have happened to you', until I wanted to scream whenever I heard the phrase.

It seemed so unfair, I had been taking the right action, but it was happening to me. I had to ask people to stop telling me it wasn't fair and start helping me to get through it. I was lost, embarrassed and depressed, but somewhere in all of that I learned that I had to let go, to accept I was now bankrupt and to allow the cogs of the system to keep turning.

Letting go of the fight was the first huge step for me, the second was accepting my situation. The system was cruel. The trustee only did what I had already been doing. Once the house was sold, they had only paid the people I had told them I owed money to. I owed less than £20 000 and altogether it cost me £60 000 in fees and costs to go through the bankruptcy. It had cost £60 000 for someone else to do what I had already been doing. I cannot tell you how much that hurt.

Later, when I would talk to the Judge who would annul my bankruptcy, he asked me why I hadn't turned up in court the day the bankruptcy was declared. I told him how I had talked to the solicitor for Aylesbury Vale Council and she had said everything was 'okay now that I had paid the £100', but it was that same solicitor who then stood up in court and said the Council never received my payment.

The Judge then told me off and gave me a piece of advice. He said I should have turned up, he would have been able to help me if only I had simply turned up.

Don't hide. Turn up. Be seen

Oh my goodness that life lesson hurt. I felt like a little kid in the Head Teacher's office at school when he said those words to me. He then went on to tell me never to trust a Solicitor! I do apologise to the many honest solicitors out there. I have since met many family Solicitors who I admire and respect, but these were the Judges words at the time and personal experience has shown me that not all solicitors are honourable. I guess we can say that about any group of people, but it always shocks me when people who up hold the law do not act in an honourable way.

I had to face my bankruptcy and accept it, in order to start to work through it. There were lots of people who helped me and around this time and I found an amazing group of women at a self-growth network called Fab Friends. This network was run by a lovely lady called Ali Soleil who to this day has always held a space for me where she sees me at my best. I felt so low and so embarrassed that I nearly didn't go to the first meeting, and that would have been a big mistake.

I text Ali and told her I was struggling and didn't want to bring my depressed energy to her meeting, but she encouraged me to go anyway. The ladies embraced me and supported me and even as I write these words I'm sitting in the home of a good friend that I made through attending that first meeting. This was another lesson in not isolating myself and in accepting help and support from others. We are not here to go through life by ourselves, we are here to share the experience, good or bad with others, but in order for our friends to help we need to reach out.

We are not here to go through life alone

Now a strange thing happened during my bankruptcy. I thought that with my house up for sale I would be downsizing to a much smaller property. I accepted that my next home would be rented but that brought its own problems. With a bankruptcy order against me I would not 'pass' the financial check, so I would have to offer to pay 6 or 12 months' rent in advance to secure a house.

My horses were staying put as I was only selling my home and not my yard, so although that limited where I could live, at least it made my search a little easier. During this period, I had also joined another networking group for women, where I met a lady called Marion who was also facing some financial difficulties of her own. We met up away from the meeting and appeared to have a lot in common. Like me, she was on a consciously spiritual path; we were both divorced, but she had a teenage daughter. We became friends. I guess we were supporting each other through a difficult time.

At some point in our conversations, we decided to share a house. Marion suggested we used a visioning process by a man called Dr Michael Beckwith. I knew of Michael Beckwith but at that point was not aware of his visioning process. Marion and I got together to use this process to manifest a new home. She had a recording of the guided mediation and all we had to do it seemed was close our eyes and follow the instructions. We had paper and pen at the ready to write down any thoughts or pictures that came to mind during the procedure.

As Michael Beckwith led us through, I could start to see a large house standing in its own grounds. It was surrounded by open fields and in one of the fields was a large lake. As I looked at the house it was like I was looking down on it from above and I could feel excitement surrounding this house. All the way through my mind was thinking I could never afford a place like this, but this was the vision I was having.

At the end of the process Marion and I wrote our thoughts down in silence. When we were ready to share, I remember saying to her,

"Well, I have no idea how we would ever afford this but this is what I've got..." I then went on to describe this large house in acres of land. Her face looked more and more amazed as I continued to speak. When it was Marion's turn to share, she read out her words and described exactly the same house! We were both in shock. It was like we had visited the same place in our shared visioning process. Excited about the house but with a strong dose of reality and our financial situation setting in, we decided to trust God and our Angels. If this house truly was for us, and it was a very big 'if', then somehow, we would be guided to it.

Well, you may not believe this but one week later we were standing in that very house! Marion had phoned an estate agent who had pointed her in the direction of someone else who knew of this house. The house was in fact an old farmhouse on an estate belonging to a local Lord and Lady. The outbuildings of the farm had all been converted to a business centre, but the house was still being rented out as a home. It had just been rewired and redecorated so it was clean and new and empty.

There were four bedrooms to the house and a family bathroom upstairs. Downstairs there were three reception rooms and a kitchen. The ceilings were high, the sash windows let in lots of light and the rooms were all big. And yes, in case you were wondering, it was surrounded by fields complete with a lake! We fell in love with it and although it was a lot of rent it seemed incredibly reasonable for its size and position. Besides, we were splitting the rent, so individually it was within our budgets. We held our nerve, negotiated to pay 12 months' rent in advance and soon found ourselves moving into this beautiful house. Even at the time it was not lost on me that my bankruptcy had led me to live in a large home surrounded by open countryside and gentle hills. It was perfect... but not for long.

I had moved into a new home with a lady I barely knew and her daughter who was a teenager. To be honest, of the two of them the teenager was much easier for me to get along with. There were signs in the first few days that living with Marion was not going to be easy.

My furniture didn't arrive at Gregory's Farmhouse until 2 days after Marion's. During those first couple of days Marion was happy and excited, but as my furniture started to arrive her mood began to change and our differences of opinion began to emerge.

I thought it was better to put one style of furniture in one room but Marion, however, thought we should have some of our own furniture in each shared room. I liked to have clear and clean surfaces, whereas she like trinkets everywhere. I wanted my desk in a certain position in the shared office, she said I was taking the 'power position'. I like order in my cupboards, a little OCD I admit, but she liked everything higgledy piggledy.

Even as I write this, these issues sound minor but believe me it became a living nightmare. We disagreed on everything. We had moved in together believing we had our spirituality in common, and the fact that we were single divorced women trying to make our way in the world. Well, we were right on the second point but very much mistaken about the first.

Saying you are spiritual is like saying you are English, there is a wide variation of personalities under the one umbrella. The furniture did become an issue. I even tried bringing an interior designer friend into the house for her to give us her non-biased view. She had no idea whose furniture belonged to who, but like me she favoured one style in one room and that didn't go down well with Marion. The end result was she felt we were ganging up on her.

By the time Christmas arrived, despite having found some moments of pleasure along the way, something happened that drew a line in the sand and the battle ground began in earnest. I'm not sure what that something was. There had been an incident about buying the Christmas tree, but I'm not sure if this was the final straw for Marion.

At this point we hadn't argued with each other, we had simply had heated discussions. Marion and her daughter were away for a couple of days over Christmas, so we agreed to have a Christmas meal together and open presents when they got back. I was hopeful that this would start a better precedence and we could have a fresh start for the New Year.

On the day that they arrived home, I'd been out visiting a friend but had arrived home in time for us to make a meal and swap presents. As I entered the house I shouted 'hello' 3 times before anyone responded. Marion came out of her office, as we had separate offices by this time,

"Oh hello" she said, "Katherine and I are just watching a film." She didn't wait for a reply, but she did firmly close her office door behind her. I could feel something had changed and I ended up spending the rest of the evening alone in our shared lounge. It felt very odd.

This was the first of many such evenings. Suddenly it seemed there was a 'me and them'. Whenever Katherine came to talk to me, Marion would find something very important and very urgent that she needed her to do. When I went into the kitchen, Marion would make it clear that she was busy but she would let me know when she'd finished.

There were no shared meals anymore, no conversations over coffee and I started to find myself living more and more in my bedroom. I want to make it clear here that I had the largest bedroom, and being enormous it wasn't difficult to spend time in my room. What was difficult, was that I was starting to feel unwelcome in a home that I paid half the rent for.

I tried to talk to Marion about this, but you cannot have a conversation with someone who keeps telling you that it is your issue and therefore nothing to do with her. She was very passive aggressive and I honestly didn't know how to have a conversation with her, so eventually I gave up.

As is often the case the straw that broke the camel's back over this situation was something very silly. In fact, it all came to a horrible end because of the way I put the knives in the dishwasher!!

Chapter 30: Mt Toubkal

I know this all sounds very childish. Marion had made it known to me that I should put the knives point-end down for safety reasons. I'd told her the reason I placed the knives upwards was because I felt they washed better this way. We had a couple of run-ins over the situation and I dug my heals in and refused to change.

I was finding life at home challenging, so I took the opportunity for some quiet time by signing up for a weekend retreat. The idea was for me to have some time out. Time to rest, time to eat healthily and time to do some walking.

Two of the ladies and myself were preparing to climb Mt Toubkal in Morocco the following month, so we were promised some trekking time during the weekend. The house we stayed in was lovely, however, there was a small problem, my phone had no signal when we were inside. On the Saturday, we went on a walk in the morning and finished at a local pub where we stopped for lunch. As we were all sitting down at the table my phone pinged to say I had a message. It was from Marion. The message read;

"Dear Karen, I hope you're all relaxed and having a lovely time but please, please, please leave the knives point down in the dishwasher in future. I don't want to go on about it, but Katherine just caught her hand on the tip of the same knife that I stabbed myself on last week. Luckily it didn't hurt but it could so easily have done. I know you have never hurt yourself on a knife in the dishwasher but when one of the sharp ones is in there sideways on - particularly that long one – and we are not expecting it, it just doesn't show up. I'm sorry to have to say anything but don't want to take the risk of Katherine doing what I did. It still hurts a lot nearly a week on. I thought I would text you now so that if you're pissed off that I've mentioned it twice now (which I guess you may be) you'll have time to get over it in pleasant company before you come home ☺ Enjoy your weekend xxx"

There was a pause as I looked in disbelief at the message and then the tears welled up in my eyes. I was supposed to be on a retreat, a time for me to get away from Marion and all the trouble that came with her. Ironically, the text was sent the previous evening. Marion had intended to upset me, intended to spoil my retreat time. However, the ladies saw my reaction and insisted that I read the text out loud, which I did.

It was greeted with howls of laughter, followed by incredulous exclaims. She's crazy, they said. They could see right through her passive aggressive approach and within minutes of reading the text aloud, the ladies had me laughing out loud at their reaction. It wasn't just me that thought this whole thing was ridiculous. All weekend the other ladies made tongue-in-cheek jokes about me deliberately trying to hurt Marion with a knife. The jokes did lift my mood but I was nervous about going home, so I stayed an extra night at the retreat.

When I arrived home on the Monday, Marion was in the kitchen and she greeted me all smiles. I said 'hello' then asked her if she had anything she wanted to say to me to which she declined. I asked her again, letting her know I wanted to say something to her, but making it clear I was happy to listen to her first. Again she declined, so I then shared my thoughts.

"I want to make it clear to you that no matter what you say to me, I intend to put the cutlery in the dishwasher the way I have always done. If, after all the time you have lived with me, you are still shocked to find the pointed part of the knives upwards, then you need to start working on your personal awareness and that is your problem not mine. I have nothing more to say on the matter."

I had used her own passive aggressive approach right back at her. Not sure this was my best approach, but I was fed up of being treated the way she was treating me. Well, not surprisingly I had unleashed the beast inside Marion. Considering 5 minutes earlier she had nothing to say, she now had a whole lot of something to say, except she didn't say it, she screamed it at the top of her voice. I joined the argument for a while, until I realised it was a pointless exercise and then I walked away.

I was shaking from head to foot as I heard the front door slam behind Marion as she left the house. I'd had enough; I couldn't live with this woman any more. No one had ever screamed at me like that, not even my Step-Mum and she hated me. I was shocked at my reaction and how my whole body continued to shake, I seemed to have no control over it. I curled up in a foetal position on the settee in the lounge and cried. I always seemed to end up crying these days; I wasn't sad, my tears were my body's way of trying to release all the angry energy that had just been thrown at me.

Through my sobs, I heard a text arrive on my phone; it was Dainan. I read his words

"Are you ok darling?" I explained to him what had happened and he offered me some healing. What would I ever do without this kind man in my life? I lay on the settee with the phone to my ear as Dainan sent his golden healing energy to me. As the healing continued my body started to relax and I felt sleepy. By the time Dainan had finished the shaking had stopped and I felt much calmer. Dainan told me he had a message for me from my Angels; they advised that my lesson was to speak my truth to Marion. I couldn't let her scream at me like that again, I couldn't let her treat me like that. It was time to set my boundaries.

When Marion returned home, I was still in the living room. I felt absolutely drained and didn't want to talk to anyone. Marion found her way to me, but now she was calmer. Actually, she was a lot calmer. She said she understood if I didn't want to talk, but she wondered if I would do a spiritual exercise with her when I was ready She said that we were just pushing each other's buttons and helping each other to grow. Now to be honest, I was not ready to hear those words. The spiritual exercise she wanted to do was to sit opposite each other and, without any words, look into each other's eyes. She wanted our souls to connect, to see the truth of who we are.

Now, I've done this exercise before. I have even done it with complete strangers at a workshop, but I was not ready to do this with Marion. I felt she'd attacked my physical body with her angry words and now she wanted to connect with my soul. No way was I going to allow her to do that. I told her I wasn't ready for the exercise or to talk and she accepted that.

As I said, by throwing all her angry energy at me she felt a whole lot better, but I was still dealing with the aftermath of receiving that energy. It would take another 3 days before I was ready to talk. There were many thoughts that ran through my head over the following days, but I suddenly saw the lessons of Spiritual growth in a new light.

Level 1 – See the good in everyone

When you consciously start on a spiritual journey, somehow you think that being a spiritual person means you ought to see the good in everyone.

I had started my journey at this point and saw the good in everyone for years, until my very good friend Mini pointed out the problems that my beliefs brought. She said that by seeing the best in someone, I was putting them on a pedestal and that one day they would fall off. It was those times when they fell off that I felt hurt because I couldn't believe what they had done or said.

In later years, I would realise this righteous indignation was part of my pattern and my hurt was coming from a situation that I was creating. It was a shock to realise that only seeing the good in people made life difficult for my friends, and very disappointing for me. Time and again I would be hurt and shocked by the actions of the people I liked. Then once someone had done something wrong I could forgive, but I found it hard to let go of the knowledge of what they had done. This resulted in me backing away from people who I felt had hurt me, and it made me mistrust anyone because I felt they'd always let me down. The truth was I held the bar too high for anyone to live up to, and that included the expectations I had of myself. This was a huge lesson.

Level 2 – Accept that everyone has a shadow side

This seemed like a huge step forward. I stopped seeing only the good in everyone and started to accept that we all have a shadow side. The problem with this level of understanding is that I made excuses for peoples shadow sides.

I would allow people to treat me badly and assume that they were just having a bad day, that it was just their shadow side and nothing personal towards me. But although I hid my feelings when someone treated me in this way, it hurt, really hurt. I got into a bad habit of accepting people's bad behaviour. Oh my goodness, I allowed this to happen to me for so many years. Over and over, I allowed the people I loved to hurt me and I said nothing. Or at least, I said nothing until it all got too much and then I would explode. At that point, my friends would wonder what had got into me! Now, with this situation with Marion I had a moment of clarity. I had learned all about boundaries and behaviour in Conversations with God, but now I was living in a situation where I had to go to the next level of understanding.

Level 3 – Accept others as they are but set your boundaries!

Suddenly, I understood the words from the Conversation with God. It was not my place to ask Marion to change, that was her path, her journey. I could accept her as she was, but I had to set my boundaries. I had to take care of me and say **You Cannot Treat Me This Way.**

Throughout my life, I had never said these words. When I lived with my Step-Mum, I could not say these words and during my marriage I had chosen not to say these words. Now, Marion was my biggest teacher. She had held up a mirror to me and pushed my buttons until I could no longer stay quiet.

Damn! Her behaviour was helping me to grow. She was right about that. Through her I'd had a moment of absolute clarity, and for that I needed to be grateful to her, but first I needed to explain to her my new understanding. I needed to explain that I now understood it was good to see the good in people, it was good to accept their shadow side, but it was never good to allow someone to treat me badly, and until I stood up and spoke my truth they would continue to do so. My experience with Marion would be my first step towards standing up to Cal, but I didn't know that then. First, I needed to have the conversation with Marion.

Three days after our original argument, I sat quietly at the kitchen table and talked to her; I explained my new understanding in the levels of growth. I explained how her shouting had made me feel and I didn't say 'you did this to me', I simply shared the facts of how I reacted. I told her no one had ever shouted at me like that before and I calmly told her that if she ever did it again I would have to leave. It wasn't a threat, I was simply informing her of the consequences if she ever shouted at me that way again. For the first time in my life I spoke these empowering words out loud; "You cannot treat me this way".

Marion and I didn't stay housemates for very much longer after that, as she chose to move out of Gregory's farmhouse shortly afterwards . However, we are still on friendly terms to this day and I have total respect for the huge opportunity she gave me to find my own voice.

Sometimes out of the most difficult situations comes our biggest lessons. I don't see Marion that often these days. Our personal challenges did not result in us becoming bosom buddies, but when we do bump into each other there is a respect and warmth towards each other that comes from facing our shadow sides together and helping each other through them. This again supported the words in Conversations with God that said that the purpose of relationships is to help us become better versions of ourselves.

It seemed that life lessons were coming thick and fast during this phase in my life. In Conversations With God, it is God who suggests we are not here to learn anything but to remember who we are. So maybe I was opening up and remembering.

Some months before I had heard one of the ladies from my networking group talking about a trek she was organising to climb Mt Toubkal. The idea was to reach the summit on International Women's Day. As I heard her talk a voice in my head said,

'You should sign up!'

'Really?' I heard myself reply. I was listening to this lady talking and at the same time I was having a conversation with myself inside my head.

'I hate being cold, I'm frightened of heights, why on earth would I want to go and climb a mountain?'

'It would be good for you!'

'Seriously, how on earth could it be good for me?'

'You won't ever know unless you sign up. Tell her you will go. Do it now.'

I argued with myself for some time but the voice in my head saying I should go was getting louder and stronger. I started to feel there was some reason for me to go. I was scared to even voice an interest, but the voice in my head wouldn't shut up.

"I might be interested" I heard myself say.

I went on to voice my fears to Sky, the lady organising the trip, but she was convinced I could do it. I took the information home and sat down with it. One of the ladies I knew who'd also heard Sky speak texted me to say 'I will do it if you will'.

Oh gosh, so much pressure. As the days passed by, the 'knowing' part inside me kept telling me that this was a good adventure for me. I had never done anything like this before, but I now found myself signing up. The trip was challenging, there wasn't a training program but the eight ladies going would meet up regularly in different combinations to walk, often taking our dogs with us.

We started to buy equipment and ironically, I think the equipment cost as much as the trip. As the trip got closer our excitement built, but so did our fear. It didn't seem long until we were sitting on an Easy Jet flight in our trekking gear heading off to Morocco. The trip didn't start well as one of the lady's left her purse on the plane and wasn't able to retrieve it, but as we pooled our resources, our trekking family bonded even more. We were met in Morocco by Ben and Jack, two Englishmen who were supporting us on our trip and of course our mountain guide. We had just over 24 hours to take in the flavours of Marrakesh before we were bussed into the Atlas Mountains to start our challenge.

Trust your guide and follow the steps in front of you one at a time

The trip was eventful from day one. There had been an unexpected covering of snow and we found ourselves walking along the side of a steep mountain without a clear path to follow. Our Mountain Guide took the lead and we had to trust that he knew where to walk so we could keep following the footsteps of the person in front.

There was a scary moment when one of our lady's nearly had a very nasty accident. She wobbled off balance and if Ben hadn't grabbed her backpack, she would have fallen down the mountainside . It was a moment that reminded us to respect where we were and what we were attempting. However apart from that moment, it amazed me that I didn't feel any fear. In fact, I felt completely at ease.

Over the next 3 days we climbed up and down these beautiful mountains to acclimatize to the altitude. I had a horrible attack of altitude sickness on the first night which wasn't nice, but Ben assured me that my body would acclimatise by the second day and I did wake up feeling much better. Wanting to leave nothing to chance however, I quietly decided to take the tablets I'd got from the Health Food Shop. I say quietly, because the tablets were apparently a natural version of Viagra and yes, I did ask if there would be any, shall I say, side effects if I took them! The knowledgeable man in the health food store assured me that there wouldn't be.

By day 3 we were used to the routine of trekking along the rocky paths, always looking out for our mules and support team that signified a snack or lunch stop. Our support team were amazing. They moved with the mules who were loaded with our bags and they set up camp ahead of us and made the most amazing meals. It was a gift to be sitting carefree on this range of mountains with my new trekking family being served gorgeous food and sweet tea.

It was also by day 3 that I found myself talking to the Mountain. I know you probably think I was losing the plot, but I promise I could hear a deep voice welcoming us and promising to keep us safe. The mountain air seemed to create a space for healing and each day at least one of the ladies would have a tearful moment, but we naturally supported each other through those moments. It brought us closer together every day.

There were people living on the mountain paths. We even saw a sign for Coca-Cola, would you believe? We had started our trip in beautiful sunshine, but as we went higher into the mountain range, the temperature started to drop and we found ourselves wearing more and more layers of clothes. Up until now, the atmosphere in the group had been light hearted, that was until we got to Summit Day.

Suddenly, everything got serious. We had arrived at the highest basecamp the night before our summit. Power was in short supply here, so the lights only came on for a few hours at night. At dinner, we were reminded of what lay ahead and the mood became very sombre as we were given ice picks to replace our walking poles, and crampons to help our boots grip on the snow. We had to sleep in our base layers so that the following morning we simply had to add layers of clothing.

We slept on the most enormous bunkbed I had ever seen. There was room enough on the bottom bunk for eight of us to sleep next to each other and when the alarm went in the early hours of the following morning, we dressed in silence by the light from our head torches.

Breakfast was a also a sombre event as everyone focused on the challenge ahead. At that point in time, it had never crossed my mind that some of us would not make it. For months, I had visualised us all reaching the summit. I'd felt the feeling of euphoria as we took a team photo to celebrate our achievements but Summit Day did not go as planned.

From the offset we were climbing, initially in the dark as we set off before dawn. Every step was a step up and the more we climbed the harder it got. We climbed for a couple of hours before Ben turned back with two of our ladies. I kept going but my legs felt like lead. Every step was harder than the one before. Disappointment started to rise in my body as our Mountain Guide tried to push the pace and I couldn't keep up, but I kept pushing, kept trying.

We stopped for a rest and I voiced my fears with another lady.

"I will come back with you if you want to stop now," she said. I didn't want to stop. I wanted the euphoria of getting to the top. We were here to climb Mount Toubkal and I ached to get to the top but another half an hour and I was done. I just couldn't keep up the pace. I'd climbed for 3 hours and I wasn't going to make it. With a very heavy heart I admitted defeat. Together with this other lady, we turned around and started the descent.

It was a very long walk. We still had another 5 hours of descent once we'd got back to the base camp that we had stayed in the previous night. The lady that I descended with had hoped we could phone for a taxi once we got to base camp, clearly the altitude was affecting her ability to think! It made me smile to think she had hoped for a taxi in the middle of the Atlas Mountains.

We made it back; 11 hours of walking up and down and we hadn't summited. Ben tried to focus on what we had achieved, but I didn't want to hear it. When the four who had got to the top finally made it home, I could hardly congratulate them. I was pleased for them, but distraught at my own lack of achievement.

The following morning, I awoke still feeling down. It was one of the lady's birthdays that day, so we were going out for a meal in the evening to celebrate and congratulate those who made it to the top.

I didn't want to be a party-pooper, so I did the only thing I knew how. I meditated and called in my Angels to help me. A feeling of unconditional love from my Angels soon wrapped me up. They got me to understand that my biggest lesson from all of this was that life is all about experiences.

My need to do everything perfectly was debilitating and if I had reached the top, I wouldn't have understood the beauty of the journey. They were telling me what Ben had tried to share the previous evening. I had climbed to 3800 metres. This was an amazing achievement. I had felt the energy of the mountains, I had bonded with this family of trekkers, and overcome altitude sickness. I had not felt afraid at any point and I had learned to follow the footsteps in front of me, one step at a time, and trust in my Guide.

On this occasion if I had reached the top I wouldn't have learned this most important lesson of life. As I realised this truth, a feeling of euphoria swept through my body and stayed with me for many months. From that moment on, whenever I doubted my ability to do anything I would ask myself,

"Can I do this?" The answer was always the same, "hell yes, I've climbed a mountain."

LIFE IS ABOUT EXPERIENCES

Chapter 31: Time to Move On

Later that year God sent me a gift in the form of a cockapoo puppy. Now, I wasn't looking to have another dog, but life was relatively quiet with a 13-year-old border collie and a 14-year-old cat and I thought that suited me.

However, my friend Cleo, who was a dog trainer had other ideas. She had just bred a litter of gorgeous cockapoo puppies. After a training class one day, I was sitting in Cleo's kitchen with some of the other dog owners when Cleo started to bring the puppies in and asked each of us to hold one.

Cleo cleverly dropped her favourite puppy onto my lap. She was 6 weeks old, had champagne coloured fur and a cute brown nose. She was the cutest puppy I had ever seen and the other dog owners teased me because my hair looked like this puppy's fur. I couldn't deny it. My curly hair did have a mind of its own. As I held this little puppy to my heart, I could feel the warmth grow inside me and a little voice in my heart whispered,

"Keep her," but my head overruled that voice immediately and when it was time to leave, I handed her back to Cleo without another thought of adding to my animal family.

The following week the same thing happened as Cleo dropped the same adorable puppy on my lap and the voice in my opening heart grew louder, but I was still trying to be sensible and say 'no'. We joked about what we could call her. As she was champagne coloured, we went through all the makes of champagne looking for a name that we could shorten until we came to Bollinger and this shortened quite nicely to Bollie.

Suddenly, this puppy had a name and the other dog owners in the kitchen started to say she was mine now. I still fought the urge to tell Cleo I would have her, but this time as I left her, I left a little piece of my heart with her.

During the following week, I tentatively told my business coach that I was thinking about getting a puppy. She played devil's advocate perfectly; the more she reminded me that successful people focus solely on what they need to do to become successful, the more I wanted this puppy.

The more she asked me,

"Is this really a good time to get a puppy?" the more my heart said 'yes'. Life had been so tough for so long, I needed something good to happen. I put the phone down at the end of my coaching session and cried. In that moment, I suddenly realised how much I wanted to keep this puppy.

In pointing out all the reasons why I shouldn't have her, in keeping me focused on not having her, I suddenly became clear about what I did want. I was starting to realise that clarity through contrast was a good process for me. By looking at what I don't want in my life, I can often get absolute clarity about what I do want. I stopped the tears, picked up the phone and told Cleo I would have Bollie.

Clarity about what we do want can often come when we first focus on what we don't want

Bollie was definitely a gift from God. She brought so much joy back into my life. She made me smile every day. She was cute, naughty, persistent and I loved her instantaneously. She got away with so much more than my 6 previous collies had before, simply because she was small and cute.

Gypsy my older dog was like the serious side of me, but Bollie was like my playful side, one I had almost forgotten about. The first couple of weeks with Bollie at home were a bit of a challenge. My elderly Gypsy didn't seem to be happy about having a puppy in the house; she wouldn't let Bollie anywhere near her and if Bollie got too close, Gypsy would pin her to the floor.

Poor Bollie, sometimes she would pee when Gypsy pinned her down, but I couldn't blame her. I may have done the same in her position! I did worry about Gypsy, but I so loved having Bollie around. After 2 weeks things started to improve. Slowly Gypsy started allowing Bollie to get closer and Bollie was always respectful and submissive to Gypsy.

After a month Bollie started teaching Gypsy how to play. My old Gypsy was a rescue animal, and as I have mentioned, a rather serious dog, but suddenly I saw her playing with Bollie and barking joyfully at her. It made me heart sing, we had turned a corner. Gypsy was teaching me a valuable lesson in those early days. She wasn't swayed by Bollie' s cute appearance, she laid her boundaries down the moment she'd arrived in the house. Bollie never took Gypsy's actions personally, she always came back for more. She desperately wanted to be friends with Gypsy and Gypsy allowed that, but on her terms.

Some three years later I'm often reminded of the benefits of Gypsy's approach. If Gypsy says 'no' to Bollie, my little cockapoo immediately respects her decision. If I say 'no' to her, she puts her head on one side, looks me in the eyes and seems to say, 'are you sure?'

I have learned the hardest way that it is better to start the way you mean to carry on and set very clear boundaries. It always makes me smile when I think about this, as a teacher I found it easy, almost second nature, to set clear boundaries for the children I was teaching. I had also found it easy to set boundaries with my animals until this cute bundle of fluff came into my life. I was blinded by her appearance, and that meant I had to be firmer with her later on. With other adults though, it has taken me a lifetime to realise just how important it is to set my boundaries.

Unless I speak my truth and let people know what is, and is not acceptable to me, they constantly break the boundaries they cannot see and I get hurt.

Good relationships are built on clear boundaries

This was something I would be reminded of when my ex-husband Cal, came back into my life a couple of years later. We hadn't fallen out or anything, I had just not heard much from him in recent years, until a phone call out of the blue.

He was in a bad way. His relationship with his second wife was heading to the divorce courts and he needed someone to talk to. My head was spinning when he first started to phone me. I hadn't expected his relationship with Nikita to last beyond a couple of years when they first got married, but when I had seen them together at Cal's Mum' s funeral the previous year, I thought I'd got it all wrong. Together with their two children they'd looked like a strong and close family.

I should have known better. Anyway, Cal started to tell me about all the bad things Nikita was doing. I guess part of me wanted to hear, and part of me wanted his relationship with her to fail since he had left me for her.

At this point in my story, I still loved him. Evidently Nikita had started going to the gym, had started leaving her children to go out, was sleeping with other men. He had plenty of stories to tell me about how she was a bad mother and wife, but the ones that hooked me in were the stories about his children.

My heart went out to them, they were 6 and 8 respectively at the time and were living in a battle ground between their warring parents. I would later find out that Cal was using these stories to manipulate me, that he had added his own perspective to make it seem like Nikita was the bad person in all of this and he was father of the year. I was aware that there were two sides to every story and even at this stage, if Nikita had accused him of something that rang true to me, I would remind him of events in our own marriage. I wasn't looking for a relationship here so I could be blatantly honest with him, although I did present my truth in a kind and gentle way.

Cal would phone me at all times of the day and night, and his drama started to become my drama. At this point, I was not setting my boundaries, Cal was playing the victim and I was facilitating that all without me even noticing. I wanted to help him, I wanted to make things better for him.

I had loved this man since I was fourteen and it hurt me to see him in so much pain. He continued with his complaints about Nikita. She had never worked, she had never shown an interest in the business, she didn't even pay the bills out of their joint account, and now she wasn't even taking care of the children properly. She was more interested in how she looked and who she could sleep with. It seemed that Cal had to do everything, and on top of that Nikita's parents would come over from Prague to stay in Cal's house for months at a time. He hated having her parents in his house. He spoke no Czech and they spoke no English.

Since his children were bilingual, he felt like an outsider in his own home. I should have been a bit more detached as I listened to Cal's complaints. I was aware that when he complained about the time Nikita spent at the gym that if I only changed the word 'gym' for the word 'horses', it was a familiar complaint I'd heard many times before. However, I continued to allow myself to get drawn into his story and started to do what I always had done with him, I tried to fix it for him. I so should have known better.

I spent some time researching solicitors. I asked my contacts for advice and we found a highly-recommended solicitor to represent Cal. I then started to read through all the communications between the two solicitors. Before Cal agreed to anything he would ask me what I thought. This all felt very familiar to me. I had always taken care of the legal stuff when I was married to Cal; accounting, solicitors, Customs and Excise, Inland Revenue, these had all been on my to-do job list.

There was even an occasion when Cal was sitting with his solicitor and had to phone me to ask the date of our divorce and then the date of his marriage to Nikita. I looked through his Form E with him after he had gone through it with his solicitor, and at every step of the procedure I held his hand and gave him questions that he needed to ask the solicitor. Cal was grateful for my help. This was something I was definitely not used to.

When I was married to Cal he was rarely grateful for anything, least of all the everyday life stuff that I took care of for him. Now, however, he seemed grateful. Together with the fact that it appeared he was taking responsibility for his children, I wondered if he had finally grown up. Whatever was happening between us, I was enjoying having him in my life again. He even took me out to dinner to say thank you. It was lovely. It was easy. Even though his circumstances were difficult, we would always laugh when we were together. I was really starting to enjoy his company and our relationship was rekindling, or so I thought.

That year Cal was taking his children, Angelo and Chiara, to his brother Teo's for Christmas. Teo had a daughter of his own, Aimee, with his wife, Eve. Joining them for the Christmas period was Cal's third brother, Sandro.

I was very happy when Cal said he had been talking to Teo and Eve and that they would like me to join them for Christmas dinner. I had a wonderful time that year; I felt like I was back with my family. Everyone, including Eve's parents were pleased to see me and made me feel so welcome. Cal's children were soon comfortable around me and Chiara kept thanking me for her present and hugging me.

When we all curled up on the sofa in the evening on Christmas Day to watch the traditional Christmas film, Chiara cuddled up to me. This little girl was so easy to fall in love with. Angelo took a little longer to get close to, but even so he was relaxed and talkative in my company. That night Cal slept downstairs on a chair so that I could stay for the night. I got to sleep in the same room as the children, which gave us a couple of hours to talk and play games the following morning before anyone else surfaced. As I drove home on Boxing Day, I felt happy and content. I had no idea why this was happening but somehow, I had found my way back into the family I had been a part of for 30 years, and it felt really good.

As I drove through the gateway and down the drive to Gregory's farmhouse something had changed. I had been happy at Gregory's, but something told me it was time to move on. The previous year had been a sad one for me as all three of my horses had died in the same year. Marcus died early on in 2015, it was sad to lose him but he was 31 years old and so it was not unexpected. Bless him his legs simply couldn't hold him anymore.

Marcus's death created an amazing moment to remember in my life. As a rule, I always allow my horses to see the body of a horse that has been put to sleep so that they know why their family member has gone. Somehow, they seem to deal with the absence better this way. On the day of Marcus' death my remaining horses, Jim and Ella and my little pony Magic were all allowed to go up to Marcus's body before he was taken away. The following day when I arrived at the yard, the horses were standing in what looked like a ceremonial straight line, staring at the space where Marcus had lain the day before. I had never experienced anything like this before. I knew elephants did this kind of thing, but I didn't realise that horses did it too. You could have drawn a straight line through their front hooves. There was a gap between Jim and Ella so I joined them, standing in silence, honouring the passing of their pack leader.

It was a very special moment; a moment when I was a part of the pack and could feel their sadness at the loss of their friend, but also feel their knowing that it was his time to go. I don't know how long the horses had been standing in line before I got there, but I joined them for about 15 minutes. They must have stood there for another hour as I mucked out the stables behind them. Yet again these beautiful horses had surprised me. It was a sad experience, but an awesome one also.

My mare Ella followed Marcus in the summer. She had struggled on and off with laminitis and her life was becoming severely limited by the short amounts of time she was allowed out in the field. Eventually I arrived at the yard to find her in incredible pain with colic. It was her time to leave us and join Marcus, yet again Jim and Magic stood to honour the spot where she had died. I knew what they were doing this time, but I guess it didn't look quite so impressive with only two of them. It was still an honour to join them though.

Jim's death was my biggest shock. I arrived at the yard one evening, a week before Christmas and he was in trouble. Somehow, he had lost his rugs and was covered in mud, so he must have been rolling in pain. He didn't seem to hear me. His eyes only showed pain. He was a big horse, 17hh and he could hardly stand. My heart stopped for a moment before I phoned the vet requesting immediate help. As I talked to the receptionist Jim made his way behind the stable block to another small paddock, I quickly finished my conversation and followed him. I was fighting to stay strong for him. I had a rule; no tears, no emotion while the horse is still alive, but I was struggling to hold myself together. As I got to Jim he fell to the floor, his legs were flailing everywhere and he was gasping trying to breathe. He was in so much pain and I couldn't get near him, if I'd tried he could have seriously hurt me. I called out to my Angels and asked Marcus and Ella to come forward for their friend, then I turned to Jim and said,

"Jim, if you need to go then you can go."

Before the words were even out of my mouth, he took one final deep breath. His legs stopped moving and he stopped gasping. My gentle giant had gone and I was distraught. I stood in the field next to him in the dark. This beautiful horse had seen me through so many bad times. He'd allowed me to fling my arms around his neck and lean into his strong warm body when life's challenges were getting too much for me. He had stood quietly as I sobbed but now as the tears rolled down my face, he lay motionless on the floor. Only Magic stood alone and silent at a distance in the field. The world as I knew it was coming to an end. The ground was moving away from underneath me and I felt very alone.

The vet soon arrived, but he was not happy.

"Well, there's nothing I can do," he said, "it's already dead!"

"Could you get someone to take him away please?" I quietly asked him.

"Well, you won't get someone at this time, but I will give you a number."

He wrote a phone number down on a scrappy bit of paper and pushed it into my hand before driving off the yard. I was in shock. I stood there in the dark, literally with my dead horse in the field beside me. I couldn't leave him on his own. I covered him in horse blankets and phoned the number on the paper. The man on the other end of the phone remembered coming to my yard earlier in the year. I heard him say,

"You don't want to leave him in the field all night, do you? It may take me a couple of hours but I can definitely be with you tonight." I thanked this kind man, relieved that I wasn't going to have to sleep in the yard.

I tried to make a coffee but the generator wouldn't work, so I sat on the hay with my dogs and the yard cat to keep me warm. As I sat there it struck me that my horse, Ella, had died on July 1st which would have been my Mum's birthday, and now Jim had died on December 18th which would have been my Grandma's birthday. I didn't believe in coincidences. Was this timing just reassuring me that it was my horses time to go. To say goodbye to one horse was hard, two horses in the same year was traumatic, but losing my third horse in the same year had caused a deep pain like I'd never felt inside my body. I was lost without him.

So, as I drove along the drive back to Gregory's farmhouse after my Christmas visit, I knew my life was changing. Maybe it is time to leave Gregory's farmhouse,

I thought. It had been my sanctuary for 2 years longer than I had intended once Marion left. I loved the house and the surrounding land, but It was a lot of rent for one person, especially as I only used half of the house. Maybe it was time to downsize and move? It also struck me as I drove towards the house that it was time to sell the yard. I already knew someone who wanted it and I had to admit the proceeds from the sale would come in handy. I seriously did not need 5 stables and 11 acres of land for one little pony.

Now, only a few days after this thought, my life began to move incredibly fast as the estate office contacted me to see if I wanted to renew my tenancy in July.

I was shocked. Thinking that I might move and then actually handing in my notice to the estate office were two entirely different things. The latter would make my thoughts a reality and I wasn't ready for that.

I waited a couple of days before I replied with an honest account of my thoughts over the last few days, including the panic I had felt when the email had arrived from the office. No sooner had I sent my reply than the land line rang, it was the estate office wanting to reassure me that they weren't kicking me out. If, however, I wanted to go, they had someone who was going to rent a business unit from them who would also be interested in the house. At some point in the conversation I explained that I would like to downsize, so if any other smaller properties came up on the estate could they let me know? As I put the phone down, I felt calmer. My tenancy didn't end until July, I had plenty of time, or so I thought.

Everything went into overdrive. The universe had provided me with a buyer for my land and when I contacted the lady to see if she was still interested, she jumped at the chance. We had lunch and started to talk practicalities and at some point she said it would be okay for Magic to stay at the yard. I wasn't selling him with the land, but she was happy to take care of him if I covered his costs, so we put the wheels in motion for the sale of the land.

In the meantime, the estate office came up with 3 properties for me to view. The first was beautiful, but no smaller than the house I was in, so not an option. The second was incredibly small; the present tenant was a yoga teacher so I thought the energy in the house would be good, but it wasn't and when I came out I just wanted to cry. This was definitely not the house for me.

The third house however, was a cottage only a couple of hundred yards away from where I was living. It was much smaller than the house I was in, but it was light and cosy and I could really see myself living there. The only problem was that the garden wasn't contained for the dogs the Lord and Lady intended to build a new house behind it, so I would be living right next door to a building site. However, I did love the inside of the cottage, so I shared my concerns but kept my options open thinking I had plenty of time to decide.

The lady from the estate office then dropped the next bombshell; the current tenants were leaving at the end of the month and the estate wanted time to freshen up the house. To this end, they expected the new tenants to move in at the end of April! Suddenly, I was facing a moving date a little over 8 weeks away. It was all getting a bit much.

Meanwhile, my relationship with Cal was still going full speed ahead, until he surprised me by asking me to go and live with him and the children as a family. He said all the right things, all the things I had wanted to hear when he left me for Nikita. He had loved me since he was a teenager and, except for the birth of his children, leaving me was the worst decision he had ever made in his life. I believed he wanted a romantic relationship with me. He was asking me to make a life with him and the children, but although we had spent more time together, he hadn't even kissed me yet.

To add to the complication, the very day after Cal had asked me to make a family with him and the children, Daniel text me to tell me he was now divorced. What was happening? I had wanted to hear Daniel say those words for years. Why was he saying them now? What should I do? Where should I go? A new life for myself at the cottage, with or without a relationship with Daniel or a new life in Gloucestershire with Cal and his children? I was torn. Everything was happening so fast.

The first thing I needed to do was sleep with Cal. I know that sounds odd, but we could always do the brother/sister relationship really well, I needed to know that we still had a spark between us sexually. The next time Cal stayed over at Gregory's farmhouse we slept in separate rooms, but the following morning he said to me,

"I was so cold last night I nearly came into your room to snuggle up with you." I assumed he was checking to see how I felt about that.

Relieved that he seemed to want the same as me, I let him know that I would have been happy if he had done so. The very next time Cal stayed at Gregory's we did share the same bed and all my worries were laid to rest.

I still had to make a decision though, and yet again the universe helped me out.

Chapter 32: Living with Cal

A phone call from Cal ultimately led to my decision of where I would move to. It had gone past 11pm when I answered the phone and I heard Cal's very shaky voice at the other end.

"I've just been beaten up," he said.

To be honest, I wasn't sure at first if he was exaggerating but as the call continued I realised he was in trouble, serious trouble. He'd phoned me just after the incident and he was sat in his van with blood covering his face, torso and his jeans. More worryingly, he had both the children in the van with him.

He told me that Nikita had been out late and he had gone to look for her. He would later tell the police he was concerned for her well-being, but I honestly don't think that was true. He could track her SUV anytime he liked because he'd hidden a phone in it. He knew exactly where she was and had a good idea what she was doing.

Her car was parked in a lay-by off the Common, not 10 minutes from their house. Either Cal was not thinking straight or he wanted his children to see what their Mother was up to. Whatever the reason, he'd bundled his 2 children into the van and had gone looking for his wife. He told me that he had found her car and, leaving the children in his van, he went to challenge Nikita, who he found unsurprisingly, in a very compromising position with a local footballer. When he tried to film them together the situation had gotten nasty and Cal ended up getting hit badly. He eventually managed to get free and ran back to his van. His poor children saw their Dad return minus his jacket, his t-shirt and a front tooth and covered in his own blood.

He wanted to drive straight to A&E, but I was worried about him driving so I encouraged him to go to his friend's house where someone could help him, call the police and paramedics and take care of the children.

This fight started a whole sequence of events. Cal was in a bad way and it seemed that his phone had recorded part of the fight. When I heard it I felt sick, Cal was screaming to be left alone and you could hear his groans as he was being hit. Cal is many things, and he may have created this situation, but I do not believe he is a fighter.

I had never been this close to violence. Listening to the recording really upset me, it seemed to seep into every cell of my body and I couldn't shake it off. With what I'd heard, it seemed to be an open and shut case, but that is not how it went.

Cal couldn't legally go back to the house while Nikita was still in it so, with the children, he moved from one place to another and my heart went out to them. The police, the solicitors and courts all got involved and the school had to be informed about what was happening, and through it all I could only support him from a distance. The result of all of this was Nikita and Cal and the children would never again spend a night in the house together.

Eventually the courts gave Nikita 48 hours to pack her personal belongings and leave. The children did return home after a week but if Nikita was there, Cal couldn't be, so I asked Cal to come to me. I wanted to take care of him; the love I had carried for him all these years surfaced and enveloped me. I couldn't walk away, his drama was now my drama.

I hated that a man I loved had been attacked in this way. Without exception, I hate violence even when it is simply part of a TV drama, but to be so close to a violent situation really upset me. When Cal arrived at my door he looked terrible; his eyes were black, his nose was swollen and he looked like he'd had the stuffing knocked out of him. His head started to hurt so badly that he literally slipped off the settee to his knees and was clutching his head in agony. I was scared that maybe there was a bleed in his head, certainly something didn't seem right.

I insisted that we went to A&E straight away. We spent hours in there before he eventually had his brain scanned to check for a bleed. The doctor assured us that there wasn't one, only the sign of an old aneurysm. It was a throw away comment, one that was intended to reassure us, but which made both of us worry more. Cal's Mum had died of a stroke, if he had an aneurysm would the same thing happen to him? The doctor played it down and I tried to reassure Cal, but I know I felt as terrified of the information that the doctor had just given as Cal did.

At some point that day as I sat in A&E, I decided to commit to a future with Cal and his children. Up to that day I had wanted to take some time and build up our relationship slowly, to give the children chance to get used to me being around. I had a million and one reasons for taking it slow, but all I could think as I sat in A&E was that life is short, and now I needed to seize the moment.

I didn't know if it would work with Cal, but I needed to give it a go. I needed to take a chance on us. I knew my friends would think I was crazy, but I had to know if life was giving me a second chance with him. As it would turn out, the universe was giving me an incredible opportunity, but it was more about claiming my freedom from Cal than creating a happy home with him. There were rocky times ahead.

From the moment I committed to moving in, Cal started to use me as a childminder for his children. Even the week before I was due to move, a time when I needed to be at home to pack, he booked work dates and expected me to cover by looking after his children. I felt nervous, but I tried to convince myself that I was just scared about jumping back into a relationship with him. There was also one more worry. Cal didn't seem to like my cute cockapoo Bollie. "What did you have to get that thing for?" he asked me when he first met her.

A few days before I was due to move in I decided to phone Cal and set my boundaries regarding Bollie.

"There is something I need to say," I told him. "I love Bollie. She has brought a lot of joy into my life and if you cannot accept her then I can't come and live with you."

The phone went quiet. That was not the response I wanted.

"Well," he said, "you know I don't like her but I'll try." I really did not like the word try. I know it can be interpreted differently, but for me the word try gives someone the option to fail. In truth Cal was keeping his dislike of Bollie as his get out of jail card, but I didn't know that then. The conversation did get better and I did still move in, but I should have listened to my own instincts.

It was only a couple of days after Nikita moved out that I moved in. I was surprised at how easy going Cal was about all my stuff arriving in his house, although most of my furniture had been 'our' furniture and so everything matched.

Cal suggested we should have separate bedrooms for the children's sake. This was not what I wanted, but I could see the benefits for the children. Therefore, from the day I moved in, we only slept together when the children weren't in the house. When the children were in the house I was horrified to discover that Cal expected me to sleep with one of them every night. It seemed as things had gone bad between Cal and Nikita the children had gotten into the habit of each sleeping with one of their parents. Now Nikita had gone I was expected to do the same. I wasn't happy about this. I didn't think it was a healthy situation for the children and I desperately needed some of my own space. However, I couldn't walk into these children's life and start changing everything and, at that point, Chiara didn't have her own bed as her

Mum had taken it. This was something I could rectify and until I did, I had to accept a child in my bed every other week.

The first few weeks were exhausting but exciting. From the moment I moved in, Cal started taking all the work he could get and I was left with the children. It was baptism by fire. Thankfully, because of my work I had plenty of tools in my parenting toolbox, but being responsible for the children 24/7 was exhausting. Trying to find food they would eat was frustrating, cooking meat when I was a vegetarian was sickening and fitting my day into the 6 hours that they were at school proved impossible.

From the moment I had arrived I loved these 2 children, but I hadn't expected to be their main carer, I thought I would be supporting Cal. It didn't take long for the children to start turning to me for clothes, food or simply some attention. That all said, I was pinching myself as I started to believe that life had given me an opportunity to experience the mothering role to these children. I felt elated when we all went out together and we would walk down the street with one child holding Cal's hand and one child holding mine, these moments were special to me. Another part of the day I loved was bedtime; Angelo hadn't been diagnosed with dyslexia, but he had real problems with reading and avoided it whenever possible. Chiara, on the other hand was a natural and had a reading age higher than Angelo's.

When the situation between Cal and Nikita deteriorated, their bedtime reading routine went out with it. I knew how important this time is for children, not just to improve their reading, but to have the one-to-one time with one of their parents. It seemed obvious to me that we needed to re-establish this routine. Angelo was not at all enthusiastic at first, but as I encouraged him to read and praised his efforts his confidence started to grow, slowly at first but it gained momentum.

Listening to Cal comment as Angelo read one night, when he said to Angelo, "That word is easy," I realised that as a teacher, a lot of things came easily to me that would not necessarily be obvious to someone else. Being able to read a word, any word, is only easy if you know how to say it. If a child is struggling in any way and hears an adult saying it was an 'easy' word, it only makes the child feel worse about themselves. It didn't surprise me that when Cal and I were both home, Angelo would choose to read with me.

The bedtime reading was helping me to get closer to Angelo. From day one Chiara was open and loving and she was more than happy to have some female company and told me all the time how much she loved me. With Angelo, it took a little longer. The turning point in my relationship with Angelo came through a horrible situation for him. One Thursday evening I was sitting next to Chiara on my bed listening to her read when Cal returned from picking Angelo up from cubs. I could hear his shouting before they got to the front door followed by

Angelo's sobs. Cal kept shouting, screaming at Angelo as they came up the stairs and Chiara didn't draw breath, she just kept on reading. I continued to listen to Chiara, but all the time I got more concerned for Angelo as Cal continued to scream at him.

No matter what Angelo had done, I didn't believe he deserved to be screamed at in this way. I went to my bedroom door and then hesitated. Angelo wasn't my child. Could I really step in? No sooner had I asked myself the question than the answer echoed in my head; YES, YES, YES. This young boy was being verbally assaulted and it had to stop. I had to stop it. I apologised to Chiara and went to save Angelo.

Screaming at a child, no matter what they have done, is verbal abuse

As Cal screamed at Angelo,

"I have had enough of your f*****g mother lying to me and I won't have it from you too." I put my hand on Cal's shoulder and quietly said,

"That's enough." He turned to me and started telling me what was wrong.

"Okay." I said, "but enough for now, I will sort it." I pulled Cal's arm gently as I lead him away from Angelo's bedroom and down the stairs.

I knew Cal wanted to go out to an open mike night and play his guitar, so I suggested he left the house. His final words to me were,

"You will talk to him, won't you?"

"Yes." I replied, knowing that I would not be having the conversation with Angelo that Cal wanted me to. Cal slammed the front door as he headed out.

With a heavy heart, I went back up to Angelo's room. where he was still sobbing. I sat next to him on his bed and asked if he wanted a hug. He didn't say anything but moved towards me as I opened my arms. When I then wrapped my arms around him, I could feel him shaking from head to toe. I wanted to cry. How could a grown man do this to a small child? But this wasn't a time for tears, I had to stay strong for Angelo. It took nearly an hour of holding him and talking to him before his body stopped shaking and it took another 30 minutes before he was calm enough to go to sleep.

Reading between the lines a boy at cubs had been bullying him verbally until Angelo snapped and threw some stones at him. Of course the bully then played victim, Angelo denied everything and consequently got into trouble. Cal had shouted at him from the minute he had picked him up. The more Cal shouted, the more frightened Angelo had become and the more he denied his actions.

That night I realised that Angelo loved his Dad, but was also frightened of him. I reassured Angelo that whatever he had or had not done that night, he did not deserve to be screamed at the way his Dad had done. I made excuses for Cal's behaviour, but promised him I would never let Cal treat him like that again and I reassured him that his Dad loved him.

When Angelo finally closed his weary eyes, I left him to sleep and made my way back downstairs. I opened the window and sat on the window ledge to get some air. As I did so, it was my time to cry. I had taken all of Cal's angry energy away from Angelo, but now I had to release it out of my own body. I didn't know it then, but that night I created a strong bond between Angelo and myself. He took me at my word and whenever Cal started to behave in a way that Angelo couldn't handle, he would come to me and say,

"Daddy is being mean to me." When I heard those words I had to stand up and protect Angelo from his own father.

The following morning I had to leave early for a business meeting, but I was worried about how Cal would treat Angelo. I didn't know what time Cal had got in that night, but it had to have been late. Before I left, I went into his room and woke him up; I had to explain to him in a way he would understand that he could not shout at Angelo that way. I told him how I had held Angelo for an hour before he had stopped shaking and I bravely said that what he'd done the previous night would count as abuse. Also, that he could not take his anger at Nikita out on his 9-year-old son. I went on to say that in the same way that Cal did not deserve to be beaten up, no matter what Angelo had done, he did not deserve to be treated the way Cal had treated him the previous night. I warned him that Angelo would become afraid of him if he continued in this way and I suggested that he apologise to Angelo.

Surprisingly Cal listened to me. I finally shared with him a rule that I had learned when I first started to teach, 'never threaten a child with any consequence you are not prepared to carry out'.

Never threaten a child with any consequence you are not prepared to carry out

Cal didn't exactly apologise to Angelo, but he let go of his anger from the previous night. I was increasingly becoming concerned about the children. Cal would constantly call their Mum bad names in front of them, he would complain about her to his friends, but he did it when the children were in the room. His mood could switch in seconds. One minute he was laughing with his children the next he was shouting at them. Also, their growing love for my dogs was making the situation worse. Chiara was drawn to Gypsy my old collie as she would lie on the floor next to her and stroke her for hours. If Gypsy was asleep, she would take a small cushion and lie it under Gypsy's head. It was so lovely to see Gypsy getting some attention, as she was often over-shadowed by Bollie, who was ultimately a dog version of Angelo. She was full of energy, she wanted to run and play and she wanted to be fussed and loved. Angelo and Bollie became inseparable. He would pick her up and turn her upside down. He would climb trees with her and play for hours with sticks in the garden.

Sometimes a dog can be the friend a child needs

Bollie was fast becoming the friend that Angelo needed at this point in his life. She loved him unconditionally and wanted no more than some time with him. She greeted him with love and enthusiasm every time she saw him, and would curl up with him whenever he watched the television. It made my heart sing to see the bond growing between them, but sadly all this bonding between boy and dog made things worse with Cal.

Cal started to complain that the house smelt of dogs. He made me get my 2 settees that we had put in the kitchen, professionally cleaned, but within 3 weeks of them being cleaned he was complaining again that they smelled. He went so far as to say people at work could smell dog on his clothes! Every time the children touched the dogs he told them to wash their hands and to reinforce this he would show them photographs of people who had caught skin diseases from dogs.

Then there were the dogs themselves, every time I left the room he would lock Bollie in the utility room. It was literally, the more Angelo loved Bollie, the more Cal hated her. Bless her, for many months she continued to try to be Cal's friend, she would wag her tail hopefully as he walked into a room. It was only when he started to be horrible to me that she stopped trying. At this point in my story the children loved to be with the dogs, but I was getting more upset about Cal's daily verbal complaints about my little dog.

Before Cal had come back into my life, I had made a list of deal breakers for any future relationship that I might be in. Top of my list was MUST LOVE DOGS. When I had last lived with Cal we had 4 dogs. I thought he loved dogs, but 10 years without a dog had changed him. He clearly was not a dog lover now. We lived opposite a beautiful common and every day I walked the dogs, often with children who would come with me, but in the whole year that I lived at Cal's house, he only joined us once.

This wasn't quite the romantic picture I had visualised when I was single. I wanted to be with a man who wanted to walk hand-in-hand with me in nature, a man who would love walking the dogs and happily do it when I wasn't there. Now I seemed to be in a relationship with a man who wanted me to help with his children, who had made me an unpaid Nanny for his children and yet a man who did not help me out with my dogs.

Furthermore, my poor cat was living in my office, not the house. Now, in fairness, my office was a huge space above the triple garage. It was large enough to take my lounge furniture as well as the office furniture and came complete with kitchenette and shower room. So, my cat Minstrel was comfortable enough, but he missed out on human company. It was becoming clear that what I thought I had signed up for with Cal, was not the reality I was experiencing.

Chapter 33: The Beginning of the End

Apart from the dogs and the amount of time that I was taking care of the children, there was another issue brewing between us. I had made the decision to sell my land where my horses had been kept.

As I previously mentioned, I had a buyer for this land and before I had even moved into Cal's, we had agreed on a price. Now Cal needed money to pay Nikita as part of his divorce settlement so that he didn't have to sell his house. He said it was because he didn't want the children to lose their home, but I know Cal, his decision was not about the children.

For as long as I could remember, Cal's house had been a status symbol for him. He needed to live in a house that said he was successful and this house had proven to be no different. Personally, I didn't like the house. It wasn't warm and friendly but it had potential. However, it did come complete with a swimming pool and a cinema room, and despite being called The Little House, it was the largest house in the area. So, Cal's house was his castle and he would do anything to keep it.

At this point in time he had borrowed money from his brother and had sold his Ferrari to pay off Nikita, but he still needed more. I'd agreed to help him out but until the day he was in court discussing finances with Nikita, I hadn't realised just how much of my money he wanted to borrow. He telephoned me during a break in proceedings to ask when the sale would go through. I said I hoped by the end of April. He pushed me hard for a date and as he pushed me it dawned on me that he was committing all the money from the sale of my land to his second ex-wife, all £200,000 of it; I told him he couldn't have it all.

I'd borrowed £10,000 from a friend on the grounds that she would get it back as soon as the sale went through and I intended to honour that promise.

"Can't she wait?" he said, heartlessly.

"No, she cannot. I gave my word and I intend to honour it." I replied. Regardless of what I said, on that day in court he promised to pay Nikita all my £200,000 by the end of April. I know, I can hear you thinking, is she mad? Of all that happened over these few months committing to lend Cal such a large amount of money was stupidity of the highest form and somewhere deep down inside I knew it.

As the sale of my land hit one delaying problem after another, Cal started to get angry with me until one evening he stormed into my office demanding to know when the money would come through, and reminding me that he was late on his payment to Nikita because of me.

There was no gratitude at what I was doing for him, just anger that it was taking so long. I swear the universe was trying to give me some time to come to my senses, but it didn't happen. That night I got angry too. I told him in no uncertain terms that he had no right to treat me the way he was. I reminded him he should be grateful that I was loaning him the money and that the sale was out of my hands. I couldn't make it happen any quicker than it was going now.

I cannot say he took on board what I was saying, but he stopped shouting at me and left my office. That night I started to feel sick about lending him the money and as the sale got closer, the feelings of nausea increased. I wanted to keep the money but I had made a promise to Cal and he had made a promise to a Judge. If I didn't honour my promise, Cal couldn't honour his. I felt trapped. I know now that it was a trap of my own making and even at that point I could have got out of it, but I couldn't see that at the time.

Listen to your intuition

My intuition was screaming at me, but I wrongly thought I had to honour my promise. It was such a shame that Cal would not honour his promise to sign whatever agreement I wanted regarding the loan. He said whatever he had to in order to get me to loan him £170,000. Since the payment was very late, when I eventually got the money from the sale in June, Cal asked me to transfer it directly to Nikita which I did in four separate payments. My fate was sealed.

Once Nikita had the money, Cal started to take advantage of our situation. He would work away for 3 or 4 days when the children were with us and when he was home, he would be out late at night playing his guitar leaving me to take care of his children. Worse still, he was arriving home so late, 3 or 4 o'clock in the morning, that the following day he would have a migraine and be good for nothing except that is, taking the children to school of course. No matter what else he did, he always took the kids to school and picked them up when he was home. He needed people to think he was a good father, but it was becoming glaringly obvious to me that he wasn't.

I'm not sure Cal could really help it, I had thought in years gone by that he seemed to have no empathy for others. Cal's life was about him and no one else and it had always been that way. I had hoped the birth of his children would have changed that, but it seemed not. When he was with other people he would praise his children, but when he was with them he didn't really see them. He had no understand of their daily needs, to the point where he could even forget about their dinner if he was already focused on something of his own.

Cal had no instinct when it came to his children and could upset them without even understanding why. Frequently he would mess up the routines I had put in place for them just because he wanted to be with them and he never seemed to understand that they needed their sleep. In fact, one night I can remember trying to get the children up to bed, they were 9 and 7 at the time and it had gone past 8 o'clock. Cal wanted their company so he delayed bedtime and when he eventually took them up, he started playing music with Angelo in his bedroom. Angelo is a brilliant drummer and had a drum kit in his bedroom. Before I knew it, Angelo was on drums, Cal was playing guitar and loud music was blaring out of the huge speakers in his room. This was not the relaxing bedtime routine I had worked so hard to achieve; this was a man who put his own needs ahead of his children's.

It wasn't the only time either; one day I left Cal in charge of the children but I deliberately didn't leave any food for dinner. Before I left to go on my speed awareness course, I told him he would have to get something in for the children's dinner before he picked them up from school. At 6pm as I came out of the course I phoned to say I'd finished and was on my way home. I duly asked what had the children eaten for their dinner, only to be told that they hadn't had any yet. He said he hadn't had time to go out shopping, but that he would go out once he'd put the phone down.

I let him go, but I was aghast. It had gone 6 o'clock and not only had he not fed his own children, he hadn't even bought any food to feed them. Not surprisingly when I got home an hour later, they were all watching a film and eating take-out pizza. I know Cal loves his children but he was not able to take responsibility for them.

To my mind, there was something wrong with him, he couldn't empathise with anyone. He had no idea what his children needed and that worried me. In the meantime, he was telling anyone who would listen how he was a great Dad and Nikita was a terrible Mum. The really worrying thing about this was that he was so charming around everyone, people around him believed what he said.

He was damaging his children by his behaviour and letting them down with his lack of understanding.

However, because he couldn't see it, he would never ask for help. Help that is for himself, he was more than happy for me to be the free help to look after his children while he went out to work, or out to play his guitar to relieve his stress. It was becoming an untenable situation.

More cracks started to appear in our relationship and when the children were at their Mum's he started 'working away' all week. It got to the point where Cal was living alternate weeks in the house, like his children, and I knew this could not continue.

I loved the children but this was not my life. I made a decision. I needed to end my romantic relationship with Cal and then talk to him about how we could make this situation work until he paid me back the money he owed me and I could leave. I thought we could remain friends, but I had no idea how he was about to treat me.

There was no reason why it had to get nasty... but it did.

Things came to a head the weekend beginning Friday 2nd September. Angelo was poorly and Cal had little patience in allowing him to stay at home and quietly let his body heal. So we all went to the outdoor market as usual on the Saturday morning and Angelo's drum teacher joined us for coffee. As we sat on the communal benches, an old lady joined us with her Chihuahua dog. Now, these are not my favourite breed of dog but it had curled up on this lady's knee and was causing no harm to anyone. Cal, however, was rude to the lady about her dog and naturally I was horrified. Why would he hurt a little old lady for no reason? That dog may have been her only friend in the world.

When the lady had gone, I challenged him as to why he would be so mean and he told me to shut up. It wasn't the only time he would tell me to shut up that weekend either; the following day as we were coming out of John Lewis car park and he was driving on the wrong side of the road, I asked him to move over and yet again, his response was to tell me to shut up.

When we arrived home, he sat at the table and Gypsy lay down underneath. Somehow, he got his chair caught up with Gypsy's paw and he started to moan about my 'bloody' dogs. I'd had enough. I moved my dogs up to the office and went back to the kitchen to join Cal and the children for dinner.

Later, Cal tried to pick a fight with me. I wouldn't argue in front of the children but after they were in bed we had a heated discussion. I tried to keep things calm, but he just wanted me to know how disgusting my dogs were. He sat cross legged with arms folded on the settee in the kitchen; it was a posture I had seen once before and I knew I was in trouble.

He talked about my dogs and Bollie in particular, however hard I tried he wasn't hearing what I was trying to say, he just wanted me to agree with him that my dogs were disgusting. It seemed to him that all our problems boiled down to the fact that my dogs were disgusting and he kept saying the words over and over. I tried to say it didn't matter what he thought about my dogs as it was clear we had a difference of opinion that could not be resolved. Then I said it;

"We need to go back to just being friends." There, I had done it, I had ended our romantic relationship. It was the end of all my hopes of what could be. I wanted to work out a way forwards but he didn't hear me. He was still stuck on disgusting dogs and in the end, I realised, I just couldn't talk to him. It appeared he had never wanted a relationship with me in the first place, so without realising it, I had just let him off the hook.

Cal came and went as he pleased from that moment on. It was a long, intense week that followed, as Cal continued to expect me to look after the children when he wasn't around. Once the children were safely back with their Mum the following weekend, I let rip at him. I couldn't help it. Once I'd started to tell him all the things that were wrong about the way he treated his children, I couldn't stop.

I went on to the way he had treated me when we got divorced. I told him to stop playing the victim and moaning about what Nikita had done. I reminded him that everything she had done; the lies, the relationship with a younger person, sleeping with someone else while she was still married to him. All of it, he had already done to me. The only difference was that she had asked for a divorce before she'd done any of it. At first, he argued vehemently with me, but eventually he went quiet and whispered,

"I love my kids. I would do anything for them."

"No, you won't," I replied, "you won't do the one thing that they need you to do."

"What's that?" he asked.

"Get help with your anger," I replied.

He looked crestfallen. All his fight was gone. I felt awful for hurting him with my words, but I knew I needed to speak my truth. I only hoped it would make a difference. It didn't.

Cal continued to come and go as he pleased and often left me in charge of the children. On the 21st of September he appeared in court with Nikita to sort out the custody arrangements with the children. To this point, they had been spending a week at their Mum's and a week at their Dad's and the court had to decide if these arrangements could become permanent. The best Cal could hope for was to get equal custody of his children and typical Cal, he got it.

When he arrived home, I was just taking the children to Angelo's football practice so Cal jumped in the car with us. As we drove to the practice ground he told me he had won. Nikita had lost on all three accounts; she couldn't have sole custody of her children, she couldn't take the children out of the country for longer than 2 weeks and she didn't get any more maintenance money for the children. Even as he started to talk, I tried to end the conversation.

"It wasn't about winning Cal, it was about what was best for the children." I was concerned that the children were sitting in the back of the car listening to his victory speech. He didn't understand how hurtful it was. At that moment, his brother phoned so he went through the whole thing again with him. Angelo and Chiara heard all of it.

The following day, I had a busy day helping a colleague launch a new networking group. As I walked in the door at 5pm, Cal walked out to go to a band rehearsal and yet again left the children with me. He made some passing comment as he left about how he would send flowers to the children's headmistress to say 'thank you' for her support. I should have known she would never get the flowers, but I was furious at that point that he never once thought to thank me!

The children had told the lady from Children's Services that they were happy at their Dad's, but I knew that was because I provided some stability for them. The Headmistress had even commented on how much better Angelo was doing since I'd arrived.

Since I had moved in with Cal, I hadn't worked with a single client, it was almost impossible to do. I would normally mentor children after school, or on Saturday, but every other week I was taking care of Cal's children and on the few occasions that I had booked work related meetings, Cal would suddenly tell me he was working and I needed to look after the kids. I know I could have said no, but he was playing Russian roulette with his children and I couldn't let them down. The relationship between Cal and I got increasingly worse. I tried to talk to him about a way forwards, but he wouldn't talk to me. I was banging my head against a brick wall.

On Sunday the 9th October the next bomb was dropped on me. Cal came home around 9pm and I had just sat down and put the TV on. When he walked in I paused the program I was watching, so we could talk, he exchanged pleasantries and then said to watch the program if I wanted to.

He refused to sit down on the settee as he claimed it still stank of dogs, so he chose to sit on a hard wooden chair instead. I resumed the program and for an hour we sat in an uncomfortable silence. At the end of the hour Cal got up to go to bed, he said good night and I told him I wouldn't be far behind him.

As Cal went upstairs I took my dogs outside for their last pee before bedtime. As I came back through the front door I heard Cal speaking on the phone to someone and he was talking about me. I heard him say,

"Yes, I got home and she was just sitting on the settee watching the TV as always." I couldn't believe what I was hearing.

He was moaning about me to some other woman. I had just spent over 12 months helping him, stupidly making his drama my drama and I had moved across the country to live with him. I had taken care of his children and supported him. Hell, I had even driven the children to and from Nikita's when he couldn't be near her without starting an argument. I had helped him and helped his children. In the bad times, I had protected his children from him and I'd put my own work to one side. I had even loaned him all the money I had and now instead of being grateful, he was moaning about me to someone else. How the hell did I become public enemy number one? I saw red. I put the dogs safely into the utility room and then rushed into Cal's bedroom.

"Whoever she is, put the phone down right now and have the courage to say to my face what you have just said to her."

His first reaction, as always, was to deny everything. I raised my voice. I'd had enough of this selfish man.

"Stop lying to me. I heard you." Eventually he promised to call the woman back and he looked at me defiantly before admitting he was now in a relationship with someone else. Of course he was, Cal could never be on his own, he always went from one women to the next.

I had taken over from his Mum, he overlapped me with Nikita, he then got back together with me before Nikita left and now he'd gotten from me what he needed, he was onto his next conquest. Every time he had played the victim to reel in the next woman. I'd fallen for it after knowing him for 40 years, so I couldn't blame the new lady in his life. I was furious.

He had every right to be in a new relationship. After all, it had been me who had taken our relationship back to friendship, although friendship was not the way I would describe it now. Yet, somehow, this felt like déjà vu, it felt like my divorce all over again. We argued for some time before he said,

"I want you to leave." He'd had it all worked out. What he wanted me to do was move out so he could move his new girlfriend in. He said I could rent a little house locally and he would pay me to come back and take care of his kids. After all he said, it was about time I started earning some money. Evidently, I had sponged off him for long enough!

Words failed me at that point. After all I had done for this man, this was how he was going to treat me. The penny dropped. He didn't want a relationship with me; he had used me to get equal custody of his kids and to not have to sell his house. Now the child arrangements were legal, and he had all my money, he didn't want me in his house anymore.

I didn't sleep that night. I felt such a fool and I felt I owed Nikita a huge apology. Without me being at Cal's, she would probably have stood a good chance of getting sole custody of her children. Since my first tentative meeting with Nikita after I took the children home, our relationship had grown. We'd been civilised to start with, to show the children how two human beings should behave towards each other, but as the weeks had gone by it had gotten easier to talk to each other. I wasn't so sure this would be an easy conversation though: I text her.

"I am so sorry Nikita. Cal has just used me to get what he wants. Now he has asked me to leave! Can we talk?"

She replied immediately and we arranged to meet at her rented house the following day. I felt so bad when I got to her door, but she made coffee and we sat down to talk. I apologised for falling for his charm. I told her all the things that had happened, how I was worried that he didn't know how to look after his own kids. Starting with his selfish behaviour to his lack of understanding of their needs, I started to share it all with Nikita. As she began to cry I thought what I was saying was upsetting her. Again I apologised, but she looked at me and said,

"Apart from my friend Sarah, you are the only one who believes me that he is not a good Dad. That's why I'm crying. It's just a relief to know someone else believes me and knows what he is like."

We hugged. We cried. We talked for five hours that day. We exchanged stories and experiences; the isolation, the constant criticism, the anger, the blame for everything that ever went wrong, the lack of emotional connection, the lack of support, we both had the same experience of being married to a narcissistic man. Speaking it out loud was both difficult and healing. We laughed together and cried some more. We remembered tough times; Cal had thrown plates at Nikita, and empty wine bottles at me. Not at our bodies, but at our feet. The broken glass or pottery didn't hurt us but his actions were intimidating. His anger was intimidating. The manipulation, the constant need to beat everyone and everything, the constant reminder that he earned the money.

That afternoon Nikita and I became good friends. Only we would ever know what it was truly like to live with this man who charmed the socks off people, but who was an emotional bully behind closed doors. Cal might have left me for Nikita, but now Nikita and I were allies. A strange thing happened at some point during that talk with Nikita. The love I had always had in my heart for Cal, the love I'd carried for him since I was 14 just stopped. It was like someone had turned off a switch in my heart.

Chapter 34: Standing My Ground

As I drove back to Cal's, I could feel a huge shift. It was a good thing but it felt like a huge void around me, like the floor had just disappeared from beneath me.

Fortunately, Cal was away for a few days so I had some time to collect my thoughts and try to decide what to do next. He arrived home the following Friday in time to pick the children up from school, but he was in a foul mood again and I felt bad that the children were once more living in a war zone. Cal worked Saturday, Sunday, Monday and Tuesday and despite all that was going on, he expected me to take care of his children. When he was home he took his bad mood out on the kids; Angelo got shouted at for being clumsy and hurting himself and Cal snatched the iPad off Chiara when she was playing a maths game.

When Cal arrived home from work at 8.30 on Tuesday evening, he first went upstairs to say goodnight to the children. He then came into the kitchen and found Bollie sitting on the settee with me. Despite the children being in the house, he screamed at me and told me to get the dog off the settee. I refused. I had played his game for long enough, lived by his rules and look where that had got me. This was my dog, on my settee and as far as I was concerned, she had my permission to be there. It was time for me to start standing up for myself, instead of accepting that while I lived in Cal's house I would be his verbal punch bag.

He threatened to throw the settee out, then he threatened to phone the police to throw me out. After all, this wasn't my house, and I wasn't sure if he could do that or not, but I hid my fears and stood my ground. The argument escalated. I pointed out that I had clocked up 44 hours over the previous 4 days looking after his children and I suggested that now we weren't in any sort of relationship he should start to pay me, just as he had offered to do when he wanted me to live locally. He saw red, he said he wasn't going to pay me anything while I was living for free in his house.

The following day he took me off parenting duty. With no thought for his children, he tried to put a distance between them and me. After school neither of the children came up to my office to see me which was very unusual. I felt sad, but accepted that these were not my kids.

At 5pm I heard his van leave and they didn't come back home until 7.30pm. As Chiara came into the kitchen, she asked me if she could have something to eat. I asked what had she eaten for dinner, but she just gave me a pleading look that said she hadn't had any anything to eat yet.

Cal rushed into the kitchen behind her with bags of pasta in his hand. It seemed he had taken the children to parents evening and then straight to Angelo's football practice afterwards. In all that time, they hadn't had anything to eat.

He could have left them with me when he went to Parents evening. I could have fed them and then he could have picked them up to go to football, but no, Cal put his needs before his children's. At 7.35 he started to cook dinner for the children. He put the plates of steaming pasta on the table while Chiara was talking to me. He kept telling her to stop talking and eat, but she said it was too hot, still he kept pushing her. Angelo sat quietly and ate but once he had got halfway through, he asked if he could leave the rest because he was full. Cal had given him a larger bowl than Chiara, so I said yes. Just as I was about to pick up Angelo's plate, Cal said he couldn't leave the table until he'd finished all of it. He shouted at Angelo until Angelo cried.

As Cal put the children to bed Angelo still had tears in his eyes and it wasn't long before I could hear Chiara crying too. My heart went out to them, this man didn't deserve to have such beautiful children. He then came back into the kitchen, turned half the lights off and told me I could only use the electricity when I contributed to the costs. With that he left to go and play his guitar. It seemed I was off parenting duties unless he wanted to go out!!

Turning the lights off in the room I was sitting in would become a common pattern of behaviour for him in the weeks and months that followed. He also turned the radiators off in the house and my office a week at a time when he went to stay with his new girlfriend. He left the underfloor heating on in the kitchen, but the rest of the house soon became extremely cold especially my bedroom. I had to wear base layers from my mountain climbing experience to keep warm and I slept in my pyjamas, bed socks, and dressing gown under a duvet and 2 blankets.

Cal's behaviour became more and more erratic. He stopped my access to his Netflix account and unplugged the Sky box so I couldn't watch the TV. You would think it was an easy job to reconnect but Cal had a complicated hub of cables which I'm sure would not pass a safety test.

I was quite pleased with myself for working out how to reconnect the dish although I always disconnected it again before he came home. The following year he got a new Sky dish which got the better of me and I couldn't work out how to get that reconnected. As well as the Sky dish and Netflix's channel, Cal also disconnected the main telephone line although I had never used it without his permission anyway.

One evening I went to Nikita's far a last-minute drink. I didn't leave the house until 8.15 and got back just before midnight. As I walked in the dark to the utility room where the dogs were, my foot kicked something. The children had been in the house with me earlier, as I was looking after them for Nikita, so I thought I must have kicked a toy.

As I approached the utility room I could see the light shining around the door. This was odd as the lights were set to turn off on the hour every hour after a certain time at night. I had discovered this the hard way one evening when I was swimming in the pool! As I opened the door to let the dogs out, I looked down and realised that what I had kicked was a mouse trap. It was complete with freshly killed mouse, but if I hadn't kicked it Bollie would have run straight into it as she came out of the utility room. I was shaking. Had things really got so bad that Cal had set a mouse trap to hurt my dog? He would know that the quickest way to get me out of his house was to threaten my animals.

Cal was supposed to be miles away at Petra's (the new girlfriend). Could he really have got someone to do this? I felt afraid for my dogs and unnerved to think that someone was watching me. This incident really shook me up, but I didn't say anything to Cal for a long time. When I did he suggested that the mousetrap had been in the space above the kitchen ceiling. He reckoned that when the mouse had got caught the trap had somehow jumped and fallen out of a hole in the ceiling. It seemed like a huge coincidence to me that a mouse trap would fall through a hole in the ceiling right at this time.

When I eventually challenged Cal over this incident, he did what I expected him to do. He accused me of going crazy. This was his plan, to make people believe I was having some sort of breakdown and acting in a crazy way. This made him the victim of my craziness, but it wasn't true, I wasn't going crazy. No matter how much he denied all the things he was doing, I knew he was deliberately being cruel to me. Instead of being grateful and coming to an agreement over the money he owed me, he was making my life hell in his house to try and force me out.

As Cal was making life in the house as difficult as possible, I decided to spend as much time as I could in my office. I hoped that this would mean life would be easier for the children when they were in the house. I had a television stored in one of Cal's garages together with some more of my stuff. I couldn't get a signal for the TV but I could attach my DVD player and watch a nice film which would be good for me on so many levels. I carried the TV and DVD player up the stairs to my office and I also found some Christmas lights to put up around the shelving unit. I made the office quite cosy and would happily sit up there in the evenings with my dogs and cat. I quite liked escaping up there, I was surrounded by my stuff, my own energy and words of inspiration and pictures that Chiara had done for me.

One day I was working in my office when Cal stormed in accusing me of having sent an anonymous email to his new girlfriend, Petra. He was raging about what I had written in this email and yet I had absolutely no idea what he was talking about. His girlfriend had spent the night in Cal's house the previous night, so if I had wanted to say something to her, I would have done so there and then.

I had said my piece to Petra some weeks previously when Cal had pushed his phone into my hand. I think he wanted her to give me a piece of her mind, but I didn't give her chance to speak. I told her I was speaking to her as one women to another, I then warned her that charming Cal was only the tip of the iceberg, and that she wouldn't know who he really was until she lived with him. I went on to say that he was both narcissist and misogynistic. I told her not to leave him in charge of her son as he wasn't responsible enough to take care of him and that I knew she wouldn't believe me at that moment , but when the doubts started to enter her head, I asked her to please remember what I had said. With that, I handed the phone back to Cal and I was done.

What decisions this woman made after that were hers to make. As far as an email was concerned, firstly, I didn't know how to send an anonymous email and secondly, if I had something to say, I would own it. It didn't matter what I said, Cal was livid. He was so angry he frightened me. Repeatedly I said I had no idea what he was talking about. He referred to things that had been said in the email as if I knew. He said everyone knew it was from me, and that I may not have had the guts to sign it but it was my language.

For a moment, he changed tactics and said if I hadn't done it, then Nikita and her friend had. They must have recorded my words and then used them to make it look like the email was from me. Interestingly, at no time would he show me the email. It would take many more months before I would get to see it, but the email had done its job. He had scared me with his anger and put doubts in my head about my friendship with Nikita. I text first Nikita and then her friend, but both of them denied knowing anything about this email. Neither of them seemed interested, but one of them said to me,

"Who benefits from this email?" Not me, that was for sure. The email had made my life even worse than it was. It became Cal's excuse for his every bad word and action against me. I didn't want his relationship with Petra to end because if it did, he would be home more often. It didn't benefit Nikita either because at this point, Nikita was looking after her children 80% of the time. Cal being away more often was giving Nikita reason to go back to court and challenge the child arrangements.

The only person it seemed to benefit at all was Cal. It gave him a reason to tell people how nasty I was, a reason for Petra to feel sorry for him. For a short-time it put doubts in my head about how genuine Nikita's friendship was with me, and Cal hated that Nikita and I had become friends. He always accused me of plotting against him with her.

Just as I was beginning to think that the email only had power if we kept talking about it, Cal's brother, Teo, phoned me. He was also angry with me about something that had been written in the email about his parents. Somehow, Cal had persuaded him that I had written the email, but this time I got angry, I'd had enough. I hadn't written it, I didn't know what was in it and I didn't care. He said whoever had written it was cruel and I replied that the only cruel person I could see at that moment was his brother Cal. He said over and over that if I didn't write it then I needed to know who had. Eventually I asked him outright;

"Teo, you have known me since you were 6 years old, do you really think I wrote this email?" If his answer had been yes, I was ready to walk away from our friendship, and from a relationship that meant a great deal to me.

Fortunately, his answer was no. He asked me why Cal and I couldn't talk. I told him I had tried and every time I did, his brother just screamed at me. He asked me to try one more time and I refused.

"You are asking me to make friends with a man who is bullying me every day, a man who I helped when he was at rock bottom and who is repaying me by trying to throw me out on the street, without paying me a penny of the money I loaned to him, so that he can move his new girlfriend into his house. I am not being cruel or mean to this man, but I will not treat him as a friend, I will not leave without what is rightfully mine. Apart from that I am done with him." As I said the words I knew they were true. The shift had taken place when I had that long talk with Nikita but now the shift was complete. I no longer felt love or hate for this man. All I could see was a manipulative bully and I was done with him.

Cal continued to find excuses to scream at me. Anything from my allowing Nikita to have the children's scooters so they could go to the scooter park with their friends, to me telling the children he had asked me to move out. In the latter case I was very careful not to say anything bad about Cal, but I had promised the children I would be honest with them, so I simply said to them that Daddy didn't want to live with my dog Bollie anymore and so we would have to leave.

The children were not stupid. Chiara said, "That's not fair, Daddy was nasty to Mummy and she had to leave and now he is being nasty to you and you have to leave." Angelo followed with,

"I think Daddy is crazy!" Out of the mouth of babes!

Although I tried to talk to Cal about a repayment plan for my money, he would not agree to anything. He wanted me to move out with £30,000 and a promise that he would repay the rest when he could. I wanted £50,000 and a written agreement to pay the rest. I had employed a solicitor to draw up a repayment plan and Cal had originally agreed to pay for this solicitor. However, as Cal got increasingly nasty, I realised that I needed someone in my corner to protect me. Whenever I talked to Cal about money, he always ended up screaming at me. He said the same stuff over and over; I was living in his house and he wanted me out. I was using him and that I was lazy. I expected him to pay for everything and I hadn't ever said thank you and finally, that he hadn't loved me for years. It was hard to hear.

I didn't love him anymore either, but it was tough to know that someone I had cared for, for so many years, wanted me out on the streets with no assurance that he would repay me all the money that he owed me.

One strange consequence of the anonymous email incident was that Petra phoned me. It seemed she had told Cal she wanted to talk to me and he had happily handed my telephone number over to her. As I answered the phone she said,

"Karen, its Petra." I told her just as I had told Cal, I had no idea what was in the email because I hadn't written it, and if I had something to say to her I would own my words and say it to her face.

Strangely, what followed was quite a civilised conversation for over an hour. I told her my truth, but said I understood that she had to make her own choice. I warned her that I could see Cal getting jealous over her relationship with her only son and that could cause problems. She gave little away. She was hung up on knowing that my relationship with Cal was over by September 8th. Clearly that was the first time he had slept with her.

I explained to Petra that Cal had not made the decision but that I had; I have no idea if she believed me. To be honest I didn't care. I can remember her saying to me,

"But I love him," and my response fell from my lips before I had time to think.

"We have all been there. I loved him for 40 years until a few weeks ago. Not any more though. Now I see him for who he truly is." The conversation ended quite civilly because she had to go and pick her son up from school.

I knew she was upset by the email, but she also loved him, so I knew that no matter what she'd said to me, Cal could work his way back into her good books. The difference was I could now see very clearly how he had manipulated people, but she still saw him through a veil of love so she was not aware of the manipulation.

If she stayed with him, I knew she was walking into a load of heartache, but if that was the path she'd chosen it was her journey and not my responsibility.

Knowing what *was* my responsibility was fast becoming one of the lessons I was learning throughout this horrible ordeal. I was not responsible for anyone but me, not for Cal or Petra, or Nikita, not even for Angelo and Chiara. It was time to look after me and make me the main priority. Besides, even if I wanted to help Nikita and the children, I had to feel strong and that would only happen if I took care of me first.

It is not selfish to take care of our own needs first. It is essential to do so

I wasn't feeling anything near strong; I felt wobbly and constantly on a state of high alert. Anxiety spread throughout my body from the minute I opened my eyes and I was starting to feel afraid of Cal and what he might be capable of. He hadn't been easy to live with when I was married to him, but we'd had some good times in those days because I'd always jumped through his hoops. Now I was starting to stand up to him and it was bringing the absolute worst of his shadow side to the surface. My new solicitor had made it very clear that the next time I felt scared, I must phone the police. It wasn't long before that situation arose.

Cal had somehow turned the heat off in my office. It was so cold up there, but I suddenly remembered that I had two oil heaters stored in the garage below. I quickly fetched the heaters and plugged the first one in near my desk.

I had just got back up to the office with the second heater when Cal yet again stormed into the office. I had forgotten that he had an app on his phone that showed him the power usage for the house. As soon as I had plugged the heater in, his phone had notified him of what I'd done.

He was furious and out of control. He saw the heater that had not been plugged in and picked it up. As he screamed at me, he swung the heater around the room. After more verbal abuse, he left the office and headed back down to the garage. I unplugged the second heater and locked the door to keep myself safe. I deliberately left the key in the door so he couldn't open it from the outside. I was shaking badly. I wanted to cry but I held onto the tears.

He came back up to the office and screamed at me to open the door; I refused to until he calmed down.

Before I knew it, he had somehow opened the door even with my key in it. He took hold of my keys and took the office key and the garage door key. He was screaming at me all the time, telling me I had to empty the office of all my stuff because he was not paying to heat and light it for me. He took the heater and as he swung it he caught the corner on the settee and a wheel fell off. As he opened the door to leave, Bollie tried to run out of the door, I put my foot out to stop her but instead caught Cal's leg.

He accused me of kicking him and threatened to get me charged with assault. I've never been so scared in my life. As he left the office I sat down and sobbed. How could this man do this to me? Why was he so cruel to me when all I had tried to do was help him? How would I cope if I couldn't get to the sanctuary of my office? What would happen to my cat? I first phoned my solicitor who didn't answer, so I then phoned my good friend Mini. She was worried for my safety and advised me to phone the police. I promised her I would but it took all my courage to do so.

The police were very sympathetic and offered to send someone round, but as it turned out there was a big accident on the motorway that night and there was no one free to come to me. It was very late by the time they phoned me back and I was exhausted.

I had stayed in the office waiting for Cal to go to bed as I wasn't sure where to sleep. I was frightened that if I went to bed in the house, Cal would come and lock all my stuff including my cat into the office. But, I didn't want to show him my fear, so part of me thought I should go to bed in the house. Besides which, the office was getting very cold.

As the children went to bed I saw the lights go on and off in the bedroom and eventually the house was in darkness. I assumed Cal had gone to sleep as well. I suggested to the police that arriving at the house so late was not in the best interests of the children, so they suggested I went to the station the following day.

I didn't get much sleep that night, but I was in the comfort of a bed. Chiara sneaked into my room the next morning to give me a hug and tell me she loved me.

As I came down the stairs, Cal and the children were getting ready to go to out. He must have been taking them back to Nikita's as he was moaning about the clothes they were wearing; they weren't allowed to wear anything that he'd bought them.

He reminded me to get my stuff out of the office. I said 'fine', but that would include the cat as I couldn't leave him in the office. He then turned and said in front of the children;

"That cat is not coming in this house. If it does I will kick it out," he then looked at me and added, "and you know I mean that." I stood up to him and politely said,

"But if I cannot get into the office, he will have to come into the house." His response was that he would leave the office open. I tried to argue that only the other day he had accused me of leaving the backdoor open and he'd been upset about the safety of his stuff.

If the office was open, anyone could go up there. His response was simply, “Tough,” and with that said, he ushered the kids out of the house and was gone.

I was very nervous as I sat waiting to talk to a policeman. Would they think I was crazy? Would they think I was wasting their time? I couldn’t have been further from the truth. The police in Stroud Police Station were always very supportive. The policeman that day took down the details of the situation, said there was little he could do, but advise Cal to give me back the key and warn him that he could not bully me the way he was doing but ultimately, he impressed upon me, how important it was that every time an incident like this happened, I should have it down on record.

The policeman also said that GDASS, the Gloucester Domestic Abuse Support Service would get in touch with me. It would take another couple of incidents before I would accept the help from GDASS, but my name was now in the system and Cal had a second complaint held against him.

Once again, as it had been when Nikita had involved the police, Cal’s home had a red flag allocated to it. If I had to phone again, they would take me seriously. I felt reassured when I left the police station and my solicitor was pleased that I had been brave and registered my complaint.

Chapter 35: Getting My Power Back

Cal continued to make life difficult. He had already removed all of my furniture from his bedroom and dumped it in the hallway. He now turned the power off to the sockets in my office meaning I couldn't watch dvd's up there, I couldn't charge my laptop, I couldn't even make a cup of coffee.

He had successfully violated my safe space. The heating was on or off depending when he was home and I continued to allow the cat to come into the house when Cal was away and the office was cold. Through all this I tried to focus on work but it was impossible, I couldn't think straight and I couldn't sleep at night.

I was determined to stay to get my money back, but I wasn't sure how long I could hold out. Cal had voluntarily repaid me £2000 at the beginning of October and offered to do the same every month. I had to ask him for the money in November and I received it mid-month, but after that he refused to pay me anymore as he said I had changed the goal posts. He even sent me a text telling me he was giving me notice to vacate his house by December 24th.

At the beginning of December, the situation took another unexpected turn. I was in the office one afternoon when a car pulled up outside the house. I knew Cal was working, so I went out to see who it was. A young black lady stood at the door of the house.

"Karen, I think I need to talk to you," she said.

I had seen this girl before as she sang with Cal from time to time. I invited her up to the office. Fortunately, that day I'd had heating so we could sit and chat quite comfortably. As she apologised for what she was about to say, my heart started to beat faster. What was I about to hear now? What else could Cal have done that would upset me. What I heard next made me laugh.

It seemed that from June to September, Cal had been in a relationship with this lady too. As it turned out, she wasn't much younger than me. She did look older close up than I had originally thought, but nowhere near as old as her actual age.

If I had still loved Cal, her news would have devastated me. After all, I had only been living with Cal for a month when he started a relationship with her. All the nights he had stayed out until 3 or 4 am started to make sense. The showers that he would take before he got into bed with me. I thought it a bit strange at the time, but it never dawned on me that he was cheating on me. The Bastard. What was wrong with this man?

He had manipulated her with his lies just like he had manipulated me. He'd said no displays of public affection were allowed because of the court case. The whole thing made me giggle. Who else would come out of the wood work now?

Cal's lies were beginning to fall at his feet. His life was in freefall. Now he had another woman on the warpath. I cannot say that I was surprised by Cal's behaviour, but this lady was not me. She was incredibly upset to find out she had been part of a 'love triangle', that he had put her in a position where she had broken one of her own values. She wanted the truth. She apologised to me, but there was nothing to apologise for. Neither of us knew about the other, so neither of us was at fault.

She did say she'd started to wonder what was going on when I had arrived back at the house early one day and Cal had ushered her out of the side door. Again, I was surprised that I had not known any of this before and was very grateful that it was not revealed to me before my love for Cal had gone. We spoke for hours. She asked if I had Petra's number and surprise, surprise I did, but only because Cal had given my number to Petra. I happily gave her Petra's number and said I would let her know when Cal was home, which turned out to be the very next day.

She didn't waste any time. Once she knew Cal was home, she phoned Petra and after a brief conversation came screeching down the drive to talk to Cal. I made myself scarce by walking the dogs, but then started to worry about her, so I came home to check she was okay. I needn't have worried. Cal was trying to use his boyish charm on her, he only went into bully mode with me.

She would later tell me she was shocked at how he'd treated me. Even then I was beginning to realise his bullying tactics were very personal to me. This new 'love' revelation caused lots of trouble between Cal and Petra, but I kept out of it. Cal had some serious bridges to mend if his relationship with Petra was going to survive.

According to this new lady, Petra wasn't so keen to move in with Cal; Cal was not happy.

In the run up to Christmas I am sure Cal deliberately kept me short of money to ruin my Christmas, but a loyal friend yet again came to my rescue and loaned me some cash to see me through. I couldn't go mad, but I could buy gifts for all the children in my life.

Ironically, I spent Christmas eve with Nikita and the children, and Christmas day with Cal's brothers and sister-in-law. I had decided not to talk about Cal on Christmas day, but he became the elephant in the room and that elephant grew bigger as the day progressed. Cal's sister-in-law had been very shocked by Cal's behaviour and had been hugely supportive up to that point, now she suddenly didn't want to talk about him, even when the two of us were alone.

I felt glad I had gone but sad at how different this Christmas felt to the last. While I was away, Cal spent the holiday home alone. I must say I was surprised he wasn't with Petra but obviously, he was still in the dog house. He did start to get the Christmas tree out of its box for the children. He did all the hard bit of putting the tree together but then never decorated it, so this sad shell of a tree dominated the lounge for the whole of the festive season.

After Christmas he seemed to calm down a bit. He started to allow the children to talk to me. He stopped turning off the heat when he went away, which I was very grateful for, but he never gave me back the key to the office. I didn't share this with many people at the time, but every time I left the office I asked my Angels to watch over my cat and my belongings and neither came to any harm and nothing went missing.

Cal was not easy to talk to, but he did start to talk instead of shout. My outreach worker from GDASS warned me this was just another of the perpetrators characters coming out, but I didn't want to believe her. She had given me a book showing me all the different characteristics of a perpetrator, as she called him, and she warned me to be careful. She even pointed out that I was in the most danger on the day that I would leave; that didn't make any sense to me.

I tried to come to a deal with Cal, while my solicitor was advising me to go to court. We were having trouble getting Cal's solicitor to respond to any emails so I would talk to him, try to suggest a deal that tied in with what he had said, but each time he had a reason not to sign.

He wouldn't secure a loan in any way and it was getting frustrating. Every time we talked he would go back to him getting beaten up, or me sending the anonymous email. I tried to keep the conversation to money but it was hard. Even though he was talking instead of shouting, he still had a need for me and everyone else to know that I was the bad person in all of this.

The last time it had happened, I broke down in a meeting with the GDASS support worker, she suggested very strongly that I find a way to leave. I had no idea how

I would do that, but for the first time I was beginning to think I can't take this anymore.

In the meantime, Cal would alternate between ignoring me and whistling as he walked passed me, to criticizing my every move. I was exhausted and I'd had enough. I felt like he was winning.

Financially I had survived because I sold my second car, my beautiful red BMW Z4. It was my fun car and as I walked away from it, I felt like all the fun had ebbed from my life. On the other hand, I was proud of myself for doing what had to be done. I desperately needed the money to live off and pay my solicitors bills.

Unexpectedly Cal paid me £10,000 as a goodwill gesture. Sadly, he thought the payment was enough to get me to leave and when I didn't, he want back into bully mode. With money in my account I took a risk and booked a trip to America to attend a Neale Donald Walsh retreat on relationships. I knew there was a strong chance that Cal would change the locks while I was away, but something deep inside me said I had to go to.

I needed time away from all Cal's emotional abuse to find my strength. Before I left I got my solicitor to arrange a meeting with a Barrister. Together we agreed that the best way forwards, when I got back from America, would be to pack up my stuff and move out and then serve Cal with a demand for all the money.

I had stayed in the house believing that I had a beneficial interest in it, mainly because I'd been in a relationship with Cal when I'd moved in and I had paid the money to Nikita so Cal didn't have to sell the house.

But Cal was clever, he had covered his tracks well. Any email he had sent to me never had any form of affectionate comment on it. Somehow every text message from him on my phone mysteriously disappeared. He hadn't allowed us to show any form of affection in public because of the children and for the same reason we had separate bedrooms.

He'd had it all covered. So, when he said we were never in a relationship, it was very hard for me to prove otherwise. I knew he had slept in my bed but he would stand up in court and deny it if need be. My barrister advised that Cal could keep me in court for years fighting the beneficial interest and there was no guarantee I would win.

The better option was to serve him for full repayment of the loan which evidently I could do, because there was no agreement between us. Even with this, Cal tried to wriggle out of it by saying I had agreed to wait for repayment as he waited to sell some land in the Caribbean. Not only was this not true, he had promised money from the same sale of land to Nikita and there was no sign of the land being sold.

I went to America and had an amazing time. At the end of the retreat Neale Donald Walsh advised us how to write a book and somehow, he unlocked a key that was the beginning of this book. Despite what happened next, I couldn't stop writing my story for the next 3 months.

I was nervous when I got back to Cal's and my heart fell when I put my key in the door and it wouldn't turn. My biggest fears had come to fruition. I had travelled all the way back from America and I was locked out of the house.

Fortunately though, I wasn't locked out of the office. I was so tired I sat in the office and cried. I spoke to my solicitor who suggested Nikita may still be able to get me in as her name was still on the mortgage. However, she did suggest that what I really needed to do was move out. I would have preferred her words to be delivered a little more gently, but a dose of harsh reality was what I needed.

The following week was a whirlwind. Nikita threatened to change the locks the next day so Cal came home. He wanted to get whatever stuff I needed out of the house and then relock it. I refused to let that happen, so when I refused to move he eventually agreed I could have a backdoor key. Once he had given me the key he disappeared again until the following Monday.

I spent the whole weekend madly packing up my stuff with no idea when I would leave, or where I would go. I hoped that when he returned and saw that I was packing he would be happy. No such luck. I should have listened to the GDASS lady. He was the angriest I had ever seen him.

When he returned on the Monday evening, I was in the kitchen surrounded by boxes. I was greeted with,

"What are you doing in here?" A bit surprised at his reaction, I told him I was packing. He didn't react well. He screamed at me that he wanted me out and that all my stuff would be going out of his house on Wednesday. I asked him where he would put it and his reply was 'in the office'. I knew it wouldn't all fit in there and I said as much. He told me he didn't care, and if it didn't fit in the office he would leave it outside on the driveway. I wasn't sure if he was bluffing. After all, when he had threatened to move my bedroom furniture, he had done it the next day, but he also had a habit of threatening me to gain control of the situation. I couldn't take the risk.

The next day I phoned Anna and asked her what I should do. Anna is great in a crisis. She is level headed and can put emotion to one side and see clearly a course of action. This is what she suggested.

- See if the auction house will store your oak furniture prior to selling it.
- Find a storage unit.
- Find a man with a van.
- See if you have any other friends with a van.
- Find somewhere for you, the dogs and the cat to go.

This friend of mine had no coaching experience, but she held me accountable by telling me to text her each time I had ticked a task off my list. It amazed me at how easy it was to do all these things. Whenever I shared my circumstances, people were falling over themselves to help me. It was a very humbling experience.

By 6pm on Tuesday, I had 2 men and a van, and a friend with a van all arriving the next day. I had a storage unit booked and an agreement from the local auction house to take all my oak furniture. I wouldn't get much for it in a sale, but it all reminded me of Cal and it had to go. The auction house was also saving me storage costs by storing it for me.

Finally, Nikita had offered me a roof over my head for the next couple of weeks. She was away with the girls for a long weekend and then the second week she was away with the children. I could have her house to myself for the next 2 weeks. Now all I had to do was stay up and finish the packing!

The next couple of days were exhausting. Ironically Cal was nowhere to be seen on Wednesday. Clearly, he had been bluffing, but I couldn't have known that. The men with the van were lovely and very supportive but my friend, Gibby, was delayed and didn't arrive with her van until 3pm. We were very tight for time to get to the storage unit by 4.15 so we sat down, had a cup of tea and came up with a new plan. The men were free the following day as well, so they would continue to load the van until 5pm and then come back the next day. Gibby and I would go over to Nikita's to look after the children for a couple of hours and then continue to pack when we got back. The couple of hours at Nikita's was a lovely diversion and some much needed light relief, but when we got back to Cal's his van was in the drive. Every cell in my body stiffened when I saw it, so much so that Gibby could feel my fear.

"Don't worry," she said, "I am not going to leave you."

Cal tried to pick a fight with me from the moment we stepped into the house. Straight away he accused me of packing one of his pans and he threatened to open one of my packed boxes to check. I started to object until Gibby stepped in.

"I've got this," she said to me quietly.

Then she protected me by standing in between me and Cal and said to him,

"Cal, I do not like all this shouting and if I have to join in you won't like it. So, if you really believe Karen has mistakenly packed one of your pans, then be my guest and open the box. But… if when you open it you do not find your pan then I expect you to repack the box exactly as it is now."

She stopped him in his tracks. Somehow, she had stood up to him and he had backed down. In fact, not only did he back down, he left the kitchen with his tail between his legs and never said another word about the so called missing pan. When she later asked if she could borrow some of his proper milk, I only had almond milk, he was putty in her hands.

"Of course Gibby, help yourself to whatever you need."

His behaviour was hard to watch. He was constantly trying to pick a fight with me and seemed to be very angry, but the moment Gibby stepped in he immediately softened and became the man I had originally fallen in love with. It was hard to see him switch from one to the other, and as Gibby pointed out to me, he wasn't angry with me; it was all an act. If he was genuinely angry he couldn't turn it off the minute Gibby was around.

His behaviour demonstrated everything the GDASS lady had said. I couldn't believe the anger was just an act. I had thought he really had an anger issue, but here he was demonstrating the opposite. He turned angry Cal on and off in a moment. It wasn't real. It was part of his bullying behaviour intended to control me. The GDASS lady was also right about him getting worse when he saw me leaving. The closer it got until I walked out for the last time, the sooner it got to him losing his control over me. The whole experience was horrid to endure, but it opened my eyes up to just how manipulative he could be.

On the second day the removals men could see the difference in my energy, now that Cal was around. They quietly took me to one side and told me not to worry because they had my back. It was a difficult time, but also a time of huge learning for me.

When the men unloaded my stuff into the storage unit, they originally left a pathway down the centre so that I could access everything, but it soon became obvious that the pathway would need to be filled. When we finally shut the door, there wasn't room for another thing and very little hope of ever finding anything until it all came out again.

Except for what was now in my car, all my stuff was now locked away and I had to walk away from it, for what would turn out to be four and a half months.

When I left Cal's on the Friday, I felt a huge sense of relief. Gibby pointed out that I didn't have to talk to him ever again. She said if he approached me in any way, I should simply tell him to talk to my solicitor.

As it turned out, I had to put this into practice that very same evening. Nikita was leaving early for her girl's weekend and Cal was delayed by 2 hours, so he couldn't pick the children up until 6pm. Ironically the children were therefore with me for a couple of hours. When Cal arrived, he very rudely walked straight into Nikita's house without knocking.

According to Nikita he had never done this before, so this bad behaviour was aimed at showing me he still had control over me. Not for long I thought.

"So, this is where you have moved to," he sneered.

"It looks like it." I replied, giving no indication that I was only here for a few weeks. "I will have my key back now then," he demanded. I could have given him the key, there was no good reason to keep it other than to say to him, you cannot tell me what to do anymore. For weeks, I had wanted to talk and he would only scream at me, or ignore me. Now he wanted to talk and I found great pleasure in saying,

“If you have anything to say to me, say it to my solicitor.” He demanded his key twice more and each time I answered with the same phrase. He then gave up and muttered something about changing the locks. I hugged the children and smiled as I watched him walk away from the house.

That man had controlled me for 40 years. I had allowed the situation to continue for that length of time, but no more. I had no home and no money, but I had control of my life back. I was exhausted but I felt good. I could finally fall into a relaxed sleep and let my body start to heal, and for the following week that is all I seemed to do. I hadn’t realised just how draining all this had been.

Getting my money back from Cal would not be easy. I would have to take him to court, but I had grown so much over this final year with him. This time I would stand up for myself and I would fight to the bitter end to show him he had picked on the wrong girl. This time I would fight to get back what was rightfully mine. I was no longer afraid of him. He was and is a cruel emotional bully. He wanted the world to see him as a nice man, but this was no nice man. This man is a sociopath, a narcissist and a misogynist, he manipulated people to get his own way so that he could be successful at all costs. This man had used and abused people to get ahead. It upset me that the situation was forcing me to do something I didn’t want to do, all in order to right a wrong. I didn’t want to take Cal to court. I didn’t want to fight with him, but he’d forced the issue and sometimes you have to stand up and be counted. Sometimes you have to do something you don't want to do, in order to defend a value that is important to you.

Sometimes you have to do something you don't want to do, in order to defend a value that is important to you

I do not blame Cal. He can only see the world through *his* eyes and what he doesn't feel, he cannot understand. He is a troubled soul who looks everywhere but inwards for his solutions.

I can remember shortly after I had stopped being in love with him my Spiritual Coach, a lovely lady called Laurelle Ronde, told me I now had to send love to him again, from my soul to his, otherwise I was sitting in victim mode. Her words were so hard to hear but I knew that when I spoke of him, I was telling people what he was doing to me. As long as I spoke of this situation in this way I was playing the victim. I had to choose my words carefully.

I knew I was not a victim, so I had to consciously choose to step out of victim mode. I started sending him love from my soul to his each evening when I went to bed. I thanked him in my gratitude journal for putting a roof over my head and giving me the chance to have a wonderful relationship with his two beautiful children.

I prayed that the Soul Contract between us would come to a successful end for the good of us both. I can never condone his behaviour, but there is no need to forgive him. He was my biggest teacher. It just took me a long time to realise that I am the creator of my own world. In order to make it better, I had to learn to say:

'You Cannot Treat Me This Way'.

Chapter 36: A Summary of Life Lessons

My journey has not always been easy, but I believe these are the lessons I have learned along the way

Who am I?

We are all energetic beings. We are much more than the solid body that we can see, and our thoughts and feelings are energetic tools that we use to create our lives whether we are using them consciously or not.

Our feelings indicate to us if we need to change something. When we are happy we know all is well, but when we feel sad or afraid, for example, we know that something needs to change to get us back to our state of happiness. In truth, we can never be happy all the time. We will oscillate in and out of that state of happiness via other emotions, and that is as it should be.

The mistake we often make is to chase happiness and fight those emotions that we have labelled bad. If instead we accept these other emotions, embrace them, allow ourselves to feel them, we will then learn from them. Only when we have heard their message will we find a way to let them go and settle back into our state of happiness. Only then will we start to understand who we are and what we want to achieve in life.

Our thoughts play an important role in creating that life. They are powerful, more powerful than most of us realise. When we are aware of that power we start to be very careful about what we are thinking. We focus on what we want and not what we don't want, we choose thoughts of gratitude and abundance in all areas of our life. We start to understand that even if we cannot see something physically in our everyday life, the first step for creating it is to focus on it being there.

As energetic beings we have a sixth sense, a sense that will often tell us who is on the other end of the phone before we answer it, a sense that warns us to avoid one stranger in a crowded room whilst drawing us to another. This sense is our intuition. It is not a gift that only a few people can connect with, we all have it, but we must learn to trust it. Your intuition is the best advice you will ever get.

Why are we here?

I believe the most fundamental reason that we are here is to experience life, although we may not all want the same experiences.

I believe we are here to be our unique selves, to grow into the people we want to be, to discover our gift and then to share it with the world.

In our early years, we start by believing that life is about the job, the house, the partner, the children and the holidays. In many ways it is, but only if the job helps you to feel fulfilled and valued, your partner helps you to experience being loved unconditionally and supported as you grow, you feel blessed to nurture your children and help them to know who they are and recognise their gift to the world, and the holiday is a chance to experience another culture, not an excuse to escape from your everyday life.

So in a sense, knowing our 'why' for doing something is what makes the experience valuable.

Know Your Own Worth

Knowing who I am and valuing my own worth has been one of the biggest and hardest lessons to learn. We are all good enough and deserving of love, although our early childhood experiences can often cause us to mistakenly believe otherwise.

My other lessons have been understanding my values and honouring them, learning to set boundaries so that others treat me with the same respect I would treat them, and taking ownership of my life and becoming the predominant creative force in it. Wisdom and clarity have grown as I have learned to believe in me.

Relationships

Relationships are the most important part of our lives because they hold up a mirror to us and help us to understand who we are. We also learn how to communicate with others through our relationships and communication is one of life's greatest gifts. We all want to have a voice, we want to be heard, but how many times do we listen and not truly hear? How many times does our body language tell a different story to our words? Communication is an art, one that we need to be able to learn if we are to succeed in this life.

A healthy relationship is based on honesty and trust, but we find absolute honesty very difficult to achieve. We often think we are telling a white lie to spare someone else's feelings, but in reality we are often worried about their response to our truth. The problem with hiding our truth is that we are then responsible for others not seeing who we are.

Learning to accept others as they are and understanding that no one has your perspective on the world except for you, are also lessons learned through our relationships. Sometimes the hardest relationships are the ones we learn the most from, and until we understand our contribution to that difficult relationship, we find ourselves having the same problems over and over again.

Parenting

Parenting can be your biggest joy, but it is also your biggest challenge.

Self-belief is the biggest key to success in our world, so helping your children to be confident is the biggest gift you can give them. Teach them not to judge others, to embrace their uniqueness and accept others as they are. Teach them to be kind and caring. Teach them to respect themselves and others, to respect animals and the earth we all live on. Teach them to be honest, to know that they have a voice and that their voice is important. You do not have to agree with everything they say, but show them that their opinions matter. Teach your children to set boundaries and to understand that decisions have consequences. Teach them that their thoughts are powerful and that their emotions are to be felt.

Give your children the gift of time, take them outside to play in nature and give them time to be children and develop their imaginations.

Be a shining example to your children of the type of person you would like them to grow up to be. They may not have the same hobbies or interests, but they will learn most from watching you

Believe in the Magic

Life has a magical aspect to it when you work with the universal laws. People and situations miraculously appear when you stay true to yourself, acknowledge your current situation and focus consistently on your goal.

Finally, I believe in God and Guardian Angels and Spirit Guides. They are my comfort, strength, support and wisdom, but my beliefs have grown throughout the different stages of my life and so my advice to you is to believe in what resonates with you but stay open minded about the rest. It is the possibilities that bring the magic.

Afterword

Since the completion of this book Karen and her legal team successfully attained full repayment from Cal of the original loan, a small amount of interest and a contribution to Karen's court costs.

Karen has now happily moved into a new home in Cheshire with her two dogs, Gypsy and Bollie, and her cat Minstrel. She feels grateful to be living in an area where she feels safe, where she can walk her dogs every day through the beauty of the local woods, where she is surrounded by the love of many dear friends and where life is full of exciting possibilities.

Printed in Great Britain
by Amazon